KISS

and

KILL

KISS and KILL

Edited by
SEBASTIAN WOLFE

Carroll & Graf Publishers, Inc.
New York

First published in Great Britain by Xanadu Publications Limited 1990
First published in the United States of America by Carroll & Graf
Publishers, Inc. 1990 by arrangement with Xanadu Publications Ltd.

Carroll & Graf Publishers, Inc.
260 Fifth Avenue,
New York, NY 10001

Library of Congress Cataloging-in-Publication Data

Kiss and kill : sensational true stories of love, lust, and murder /
    (edited by Sebastian Wolfe). – 1st Carroll & Graf ed.
        p.   cm.
    Includes bibliographical references.
    ISBN 0–88184–624–4 : $18.95
    1. Murder-Case Studies.   2. Crime passionel-Case studies.
    1. Wolfe, Sebastian.
    HV6513.K57   1990b   90-43433
    364.1'523--dc20   CIP

Manufactured in Great Britain

CONTENTS

Introduction

Nobody knows how cruel fate can be,
How close together love and hate can be. . .

Sometimes it takes a rather trite lyric to express a universal
truth, though this one had the god fortune to be sung by Billie
Holiday.

Love and hate can be as close as life and death, and this
book explores what happens when relationships go sour and
one half of a couple turns against the other. The impulse to
kill one's spouse or lover is not exactly unknown, of course.
Thankfully, it isn't often carried out, butit is behind most of
the murders that do occur; police investigating such crimes
usually look first at the victim's nearest and dearest, and they
are usually right to do so.

The candidates for inclusion in *Kiss and Kill* were therefore
legion, so to impose some order on this murderous multitude
and to give the book a structure I have classified the cases
into types, broadly following F. Tennyson Jesse's masterful
analysis in her classic study *Murder and its Motives*, omitting
only the category 'Murder from Conviction' as it does not
really suit this subject-matter, and substituting 'Killing for
Self-Preservation', which does. It is, I believe, a useful way
of looking at these things.

Under 'Killing for Gain', for example, there is a classic
murder-for-money case with all its touching domestic details,
but also the truly bizarre career of Landru who made an
industry of it and whose activities pose some still-unanswered
questions. 'Killing for Revenge' presents the redoubtable
Cordelia Botkin, the prototype of many subsequent mistresses who got some distinguished public figure embarass-

ingly involved in an illicit sexual tangle – except that Cordelia was no bimbo. 'Killing for Convenience' encapsulates every romantic triangle there's ever been, though few women blow up an entire passenger aircraft as 'Madame Le Corbeau' evidently did.

Jealousy is another hugely powerful motive, of course, and under this heading are a man and a woman: Buck Ruxton, driven to anguish by his wife's (probably imagined) infidelities, and Ruth Ellis who was mercilessly hanged for what, anywhere other than in gloomy, moralistic postwar Britain, would have been understood as a crime of passion. 'Killing for Lust' is the grimmest section of all, recounting three cases where women were unlucky enough to become involved with psychopathically cruel – but very plausible – men, though at least one of them seems to have been a willing accomplice. Finally, in 'Killing for Preservation' there are two extraordinary cases where murders were committed by people who were being threatened: Madame Fahmy by her appalling husband, and someone who had fallen into the meshes of scheming Zeo Zoe Wilkins – a lady as extraordinary as her name.

From a substantial collection I have selected the very best accounts of these crimes that I could find, and I trust that the names of the writers will be commendation enough for the excellence of the stories. My thanks to all of them.

And be careful who you kiss.

-- SEBASTIAN WOLFE

Part 1

KILLING
FOR GAIN

ALAN HYND

The Case of the Burning Bride

Somebody set a woman on fire before dawn in a lonely neck of woods in Union County, New Jersey. The victim had been murdered with a single bullet shot into the crown of her head, so that it took a course straight downward inside her body and came to a stop in her stomach. Then she had been saturated with gasoline and turned into a human torch. When the cops found her she looked like a passenger in an airplane that had made a one-point landing; she was completely unrecognizable. Only parts of her shoes, a small piece of clothing here and there, some cheap costume jewelry, her bridgework, and a small patch of skin on one cheek had escaped the flames. There were, nonetheless, certain physical clues, and just as important, certain deductions to be lifted from the scene of the crime, which, added up, were more than sufficient for a solution.

Yet, after ten days, all the prosecutor's detectives had succeeded in doing was transporting the remains from the spot where they had been found to a morgue in the nearby city of Elizabeth. The prosecutor—one Abe J. David—sent out an SOS for the Pinkertons. The man who took over was William A. Wagner, assistant superintendent of the New York offices of Pinkerton's National Detective Agency—a sharp, clean-cut fellow in his middle thirties. Wagner spent an hour with the corpse; at the end of that time he had reached certain tentative conclusions. The victim was middle-aged. She was Polish. She had come from the coal regions of

3

Pennsylvania, a few hours away. She had been involved in a romance.

'How,' asked the prosecutor, 'do you figure things like that?'

'This patch of skin from the woman's face,' Wagner explained, 'isn't exactly white; it's more on the yellowish side. The skin of Slavic people has a yellowish tinge. The contours of the woman's face bear me out. Her cheekbones were high and prominent—another characteristic of the Slavic races.'

'So you figure,' said the prosecutor, 'if she's Slavic she comes from the coal regions because there are so many Poles over there.'

'Exactly,' said Wagner. 'Now about the romance business. That patch of face skin was heavily rouged. A middle-aged, middle-class Polish woman from the coal regions wouldn't rouge her face heavily unless there was a man in the picture.'

'Middle-class,' said the prosecutor—'how do you figure she was middle-class?'

'From the cheap jewelry and shoes, and from the texture of remnants of her coat and dress. The jewelry's dime-store stuff. Most of it's new. That's another thing that makes me believe this woman was interested in a man—all that new jewelry. She was making herself as attractive as possible.'

The victim's shoes, black patent-leather oxfords, size 6c, bore a complete serial number. Part of the hem of the woman's dress was intact. It bore evidence of having been repaired. 'The stitches in the repair work,' Wagner pointed out to the prosecutor, 'are not the work of a tailor, but of a dressmaker or a seamstress. She could have repaired her own clothes.' There was evidence that the victim's coat had been of black satin and monkey fur—one of the more revolting vogues of the Twenties.

The serial number in the shoes turned out to be that of the Friedmann-Shelby Shoe Company of St. Louis. The shoes had been shipped to an unrecorded destination two years previously. The shoe company had long done business with wholesalers in the Pennsylvania coal regions, especially with its cheaper product. The first clue to be run down, then, was at least compatible with Wagner's broad theory.

Wagner got up a police flier. He incorporated in it all the known facts and deductions. Then he set out on a tour of the Pennsylvania coal region. He covered such towns as Reading, Scranton and Wilkes-Barre, with all stops in between. He papered the territory with his fliers. He talked twenty hours a day with police chiefs, sheriffs, dentists, shoe and clothing salesmen. When he had done everything he could think of, Wagner crossed his fingers and returned to New York to sweat it out.

Wagner was hardly damp when the chief of police of a little Pennsylvania coal-mining town—Greenville, not far from Wilkes-Barre—long-distanced the Pinkertons with a hot rumble. A couple of Greenville housewives had walked into the chief's office, after having taken a look at Wagner's flier posted on a local telegraph pole, and said that the flier seemed to describe a friend of theirs. The heavy rouge, the black satin and the monkey fur, the nonprofessional alterations to the clothing, and the romance, all seemed familiar to the two housewives. The friend of the women—a Mrs Mildred Mowry, a middle-aged Polish widow—had dropped from sight after marrying a man she had located through an advertisement in a matrimonial magazine.

Wagner summoned the missing woman's friends—a Mrs Dodds and a Mrs Straub—to New Jersey. The remains of the torch victim were taken from the morgue icebox where they had lain for two months now. The ladies from Greenville made an immediate identification. Wagner had now reached the point where he was starting from scratch. The identification was the X factor that was to mark the difference between a solved and an unsolved case.

Wagner had the Greenville women fill him in on Mildred Mowry. The woman had been the widow of a miner named Jake Mowry, who had died ten years previously. Millie, as her friends called her, had come into a few thousand dollars in insurance upon her husband's death. She had sold her home, which netted her a few thousand more, and went to live in a rooming house. She earned her living by doing sewing, mending, and needlework for the townfolk; her little fortune, about six thousand dollars in all, remained intact.

As the years of widowhood passed, Mildred Mowry, reaching fifty, found herself in the grip of an overwhelming biological urge. She decided to insert an advertisement in a matrimonial magazine for a husband.

In her ad, which appeared in July, 1928—some seven months before she became a human torch—Mildred Mowry mentioned that she had about six thousand dollars. The ad drew an immediate response in the form of a well-dressed, fiftyish little man with prematurely white hair, parted severely in the middle, and rimless nose-glasses on a sensitive, almost feminine face. Mildred Mowry, rouged to the ears and fluttering like an aspen leaf, introduced her prospective husband to her friends Mrs Straub and Mrs Dodds as Doctor Richard Campbell, a big New York surgeon. Doctor Campbell, who was in the habit of chewing cloves, disclosed that his specialty was intestinal surgery. 'You might call me an inside man,' he said to Mrs Straub, laughing quickly, the while displaying a strong set of large, yellow teeth.

Some of Mrs Mowry's acquaintances in Greenville were just a little suspicious of the doctor, who checked into a local inn while conducting his courtship. They wondered how it was that a big New York surgeon would come to the coal regions for a wife, and, more to the point, how any man with any sense of discrimination whatever could, after meeting Mildred Mowry in the flesh, remain interested in her.

There appeared to be, moreover, a basic incompatibility between Doctor Campbell and Mrs Mowry. The lady, although taking an occasional sip of homemade elderberry wine, was bitterly opposed to overindulgence in strong drink. Dr Campbell claimed that he was always chewing cloves to deaden a toothache. Mrs Mowry, trusting soul, believed him. The more objective students of the doctor, however, questioned that even the most severe toothache would cause him to lurch, as he frequently did late at night when making his way to his room in the inn.

Doctor Campbell's courtship was mercurial and spectacular. Although the inn where he was stopping was only down the street from where Mrs Mowry lived, he sent her telegrams at all hours of the day and night. He woke her up in the morning with messengers bearing roses. He told friends of the bride-to-be that she set him on fire—a remark that caused them to wonder, on a later day, if they had heard him quite correctly. Mrs Mowry flounced about town, intoxicated by the wine of her romance with—as she insisted upon calling Doctor Campbell—Dicky Boy.

She was a new woman. She was, for one thing, awake most of the day. That was unusual for her. Mildred Mowry loved to sleep. She was in the habit of dozing off in the middle of a parlor conversation.

Doctor Campbell turned out to be not only a man who knew his way around the alimentary canal but one who was making money hand over fist in Wall Street. The great Wall Street crash was, in the summer of 1928, more than a year away; there were only two types of people in the country—those who were cleaning up in the market and those who needed their heads examined. One rainy Sunday afternoon, Doctor Campbell, Mildred Mowry and her friends Mrs Dodds and Mrs Straub were in the living room of Millie's boardinghouse, sipping weak tea and munching homemade cookies, when the talk took a fiscal turn. Millie said that the bank was paying her three per cent on her savings.

'Why,' said Doctor Campbell, 'the bank ought to be *indicted* for *cheating* you! They're using your money to make anywhere from two to five hundred per cent in the market. You should be making that money yourself, Millie darling.'

A few days later, Mrs Mowry withdrew her cash from the bank and gave it to Dicky Boy to invest for her. Mrs Mowry couldn't lose. 'If anything *should* go wrong,' she explained to Mrs Straub, 'Dicky Boy says he'll make it up to me himself.'

Late in August, a month after Doctor Campbell had first integrated himself into the Greenville landscape, he and Mildred Mowry stole away in the night, if not like two Arabs at least like two fiftyish adults who weren't acting their age.

Mrs Mowry left a note for Mrs Straub. 'We couldn't wait,' she said. 'Will write.'

A couple of weeks later Mildred Mowry-Campbell, as the lady was calling herself at the suggestion of the doctor, wrote to her Greenville friends from New York. Doctor Campbell had a large practice on fashionable Park Avenue. She and the doctor were, however, staying at a small residential hotel while his apartment, where he lived and practiced, was being redecorated. She saw very little of the doctor; he was busy from early morning to late night calling on patients, operating in several hospitals, and going out on consultations, often all night.

In October, some six weeks after her marriage, Mrs Mowry-Campbell returned unexpectedly to Greenville to reoccupy her old room in the boardinghouse. Her return, she went to great pains to explain, was temporary. Doctor Campbell had gone to California to take out the gall bladder of Tom Mix, the movie cowboy, and to perform an exploratory operation on Cecil B. DeMille, the spectacle maker. 'Dicky Boy doesn't know exactly when he'll get back,' his bride explained. 'He says there's no telling *what* he'll find when he opens up Mr DeMille.'

Two months later, toward the end of December, Dicky Boy was apparently still so busy looking around inside Mr DeMille, and so intent on what he was seeing there, that he didn't get around to any Christmas shopping for his bride. Mrs Mowry-Campbell was putting a brave face on things; her friends were sure that the doctor had done her wrong.

On the first day of February, 1929, some five months after her marriage, Mrs Mowry-Campbell announced that Dicky Boy had returned to New York from California and sent for her. Mrs Straub went to the train with her, doubting very much that her friend Millie had ever heard from Doctor Campbell and suspecting that she was going to New York to hunt for him. Two days later, on February 3, Mrs Straub received a letter from Millie. Everything was all right, the letter stated; Millie would write again soon.

Mrs Straub took the letter to Mrs Dodds. 'There's something mighty fishy going on,' Mrs Dodds said to Mrs Straub.

'The return address on this letter is 607 Hudson Street, New York. I thought Millie said the doctor lived on Park Avenue and that he was getting his apartment all fixed up right after they got married.'

Mrs Straub decided to keep the letter. She never heard from Millie again. Now, some three months after Millie had written, Detective Wagner studied the letter, which the addressee had brought to New Jersey with her.

The Hudson Street address on the letter turned out to be Laura Spelman Hall, a YWCA. The register there showed that Mrs Mowry-Campbell, of Greenville, Pennsylvania, had checked in on the morning of February 2, and checked out on the afternoon of February 22. This latter date was the afternoon before the bride was found burning across the Hudson River in New Jersey. The deductions to be drawn from the register dates were simple: the bride had come to New York to hunt for her husband; she had, after almost three weeks, somehow located him.

A clerk at the YWCA partially corroborated Wagner's suspicion that Mrs Mowry-Campbell had caught up with her husband before checking out. During her entire stay at Laura Spelman Hall, she had impressed the personnel there as an individual with a burden on her mind—until the afternoon she checked out. Then she had undergone a noticeable change; she had been smiling, lighthearted, unworried.

Wagner now resorted to a series of connected deductions, stemming from his theory that Mrs Mowry-Campbell had left Laura Spelman Hall happy because she had found her husband. Campbell had put a face on things; somehow he had made an excuse to his bride for his long absence and silence and assured her that everything would be all right. That was why she had been so happy when checking out.

Now, putting himself in the position of a man who found himself in the spot where Campbell had found himself, Wagner tried to decide what he would have done between the time he had picked up the woman one afternoon and the time he had set fire to her before dawn the next morning. Wagner already knew certain things about Campbell. He knew he had told his bride he was a doctor. He knew he had told her he had an apartment on Park Avenue. Both of those statements had probably been lies. That being so, it would have been natural for the man to have ridden his bride around in an automobile on the pretext that he had to call on patients, the while trying to make up his mind just how, where and when to murder her.

Wagner recalled that Mrs Mowry-Campbell had been in the habit of dozing off. Campbell would have known that. He would have driven her around until she fell asleep. After she had dropped off, he had shot her, probably not far from where he later removed her body from the car and set fire to it.

The Pinkerton detective had, all along, been puzzled by the fact that the bullet that had killed the bride had been fired straight into the crown of her head, so that it had traveled a straight course and remained inside the body. The explanation for the path of the bullet now occurred to him. The woman had been shot, probably while dozing, while in Campbell's automobile. Her murderer had been careful to shoot her in such a way that there would be no bullet hole or bloodstains in his car after the job was done and the body removed.

Campbell had been a man in his fifties. He had probably been married. He quite possibly had a wife and family in or around New York. That would have accounted for his absences, on 'consultations,' all night just after he had brought the former Mildred Mowry to New York immediately following their marriage. His marital status would also have increased the ex-Mildred Mowry's stature as an obstacle.

The murderer, Wagner deduced, was no doubt well acquainted with the region where he had disposed of the body. There were, closer to New York than Union County, New Jersey, and far more accessible, spots in Westchester County, adjacent to New York City, and on Long Island and Staten Island, where a man could just as well have done to a woman what Campbell had done to the woman from Pennsylvania. Campbell, then, may even have lived in Union County.

Wagner got on the long-distance phone and called the chief of police in Greenville. Here was one small-town police chief who was on his toes. He had, after Mrs Straub and Mrs Dodds had departed for New Jersey to make an identification, gone to Mrs Mowry-Campbell's room in the boardinghouse and examined it. He had found a series of letters to the bride from the groom—all written following the woman's return to Greenville after her marriage—and he was all ready with an intelligent digest of the communications when he heard Wagner's voice on the phone.

Doctor Campbell's letters to his wife bore two return addresses—office numbers in buildings on West 42nd Street and on Fifth Avenue, New York. The letters from West 42nd Street had been mailed in November and December, and the ones from Fifth Avenue during January—the month before Mrs Campbell had come to New York. Through the doctor's purple prose of endearment ran one basic theme: don't come to New York. Dicky Boy had made one excuse after another, each one leaner than the preceding one, to keep his bride away from New York.

Wagner found the West 42nd Street and Fifth Avenue addresses to be those of mail-receiving services—outfits which, for a fee, permit use of their offices as mailing addresses for clients availing themselves of the service. The client calling himself Doctor Richard Campbell had been a furtive character. Just before terminating his arrangement at the West 42nd Street service in December, he had seemed to fear that somebody might call at the office of the service and ask for him. 'If anybody comes,' he told the people who ran the place, 'say you haven't seen me lately. Say I've left for China. Say anything.'

Upon making arrangements to get his mail at the Fifth Avenue service in January, Doctor Campbell seemed even more fearful that somebody would come in and inquire for him. As a matter of fact, somebody did, several times in February—a woman who answered the description of the middle-aged bride. The caller had put in her appearance between the first part of the month and Washington's birthday—the period during which Mrs Mowry-Campbell was registered at the YWCA. She had asked hopefully for Doctor Campbell at first, and then, as she continued to visit the place and found that she had missed him, she became visibly dejected.

Doctor Harvey Crippen, the London murderer, had been a very contained man, except for one thing. When he was excited, his Adam's apple bobbed up and down. Dr Richard Campbell had an Adam's apple that did precisely the same thing. The doctor had worn high choker collars that covered his Adam's apple, but the apple had behaved like a bobbin on a sewing machine when the doctor was told that a middle-aged lady had been inquiring for him.

Another part of the picture was in focus for Detective Wagner now. Mrs Mowry-Campbell had hung around the building on Fifth Avenue where her husband had received his mail and finally personally contacted him. Then he had driven her around until she fell asleep, and murdered her. But where was Doctor Campbell now? If Wagner couldn't find his man at the end of the trail, perhaps he would have more luck at the beginning of the trail.

Neither Doctor Campbell or Mildred Mowry had ever mentioned where they had been married. From all Wagner could gather about the woman, she wouldn't have stood for a relationship without benefit of clergy. Where, then, would a pair of middle-aged lovers, stealing away from the coal regions in the middle of the night, go to get married? The logical answer seemed to be Elkton, Maryland, a Gretna Green only a few hours distant.

Elkton it was. Wagner was interested in just one item on the application for the marriage license that the pair had filled in—Doctor Campbell's home address. The groom had given it as the 3700 block of Yosemite Street, in Baltimore.

The Baltimore address was a vacant lot. That in itself was a clue. A man had to know the neighborhood pretty well to know the number of a vacant lot. Pinkerton operatives canvassed several blocks of Yosemite Street. Finally there emerged in their mind's eye the figure of a little man with sensitive face, pince-nez and prematurely white hair, parted severely in the middle. He had a few years previously, lived in a rented house on Yosemite Street. He hadn't occupied the dwelling long. He had been a furtive sort of man.

His neighbors had never learned precisely what he had done for a living. His name had not been Campbell; it had been Close—Doctor Henry Colin Close. Wagner located the landlord who had rented the house to Doctor Close. The landlord knew but two things about Close: the man had previously lived in Salisbury, Maryland, not far from Baltimore; his Adam's apple had bobbed up and down when he was inwardly excited.

The town of Salisbury sounded vaguely familiar to Wagner. He had, sometime in the previous year or two, heard the name Salisbury, or read it in the papers, in connection with a murder case of some kind. Now a bell rang in Wagner's mind. He had read the name Salisbury in connection with another murder right in New Jersey—that of Margaret Brown, a New York governess, who, after being wooed and won by a stranger, had wound up, just like the woman from Greenville, as the hot core of a torch. All that had ever been learned about Margaret Brown's murderer was that he had represented himself to the governess as a Doctor Henry Ross, a practitioner of Salisbury, Maryland.

Wagner hunted out friends of Miss Brown's who had briefly glimpsed Doctor Ross during his courtship with the governess. Doctor Ross tallied to the eyelashes with Doctor Campbell. Even his Adam's apple had bobbed up and down. Wagner was on his way to clean up not one murder but two. He had started behind scratch; now he was about to wrest a killer from the thin blue air.

Wagner slept on his problem. He was shaving one morning when he was visited by the thought that a man who had committed two torch murders might very well have constructed some sort of an official record for himself before turning up in New Jersey with gun and gasoline.

Wagner's man, under half a dozen aliases, including his real name of Henry Colin Close, had a long record. The Chicago police department had a plump dossier on him. Close, a native of Colorado, was now in his fifty-ninth year. He had studied medicine as a young man, but had not gone through with it. Liquor and woman were too attractive. He started out as a forger in California and wound up in Folsom. Then he came to New York, got a job as office manager for a construction firm, and maintained three different women in three different apartments simultaneously—quite an accomplishment even after being able to stand the expense. Close had been obliged to swindle his employer to hold up the fiscal side of his affairs and, caught, was sentenced to a term in Sing Sing.

Close was forty-two when he got out. He turned up in Omaha, loaded with fake credentials, and became educational director for the Union Pacific Railroad. He got himself engaged to five girls simultaneously in Omaha and left town when he saw feathers and smelled tar. After that he turned up in Chicago as a publicity and promotion expert. Some of the projects he promoted smacked so strongly of fraud that Close was, in a way, continuing his criminal career. A married woman probably saved Close's life in Chicago; she told him that her husband had just found out about them, and Close left the city.

Close's record stopped ten years short of 1929, when Wagner wanted him. Wagner searched vainly through telephone and city directories of every city and town in northern New Jersey for his man. He wondered if Close was still engaged in public relations work. Close's specialty had been promoting real estate developments.

Wagner looked through the New York papers for such developments. He began to canvass them by telephone. One of them employed a promotion expert named Campbell— Henry Campbell. As the man's description came over the phone, Wagner knew that, at long last, he had his man. Henry Campbell lived in Elizabeth, New Jersey. Wagner whistled when he heard Campbell's address. It was an apartment house right around the corner from the morgue where his bride's body had been identified.

Wagner called at the Elizabeth apartment. Campbell was in New York, handling a promotion of some sort. He had a wife—a fine woman who knew nothing of his criminal past and who considered him a devoted husband. She had been married to him for nine years and borne him two children. She knew that her husband had been in financial difficulties but it had never occurred to her that he had been engaged in criminal activity of any sort. Now that she thought of it, though, he had acted very strangely when the body of the torch victim had been brought to the morgue right around the corner. He had seemed overly interested in developments; he had sometimes phoned her from New York to ask her if there was anything new about the corpse around the corner. Then, when the body had been identified, Campbell had not been able to sleep.

They were waiting that night, Wagner and the detectives from the prosecutor's office, for the little slayer when he came home from work. His Adam's apple began bobbing when he saw the strangers. He wouldn't admit a thing about the first of the torch murders, but he couldn't unburden himself of the details of the second one quickly enough. Wagner's deductions had been correct. Campbell had married the woman from the coal regions for her cash. Mildred Mowry-Campbell had caught up with him at the second mailing address.

'Gentlemen,' said Campbell, 'you can imagine how I felt when, after trying to duck this old dame, I found her that afternoon tapping me on the shoulder in the lobby of the building where I got my mail, calling me *Dicky Boy*.' A reluctant bridegroom, to be sure.

Campbell had driven his bigamous bride around the bleak New Jersey countryside all evening and late into the night, putting her off by saying he was calling on patients. Actually, he was stopping in to say hello to friends in various parts of Union County. Then, in the small hours of the morning, he did the lady in, just as he was done in himself, one night a year after the murder, in the chair where sitters sizzle in the big cage at Trenton.

H. RUSSELL WAKEFIELD

Landru: A Real Life Bluebeard

Many Bluebeards, mass-murderers, flourished before Landru, and not a few have appeared since—the United States has produced several characteristic specimens—but *his* ill-fame has exceeded that of all his rivals and competitors, and the bibliography devoted to him has been far more copious. He has come to be regarded as the archetype of serial butchers in fact, as Bluebeard is in fiction. Several causes, artificial and natural, contributed to this. Landru was the first great piece of sensational news in the post-war period, and the ears of the world were tickled to hear that all the time they had been killing for country, one sly little fellow had been killing for cash.

There is no doubt that the French authorities deliberately encouraged the Parisian press to 'splash' the Landru affair as vigorously as possible, so that, by inoculating the public with what was called 'Landru Fever,' attention might be distracted from the Peace Conference which was maturing unfavourably for France. Again Henri Désiré was physically almost a freak, and psychically and morally a strange, enigmatic person. A small, meagre body was topped by a disproportionately, almost completely bald, head, yet dangling from his chin was a great brown wispy beard of which he was ludicrously proud. Such growths came to be known as 'Landrus,' and in very many cases were hurriedly removed by their owners. His nose was very long and oddly shaped, and the skin stretched almost, it seemed, to breaking point across the bone. His eyes were deep-set, small, flickering and black—'Monkey's

Eyes,' as they were well described by a witness at the trial. So eccentric was his appearance that he would certainly have been stared after in the street in England, and though not so strange to French eyes the sister of one of his victims said, 'When one has seen that man one never forgets him, for he is like no one else in the world.'

As for his character, his psychic make-up, it requires some study to distinguish the Landru of deliberately concocted legend from the Landru of fact. This much is certain, he was an utterly brutal and rapacious monster. He was, within a limited range, cunning and far-seeing, very glib and insinuating, extremely pertinacious and energetic. The French press attempted to establish that he was a brilliant wit, possessed of masterly intelligence, a Lord of Crime, irresistible to all women, who were hypnotised by his brilliant, cavernous eyes. All this is fantastically exaggerated. He had a certain capacity for impudent repartee, the sign of a superficially quick brain, but he showed in many ways that he was mentally costive and doltish. He was only found attractive by a very undiscerning and unexacting type of woman, the middle-aged or elderly widow, bereft and derelict, chafing at her dreary existence, and finding a last solace and hope in matrimonial advertisements. Sharp-eyed and experienced persons of both sexes summed him up quickly as a 'Wrong-Un', probably dangerous, and proclaimed the fact, loudly but ineffectually, to their infatuated relatives.

That which will probably secure for the Landru case a permanently prominent place in the annals of criminology is the element of mystery surrounding his crimes. Why did he choose such victims? How many were there? How did he murder them? And greatest of all, how did he dispose of their bodies? We will return to these puzzles later. Firstly we will sketch his career. Landru was born in 1869 of humble parentage. Whether he inherited a criminal taint from further back is uncertain, but he did not do so from his father or mother. In fact, his father was so horrified at finding he had sired a thief that he killed himself long before his son became an assassin.

Young Landru had a decent elementary education, performed his military service with credit, married, and apparently attempted for a time to earn his living honestly. But he was eventually swindled out of a deposit which he had put down, and this both souring and inspiring him, he took to crime. At first he was merely a petty pilferer, but soon turned his hand to that type of 'racket' which he pursued with great energy till he was finally laid by the heels. He got into touch, usually through matrimonial advertisements, with women, almost invariably widows, who were possessed of some property. If they were sufficiently gulled he filched that property and disappeared. At his arrest in 1919 the names of 283 women were found amongst his papers. His advertisements always read somewhat as follows:

'Gentleman, aged 45, unmarried, living alone, possessed of 4000 francs, wishes to marry a lady of about his own age and circumstances.'

These he inserted in a big Paris daily. In other words, he was the meanest and lowest type of confidence trickster. And he was hopelessly unsuccessful. He was first arrested and convicted in 1900, and from then till 1914 he was continually in and out of gaol: so much so that in the spring of the latter year he was condemned by default to banishment to the New Caledonia penal settlement as an habitual criminal.

When war broke out Landru was still on the run, and remained so till April 12th, 1919. But for the dislocation and impoverishment of the Paris police force he would undoubtedly have been apprehended long before. He was a minor profiteer as he confessed in his famous saying, 'The war has ended too soon for me!'

Landru's consistent failure to succeed in his chosen career, the realisation that that failure was invariably due to the venom of his dupes, the knowledge that the horrors of life-long exile would be the consequence of one more failure, turned Landru into a serial-murderer. He saw that if he was to escape life imprisonment he must eliminate the dupe who would otherwise betray him. It was a perfectly logical and dictated conclusion; and, having come to it, he almost at once applied it.

Some time in the spring of 1914 Landru had established a connection with a Madame Cuchet, a widow with one son who had applied at his garage for a job. It should be said that Landru at one time or another owned or rented an amazing number of small places in and around Paris; lodgings, small houses, 'hide-outs' and garages. And he made use of at least as many as a dozen aliases, 'Cuchet,' 'Petit,' 'Forest,' and 'Guillet' being his favourites. He was also, according to his own account, a man of most versatile accomplishments. He was an engineer, consul, secret service agent, inventor, civil servant, manufacturer, sales manager. The garages were only such in name, being used for housing the loot from burglaries; Landru being also in a small way a receiver of stolen goods.

Madame Cuchet was a typical Landru 'prospect.' She was about forty, formerly a hand in a factory, an impulsive simpleton who speedily became infatuated with 'M. Diard,' an opulent engineer. One of the things which impressed her was his distinguished manner of wearing the violet ribbon of an 'Order' which the engineer had both created and bestowed upon himself. Her married sister was anything but attracted by M. Diard, and in company with her husband, she actually broke into his decrepit villa at Chantilly and ransacked his bureau, with the result that she discovered his name was Landru and that he was in dubious communication with dozens of women. Even that didn't produce any lasting effect on Madame Cuchet, who was soon completely in Landru's power once more. He forced her to take a villa at Vernouillet on the outskirts of Paris and pay six months' rent. This house was called 'The Lodge.' Landru took her and the boy there on December 8th. They were seen in the garden on January 4th, after which she and her son were seen no more.

Landru probably secured about 15,000 francs from Madame Cuchet, and it should be remembered the franc was never de-valued during the Landru period. Madame Cuchet's relatives had become 'fed-up' with her and bothered little about her disappearance, though they reported it to the police, and a drowsy inquiry was still being made into her whereabouts in 1919.

Landru, made confident by this remunerative and encouraging success, speedily followed it up. He next turned his attention to a Madame Laborde-Line, a widow with a little money. As 'M. Cuchet' (with fatuous recklessness he had adopted that alias) he made love to her, secured her property, took her to Vernouillet and killed her in June. There were no inquiries into *her* fate, for no one in the world cared whether she lived or died.

It was now the turn of a Madame Guillin. She was a widow aged fifty-one, with about 23,000 francs. She replied to an advertisement, met a 'M. Petit,' a consul; was attracted by the prospect of sharing a diplomatic career in Australia, went to The Lodge, on August 4th, and was certainly killed that night. Landru secured some of her money by forgery and sold her furniture. The forgery was palpable and the bank grossly careless, but, of course, war was the excuse.

So, within six months, Landru had murdered four persons, and no trace of their bodies, not a bone or a tooth, was ever discovered; an astounding performance never wholly explained. It is true that some false hair, believed to be Madame Guillin's was found in a garage; Landru's collector's instinct was as highly developed as a jackdaw's. Although he had done marvellously well at The Lodge, he decided to make a move. For one thing, the neighbours were becoming more than a little inquisitive, and he fancied the police were also. He wanted something more secluded, less over-looked, and he soon found a suitable slaughter-house near the village of Gambais in the department of the Seine. This was the Villa Hermitage, situated on a little-used side-road. Besides a couple of camp-beds, about the only furniture he installed there was a small stove, the famous 'Poêle,' concerning which one day all Paris was to talk and joke, and which faced Landru all through his trial.

The first fuel for this stove was provided by a Madame Héon, a widow, needless to say, but a surprising choice, for all she possessed was a very little money and some cheap furniture. Apparently—and it is significant—this was the best

Landru could do. He was 'M. Petit,' head traveller for a big South American firm, at the time. He took her to Gambais and she 'evaporated' as the French put it, early in December. Some time before he had been courting a Madame Collomb, widowed typist aged forty-four with some 8000 francs. She was of superior education and social standing to Landru's other victims and he had the sense to realise it, and woo her with more delicacy and finesse. He had dropped her for a time while he was busy with Madame Héon, but resumed his amorous protestations. She responded in spite of the violent protestations of her mother, Madame Moreau, who formed no two opinions about 'M. Fremyet' being a crook. He had first introduced himself to her daughter as 'M. Cuchet,' and Madame Moreau was anxious to know the reason for this metamorphosis. Landru replied that it was for the purpose of securing a double war indemnity, a peculiarly inept and dangerous lie, for it stamped him on his own confession as a trickster.

Madame Collomb, however, who shared Madame Cuchet's blind infatuation, went with him to Gambais on December 27th, and was certainly murdered within a few hours. But her mother and other relatives began a hunt for her and him which was largely responsible for his arrest long after. A wiser rascal would have spotted that red light, but he was primed with audacious self-confidence by now and was sorely in need of that 8000 francs.

The next episode has never been quite explained. It concerns Andrée Babelay, a penniless young servant-girl Landru picked up in the Metro. She was physically attractive, yet he killed her at the end of March. Why? Several explanations have been given, but the most likely is that she was too dangerously inquisitive and found some papers concerning former victims in a desk. Landru at his trial, worn out and desperate, blurted out a hint of this to the consternation of his counsel. So he disposed of her for safety's sake.

It has been suggested that Landru was a sadist who killed for the fun of it, but it is very improbable. He murdered for business reasons and no others, and even for him the disposing of a body must have been an arduous and unwelcome ordeal. Almost certainly Andrée was removed because she knew too much.

Landru had known his next 'fiancée,' Madame Buisson, for some time. Perfectly true to type she was a middle-aged widow with some money. Landru took up with her again, got hold of her money and slew her on August 19th. Some time before he had become acquainted with a Mademoiselle Fernande Segret, who served in a shop and sang at cheap cabarets. He seems to have become genuinely attached to her, and in this he was in the tradition, for these mass-butchers often form quasi-permanent connections of this sort, the objects of their affections being in no danger of death. The Parisians made her the comic relief of the affair; Landru in love being considered great fun. This was intensified when an enterprising publisher put out her Memoirs, which are incredibly naïve and beautifully reveal one side of Landru's character. She was never in love with him, but he seemed to be a man of means and prepared to spend a gratifying amount on her. One of the secrets of Landru's success was his power to control his avarice. When he realised it would pay him to spend money to make an impression or inspire confidence, he did so readily, whether his ultimate objective was plunder by assassination, or the cajoling of a pleasing mistress.

In May Landru had met a Madame Jaume, a devout Catholic, separated from her husband, aged thirty-eight with about 2000 francs. Her association with Landru is somewhat of a mystery, for she was a quiet, hard-working woman. Probably she was bemused by loneliness. It is said that Landru told her some fantastic lie about getting her marriage annulled at Rome. In any case, she became his mistress. On one occasion he went to church with her and put two sous in the offertory box. This he recorded in his notebook, but it is improbable that this donation was recorded to his credit in the celestial ledger of ultimate rewards and punishments, for he killed her the same night. Incidentally, he took a single ticket to Gambais for her and a return for himself. This also he recorded and lived to regret it.

Madame Pascal was the next. Why he picked her out is obscure, for she was a woman of sporadically easy virtue with no money. She was not physically unattractive, which may be the explanation. He murdered her after some months and secured eight francs in cash and thirty from the sale of her false teeth and umbrella. Her murder seems quite pointless, but she may also have known too much.

With the disposal of Madame Marchadier Landru's guerrilla warfare against Society came to an end. She was a retired courtesan who had invested her savings in some shabby lodgings and furniture. He strangled her and her two dogs at Gambais on January 13th, 1919. Unknown to Landru the hunt was closing in on him. The relations of Madame Collomb, to whom he was 'Cuchet,' and those of Madame Buisson, who knew him as 'Fremyet,' had never given up the chase, and they went separately to Gambais and interviewed the mayor. He advised them to get into touch with each other and then go to the police. They did so and found that inquiries were still being made for a Madame Cuchet, a very suggestive identity of names. She had disappeared with a M. Diard. The authorities appointed Inspector Adam to investigate; a happy choice, for that astute officer soon came to the conclusion that this trinity were one, and so reported to his superior, M. Dautel, who happened to be searching for an engineer named Guillet, wanted for fraud and theft.

A few days later Inspector Adam was informed by Mademoiselle Lacoste, the sister of Madame Buisson, that she had seen Fremyet in a shop, had followed him, but lost him in the crowd. However, he was easily traced and arrested the next morning in Fernande's bedroom in the Rue Rochechouart. Then was verified, what before had been suspected, that this composite individual was M. Landru, wanted for five years. He was at once accused of the murders of Mesdames Collomb and Buisson. He attempted to protest, saying, 'That would be a matter affecting my head!' No doubt the terror of the guillotine had haunted him ever since 1915. There is no space here to tell of the versatile and laborious investigations which ended in his trial at Versailles. Of course The Lodge and the Villa

Hermitage were rigorously searched. Nothing whatever was found at the former, but from Gambais the experts bore away small sackfuls of calcined bones grubbed up from the garden and sifted from the stove. Many of these bones, the experts declared, were human, probably female, and certainly from at least three persons. This must be emphasized, for these discoveries were ruthlessly ridiculed by those who pretended to believe in Landru's innocence. But there is no reason whatsoever to doubt this evidence. Landru's garages and 'hide-outs' were likewise searched, and, besides the loot from many burglaries, much valuable material relating to the missing women was discovered; intimate papers, identity cards, clothes, and *two waxed cords*.

From now on the Landru case began to be a world sensation, and in Paris to jostle the Conference off the front page. The central figure of it was now submitted to the ordeal of the *Instruction*. This is a purely Gallic institution, a form of desultory Third Degree in which a judge, in this case, M. Bonin, supported by experts, cross-examines the accused concerning every detail of his supposed crimes. He can have the assistance of counsel, but every word he utters may be brought up as evidence against him at his trial. Landru was actually badgered and baited day after day intermittently for eighteen months! The most damning evidence against him was found in his pocket, the celebrated 'Carnet,' a little black notebook. On the inside of the cover was written:

'Cuchet, J., idem, Brésil, Crozatier, Havre, Buisson, A. Collomb, Babelay, Jaume, Pascal, Marchadier.'

And there were many cash entries such as:

'Invalides Frs 0.40.'
'One single ticket.'
'One return ticket.'

Amongst his papers were found also the carefully docketed descriptions of 283 women. Some were marked: *To be replied to*. Others, *File away. Keep in reserve; to be seen later. Probably has money* . . . and so on.

Now at first the identities of Brésil, Havre, Crozatier and Jaume were a mystery, but eventually they were found to stand for Madame Laborde-Line, who came from the Argentine, Madame Héon, who came from Havre, Madame Guillin, who lived in the Rue Crozatier, and, of course Madame Jaume. Landru was mercilessly interrogated about every entry in this diabolical notebook. He often attempted some sort of feeble explanation, but for the most part he adhered to his policy of *Mutisme*, as the French called it; a rigid refusal to answer save by some such retort as, 'You find these women; its your business. I know nothing about them. You say I killed them. Well, find the bodies!'

He appears to have been under the impression that he could not be convicted unless at least one body was discovered, and the tale told by the bones was a severe shock to him. At the end of this laborious inquisition he had admitted nothing, but M. Bonin was able to reveal that he had no positive defence whatsoever. He had no explanation for those devastating entries about single and return tickets, each one of which coincided perfectly with the known date of a disappearance. This ruthless interrogation, and the severe gastritis which afflicted him in prison had sapped his vitality and subdued his resilience. By the time of his trial he was but a shadow of his former fighting self.

He was tried at the Versailles Assize court from November 7th-30th, 1921. From beginning to end it was regarded as a great public entertainment, and competition for the gratuitous publicity attached to it was very keen. Conseiller Gilbert was lucky enough to be appointed President, but he was not so happy a little later, for the press 'roasted' him mercilessly. The Avocat-Général led for the prosecution, and Maître de Moro-Giafferi for the defence. M. Moro-Giafferi is still to-day, as he was then, the most brilliant pleader in France, a fact which makes the Landru case seem very much a contemporary affair.

The procedure of a French criminal trial seems strange to us. Every detail of the accused's past, however prejudicial to him, is raked up and related to the jury. The rules of evidence are, to say the least, elastic, and there is no judge in our sense of the word. The President is simply an agent for the prosecution who does not pretend to impartiality and is professedly out for a conviction. He cross-examines the accused as harshly as the counsel for the prosecution, and does no summing-up. Both President and counsel vehemently proclaim their conviction of the accused's guilt, which presumably must powerfully influence the jury's mind.

The conduct of the 'audience' made the proceedings a scandalous farce. The court was hopelessly overcrowded, and fiery affrays to enter it went on continuously. The mob jostled and shouted, ate and drank, made love, and at times threw the court furniture about. The President soon gave up any attempt to keep order. One of his few interventions was humorously infelicitous. When Fernande stepped into the box the rabble raised a lusty bellow of delight. 'Silence!' shouted the President. 'You are not in a theatre!' Immediately after Fernande was asked her profession. 'Lyric-Artiste,' she replied. Whereupon the rabble roared the more. It was the raucous, hysterical mood of demobilisation.

The trial itself was dull. Landru himself provided very little of the hoped-for amusement. Most of the time he seemed lethargic and bored. He tried a few feeble jests, the best, perhaps, being when he saw the women, many of them famous and notorious, struggling for admission. 'Any lady,' he exclaimed, 'is welcome to my seat.' It is recorded that not a few of these ladies behaved with hardy shamelessness, blowing kisses and making indecorous gestures to the butcher. Each case was thrashed out as it had been at the *Instruction*. Many of the witnesses were weeping, and some violently upbraided Landru to his face, at which he shrugged his emaciated shoulders. When the last had disappeared, the Avocat-Général made an impassioned demand for the guillotine, and de Moro-Giafferi uttered an eloquent but hopeless plea for acquittal. It is said he was himself convinced of Landru's guilt. He tried to maintain that his client was a White-Slaver who had smuggled the missing women to South America. But White-Slavers are not concerned with elderly widows, and the suggestion received a ribald reception. His other points were ingenious but equally unconvincing. The jury came back after two hours and found Landru guilty on every main count. That they recommended him to mercy may be attributed to the emotion of the moment.

Landru was, of course, condemned to the guillotine. An appeal was vainly made to the High Court, and Landru's last hope was in the clemency of the President of the Republic. This was refused and the execution took place on February 25th, 1922. Extraordinary as it may sound, thousands from all over France flocked to Paris in hope of witnessing the horrible scene. However, the authorities frustrated this ambition by closing the area round the death scene at the prison. The executioner and his assistants arrived at dawn and set up 'The Widow,' and soon after Landru was roused by the entry of officials and his counsel to his cell. He died bravely, waiving aside rum and cigarette, indignantly refusing to hear Mass; still more indignantly refusing to confess. It is said that his last words were, 'Ah, well! It is not the first time an innocent man has been condemned!'

So Landru shed no light on the problems of his case. Were these ten women and a boy the only persons he slew? When the scare was at its height he was credited with the elimination of scores. There were sixty unidentified women in the Morgue. Bodies were turning up all over France. What more probable, what, indeed, more certain, than that the Monster of Gambais had been instrumental in their taking off? Against that plausible supposition must be set the fact that Landru was almost insanely business-like; he recorded the pettiest detail in his *carnet*; and therein were the names of eleven persons whom he undoubtedly killed. Had he murdered others, one feels convinced he would have recorded their names also. Furthermore all the stuff discovered was traced to one or other of the eleven.

The writer has examined the problem to the best of his ability, and while it is certainly true that some difficulties would be resolved by the assumption that Landru killed other persons, there is not a particle of evidence that he did so. His choice of victims presents problems, but only if it is taken for granted that he was an exception to every other man in being a perfectly consistent human being, a miracle of coherence; and secondly, if the myth that he was irresistible to women is substituted for the reality that the vast majority of them considered him repulsive and dangerous. He must have received many uncompromising snubs and rebuffs—a few authentic instances are known. His supreme ambition was to find a really wealthy victim and retire from his nerve-wracking business. He never succeeded. He secured about forty thousand francs all told, and most of this was obtained at Vernouillet. At Gambais by comparison he did very badly and was always hard-up. He hunted the Héons and the Marchadiers because he could get nothing better, and the fable of his catholic and invincible charm is merely an essential ingredient of the legend.

What was his mode of murder? One of his few indiscretions was committed when he was taken down to Gambais by the police. When the bodies of Madame Pascal's cat and the dogs were dug up, they were found to have been strangled by string nooses. When he was asked why he had adopted that method, he replied that it was the most merciful way. Strangling is, of course, a most agonising death. Why did he tell that dangerous lie? How did he know anything about it? Remember too, the waxed strings found amongst his possessions, which, once they have encircled the victim, automatically do their work. The police, of course, received many anonymous letters and one signed, 'Alberte' stated that the writer having been imprudent enough to visit Landru at Gambais, found a small cord twisted into a lassoo under the bolster. There was also the tale of another flighty female who made a similar discovery. One is inclined to suspect their authenticity, for there were many would-be wits who thought it a good joke to mislead the police. But there is little doubt that Landru used this easy, swift and bloodless method.

The problem of his disposal of the bodies is the great puzzle in the case. Firstly, it must be emphasised that he *did* dispose of them somehow. This sounds excessively obvious, but in France there was and still is a school of thought, if it can be dignified by that term, which ridicules all the methods suggested. At the trial evidence was given, and firmly adhered to, that at certain times, both at Vernouillet and Gambais, the most pestilential and stinking black smoke came from the villas and caused much curious comment. And human bones were found in the stove. Furthermore, experiments were made with it, and it was shown that it would consume surprising quantities of meat in a short time. There is not the slightest doubt that Landru could have ridded himself of parts of his victims by this means, and there is the strongest evidence that he did so. Those who ridicule this evidence seem merely perverse and frivolous.

Again, there are several large, deep lakes and ponds in the Gambais district, and testimony was given at the trial that pieces of human flesh and in one case a whole body in a sack, were either hooked by fishermen or observed from the bank. It may be remarkable that such discoveries were not reported to the police at the time, but the French country people are notoriously adverse to minding other people's business if a visit from a gendarme or public ridicule may result from so doing. A most reputable witness, an army doctor, stated that one evening after passing the Villa Hermitage from the chimney of which foul smoke was pouring, he was overtaken by a little man with a long beard who, thinking he was unobserved, drew a large parcel from the small lorry he was driving and threw it into the *Étang des Bruyères*, a large pond near Gambais. There was no known murder about this time, but who can doubt that it was Landru? The scoffers want to know how he, who had no knowledge of anatomy, managed to cut up these bodies so adroitly. Well, a battered saw was found in the Villa Hermitage and practice makes more or less perfect even in the dismembering of bodies.

It is possible that Landru employed other methods both of murder and disposal—he may have buried portions in the big woods round Gambais, but it is as certain as anything can be in this doubtful world that Landru strangled some of his victims, burnt parts of them and threw the less combustible portions into ponds and lakes. Nevertheless, it is a perplexing fact that Landru was able to solve the greatest problem which confronts the murderer, not once, but ten times. When it was searched, no suspicious circumstance whatsoever was found at The Lodge, and though a considerable time had elapsed since he was there, it is remarkable, for it was the scene of four of his murders.

When he was arrested it is known Landru was hoping to inveigle another woman to Gambais within a few hours. Yet when it was closely examined, the villa revealed not the slightest trace of preparation for another murder. Landru took his secret—perhaps quite a simple one—to the grave, but he will always be remembered for having solved almost to perfection the murderer's hardest problem. It is quite certain he worked alone. He seems not to have had one single male acquaintance. That horrid spider spun his web and snared his prey without assistance, in its way a considerable achievement. He was a known criminal on the badly wanted list. His appearance was perilously distinctive. The victims he chose had in several cases suspicious, intelligent and energetic relatives. Yet he kept his liberty for five years and committed eleven major crimes in that period. But it is significant that once the Paris police resumed their peace-time efficiency Landru was soon picked up, and his crimes proved against him. The war had finished too soon for him.

Part 2

KILLING FOR REVENGE

EDWARD H. SMITH

Cordelia Botkin's Candy

The terror of poison must be vastly older than civilization, older than the first false dawn of human knowledge. The grazing herbivore avoids noxious weeds and grasses and makes long expeditions in quest of fresh water, when the usual source of drink has been polluted. The more intelligent carnivores can be got to take poisoned bait only under the stress of irresistible hunger, and even the humble and pestiferous sparrow is not easily beguiled with arsenated or strychnized grain. Ancient experience has taught the beast and bird to shrink from the secret and mysterious agents of death.

Man must have come by his primitive knowledge in the same way. Long before he can have assumed the characteristics that are now generally described as human, the members of the genus assuredly suffered countless tragedies as the result of contacting and eating baneful herbs, berries, shrubs, and fruits, into whose fibres the heartless mother, Nature, had infused her furious distillates. Generation after generation the ancestors of the race must have seen their fellows writhe in sudden torment and sicken and die mysteriously. Such deaths were not as the ordinary results of wounds and accidents and creeping age. There was about them the black cloud of unfamiliarity, inexplicability, and occultness. Perhaps, as some students of primitive psychology assert, the dawn men interpreted these phenomena as the work of demons and spirits and saw in them the workings of some malevolent will or force of evil. Certainly, however, man came in time to connect the results with the proper causes and to remember and avoid the sources of his undoing. So the first notes on poisons came to be formulated on the tablets of the aboriginal mind.

What use man made of this tragically acquired learning, once he had clawed and fought and bled his way to the purlieus of the civilized state is the material of a sinister history. In the lowest savage cultures ever studied the attitude toward vegetable and some other poisons has already changed from a negative to a positive one. The juices of noxious plants are used to tip the arrows and darts, while the venom of serpents and marine animals, such as the sting ray, is smeared upon knives and spears or upon the points of sharpened reeds and sticks set into the path of the advancing foe. The shaman, the medicine-man, and the barbarian king have learned how to put doubters, rebels, and rivals out of the way with secret extracts and preparations; how to throw subjects into spasms, slumbers and maniac moods; or how to rob the warrior of his caution and goad him to desperate courage with strange ferments and subtle electuaries.

Indeed, poison early in history becomes the strong and terrible ally of princes and of states, though it also displays a more than occasional turning upon its lords, and in some epochs seems more occupied in emptying than in preserving thrones. In Athens the hemlock was the portion of political and social offenders. In Rome a whole assortment of poisons, usually self-selected and administered, was at hand for the loser in any close struggle for power. Mithradates of Pontus tried to immunize himself against the effects of poisons, of which he stood in constant dread, and the official food-tasting slave has been an important and unfortunate functionary at the table of many a tyrant, Eastern and Western.

My purpose is not to attempt even the briefest sketch of poison history, for the subject is too complex and vast. The real purpose of these remarks is to show the strange working by which poisons have continually evolved out of the hands of the strong or the dominant into those of the weak or subject. Used first by lords and potentates to awe the ignorant and destroy the dangerous, they almost invariably succeeded in passing into the hands of plotters and regicides. As a matter of fact, such instruments of murder belong properly to the equipment of the frail and timid, to those who have not the strength or the courage to measure themselves with their foes in open and 'honourable' combat. It is, accordingly, not surprising to find that poison has been in all times the favourite weapon of women. Its use by them has, at various times and in many lands, been so common as to have created special legislative enactments, peculiar political situations, and even the formulation of ritualistic usages and social customs.

Suttee or widow burning, which even to-day has not quite disappeared in India, in spite of vigorous British action for its repression and a most industrious campaign of education, extending over a whole century, is the most striking example of this last phenomenon. Suttee was a quite inexplicable custom until Western students began to penetrate into the conditions of earlier Indian life. It was soon found that in this land of mysterious and subtle poisons, some of which are still said to be strangers to the pharmacopoeia, enslaved womanhood had habitually resorted to the employment of those most silent, effective, and accessible weapons which demand of their user no strength and very little skill. Older and otherwise undesirable husbands were perishing in great numbers at the hands of youthful and errant wives. Poison vendors were prowling every lane and skulking in every thicket. Despairing of any palliative measures, the dominant maleness of India decreed that every widow must expire on her husband's funeral pyre, and every man's friends and neighbours saw to it that the rule was inexorably enforced. Husband poisoning rapidly declined as a feminine vagary, but the custom of suttee remained for many centuries after its origin and significance had been lost.

Similarly in Italy and France, in the late seventeenth and early eighteenth centuries, there were epidemics of husband and lover poisonings, and there arose several organized schools of women poisoners. In France the climax of the drama was reached in the career of the celebrated Marquise de Brinvilliers, who is so well known that she requires no

more than a reference. Almost as notorious was the great
Neapolitan poison lady, the dread Toffana. She is said to
have begun her career in Palermo in 1650, when she was
a girl. In 1659 she was certainly well established in Naples,
whence she sent out her famous liquid in little vials which
bore the name or picture of St. Nicholas of Bari, the patron
of a healing spring. Her product she called 'The Manna of
St. Nicholas of Bari,' 'Aquetta di Napoli' or 'Aqua Toffana.'
It was advertised as a cosmetic and cure for blotches and
pimples, for which purpose it probably was useful, since
it was simply a distillate of arsenic. Thus, in the guise
of a saintly panacea or a harmless cosmetic, this dreadful
poison was freely distributed among women of the upper
or prosperous classes in southern Italy. At least six hundred
poisonings were finally traced to Toffana's magical water,
nearly all the victims having been inconvenient husbands,
long-lived relatives who stood in the way of inheritances,
rivals or lovers whose fancy had begun to stray. Toffana
took refuge in a convent, but she was dragged forth by
the temporal authorities in 1709, over the bitter protests
of the Church, which resented the invasion of its right of
domicilage. She was strangled and thrown into the courtyard
of the holy house from which she had been taken. And her
death was naturally followed by the wholesale executions of
ladies who had used her products.

   The successors of La Toffana were many. One of the most
remarkable of them was Hieronyma Spara, the head of a
secret society of women in Rome, most of its members being
young wives of the aristocratic class. It was soon discovered
that the Spara woman was reputed to be a sorceress, and that
she thrived by supplying the no doubt lovely members of her
society with poisons for the removal of spousal afflictions.
She was tortured on the rack, without revealing anything;
but one of her younger and softer votaries, yielding to the
agonies of the inquisition, revealed the whole plot and was
hanged together with the sorceress and twelve other ladies
of the haut monde.

   With so much of the background of the feminine employment of toxic weapons before us, we may skip the intervening

and arresting spaces of time and come down at once to modernity.

On the afternoon of August 9, 1898, the little grandson of ex-Congressman John Pennington of Delaware, went to the post office of the capital city of Dover and took home to the family a number of letters and a small package which had come from San Francisco by registered mail, addressed to the boy's aunt, Mrs John P. Dunning.

After the evening meal the family appeared on the front porch, with the evening newspaper, the late mail, and the package from California. Mrs Dunning glanced at the headlines and saw that there was no arresting news. Cervera's squadron had been destroyed more than a month before, and Santiago had surrendered two weeks later. In Porto Rico, where her husband was sojourning as the war correspondent for the Associated Press, there was little more of fighting and consequently little danger to the gentlemen of the press. Mrs Dunning passed the newspapers to the others and turned her attention to the package which had come to her through the mails.

It proved to be, when cleared of its wrappings, a box containing chocolate creams, above which was laid a new handkerchief and a bit of notepaper on which an unfamiliar hand had written: 'Love to yourself and baby. Mrs C.'

Mrs Dunning regarded the note with perplexity. She had numerous friends in San Francisco, for she had lived in California for several years; but she could not recall a 'Mrs C.' Neither could she identify the handwriting, but that gave her no pause. She had left the West a number of years before to return to the roof of her father in Dover, and it might easily be that some old friend had thought of her after a long lapse and decided to send her a little reminder. She tucked the handkerchief into her bosom, thought kindly of the unknown friend in San Francisco, and passed the candy to her sister, Mrs Deane, and to the Deane children.

While these four were nibbling the candies on the veranda, two young women of the neighbourhood passed by under the trees and were asked to join. They were the Misses Bateman and Millington, and each ate two or three pieces of chocolate creams. Then they went their way on an errand. The children, too, were not permitted to have more than a very little. The creams were rich and not good for young stomachs. But Mrs Dunning and Mrs Deane placed no such restrictions on themselves. They sat late, chatting and munching at the gift candies. At last they rose and went to bed.

In the middle of the night Mrs Dunning was awakened by cramps and an overpowering nausea. She pulled herself out of bed and staggered toward the bathroom, only to find her sister and the two children ahead of her, likewise in pain.

As the sufferers grew cold and weak, a doctor was sent for, and the two women and two children were packed off to bed, treated with the stomach pump, and plied with antidotes and stimulants. In the morning it was found that the Misses Millington and Bateman had been similarly afflicted, and the connection between the seizures and the box of candy was established.

The young ladies and the children recovered, but on the eleventh Mrs Deane died, and on the twelfth Mrs Dunning. Autopsies revealed lethal quantities of arsenic in the viscera of both, and pieces of the candy, when submitted to a chemist, were found to be impregnated with the deadly white salt.

John P. Dunning was immediately summoned home from Porto Rico, and an investigation of the affair begun. The father of the dead women and their other relatives in Dover were alike mystified. That either Mrs Dunning or Mrs Deane, or, for that matter, any other member of the family should have a mortal enemy capable of filling candy with poison, seemed entirely out of the question. Yet ex-Congressman Pennington eventually recalled that Mrs Dunning had received an anonymous letter a good many months before from San Francisco, in which she was told that her husband, who was then doing newspaper work at the Golden Gate, was having an affair with another woman. Mr Pennington felt certain that the note in the box of candy and the anonymous letter of earlier date had been written by the same hand. Such a recognition was regarded as an almost hopeless clue.

Things were in this state of befuddlement when Mr Dunning arrived from the West Indies, took one look at the slip of paper, with its few friendly words, and declared that he knew who had written it, and who had sent the candy. Broken with grief and abased with shame, the husband of one of the two victims of this infamous poisoner began a long and strange story which was made more difficult by the fact that it was, in the main, a confession of his own peccadillos.

Dunning had married Miss Mary Pennington in February, 1891, at her father's home in Dover, and soon afterward he had taken her to San Francisco, where he was employed. There, in the following year, a little daughter was born, and there, too, by a chance meeting in a park was laid the first stone of this tragical structure.

On a dateless, but well-remembered afternoon in the summer of 1892, Dunning went strolling in Golden Gate Park, with his eyes not turned altogether inward, nor his heart fixed quite exclusively on his wife and the little inheritor of his name. A woman sat on a bench in the tingling sunshine, gaily clad, indolent and inviting. She looked at him with provocative eyes, and he raised his brows and his hat. She did not deny him, and there was a meeting.

The woman, who proved to be more maturely alluring than youthful, told her chance admirer that she was Mrs Curtis and blessed with a husband who had considerately betaken himself to England. Later, when she came to know Dunning better, she confided to him that she had beguiled him a little in the beginning. She was really Mrs Cordelia Botkin, and her spouse, far from having crossed any seas, was no further away than Stockton, where he lived with his and her nearly grown son. Quite palpably there was a rift in the domestic lute, for she went seldom to the San Jaoquin Valley, and her presumptive lord and master came not to San Francisco. She was thus free to conduct an affair with Dunning, and this she did.

She took a room in a house in Geary Street, and Dunning, deaf to the urgings of conscience and morals, provided himself with quarters in the same building, that he might be convenient to his charmer. This open relationship was, of course, not possible until after Mrs Dunning had got out of the way. He appears to have met the woman only clandestinely for a good many months. Then, however, his wife took the baby and went back to Dover. She had suspected, if she had not been able to prove, her husband's indiscretions, and she was weary of his neglect. The husband seems to have offered no objections to her return to her father's roof in Delaware.

Indeed, as soon as the wife was gone East, he was openly with Mrs Botkin almost daily, at race tracks, restaurants, theatres, and in other public places, and the two resided together in Geary Street, as already described.

This association, strangely enough, continued for more than five years, and it was not until toward the end that Dunning apparently turned his eyes outward upon still other women and showed a cooling toward the charmer who had displaced his wife and child.

On March 8, 1898, almost six years after his meeting with Mrs Botkin, Dunning made the break. On that day he was appointed war correspondent by the Associated Press and ordered to depart at once for Porto Rico. The same night he broke the news to Mrs Botkin, and she insisted on going with him, even on accompanying him to the West Indies. Dunning, now thoroughly finished with this romance and probably more interested elsewhere, resorted to the inevitable frankness of satiety, which figures so largely in femininely conceived novels as downright brutality. He told the lady bluntly that he was going alone, that he would never return to California, that he hoped to make up with his wife—in short, that he was done. She followed him tearfully across the bay to his train and left him only after a scene.

Dunning repeated all this to his father-in-law and the authorities in Dover, deploring and lamenting, as he recited. He had never dreamed that the woman bore his wife any malice; that she was capable of a crime; that she might resort to such diabolism. But the handwriting was unmistakable.

A detective was immediately sent from Dover to San Francisco, where he went to work with the California police. Mrs Botkin was arrested in Stockton, where she had been living with her husband and son for some time, a reconciliation having evidently been effected after the departure of Dunning for the war. She was locked in the county jail, and the investigation of her acts went forward with astonishing rapidity. On the day after her arrest, the detectives found that the candy had been bought in the shop of one George Haas, who conducted a sweets store in Market Street. Two of his clerks, both young women, immediately identified Mrs Botkin as the woman who had bought the box of candy of them some ten days before its delivery in Dover. They specially recalled that she had asked to have it put into a fancy box, not containing the name of the store, and that she wanted the box not quite filled, as she wished to enclose something else.

Mrs Botkin, if it was she, had planned so poorly that she had even neglected to remove the tag from the handkerchief. Accordingly this enclosure was easily traced to a linen shop, where the clerks also identified Mrs Botkin as the purchaser.

A woman who was acquainted with Mrs Botkin came forward and testified that she recalled a conversation, late in July, in the course of which Mrs Botkin had inquired about the effects of various poisonous drugs, and had also asked if one needed to sign his name in sending a registered package through the mail.

Next, a porter and a clerk of the Hotel Victoria, where Mrs Botkin had been living for months after Dunning's departure, went to the prosecutor with a torn piece of gilt seal, which they had found in room 26, occupied by Mrs Botkin. This seal, it was shown, had come from the Haas candy store and had been used on the box of candy when she bought it.

Handwriting experts also were called in, and they decided that the lettering on the note sent to Mrs Dunning was the same as that shown in various love-letters written to her husband and signed by Mrs Botkin.

By a peculiarity of fate, one of those unforeseeable and miraculous-seeming coincidences, which have so often betrayed the most subtle of criminals, another link in the chain of evidence was formed. At the ferry post office in San Francisco was a clerk named John Dunnigan. On August 4, he had received the registered package and had remembered it clearly because the addressee, Mrs John Dunning, possessed a name so much like his own. It was shown that Mrs Botkin had left San Francisco for St. Helena on the day the package was mailed, and that she was therefore likely to have stopped at the ferry post office to mail the deadly gifts.

Finally, however, came one Frank Grey, a druggist employed in the Owl Drug Store, who identified Mrs Botkin as the woman who had bought two ounces of white arsenic from him some time before the events related, saying that she wanted to clean a hat with it. He had offered her other substances and mixtures, which he had told her were better fitted for her purpose, but she had insisted on the arsenic.

All this evidence was piled up before the trial as grounds for asking the extradition of the accused woman from California to Delaware. When it came to the point of removing her from the State, however, her attorney interposed the objection that she was not a fugitive from the Eastern State. On this pleading it was decided that she must be tried in California.

The trial was called on the morning of December 9, 1898, exactly four months after the receipt of the poisoned candy in Dover. Mrs Botkin's attorney made a spirited defence, trying first to show that identification was a weak kind of testimony, and, second, to impeach Dunning and cast the blame upon him. The cross-questioning of the errant husband of the victim reached dramatic proportions when, on December 19, he was commanded to give the names of other women besides Mrs Botkin with whom he had been intimate, he having admitted the impeachment. Dunning refused to answer, though commanded to do so by the court. He was thereupon committed to jail for contempt and remained incarcerated some days till the question was withdrawn. All this fireworks display availed nothing, however. Mrs Botkin was convicted on the last day of the year save one, and on February 4, 1899, she was sentenced to prison for the rest of her life.

Under the system in vogue in California in those days, it was not necessary for a woman to serve a prison sentence in the State's prisons at Folsom or San Quentin, especially where an appeal was pending. The servitude might be endured at any jail in the county of conviction. So it happened that Cordelia Botkin was permitted to begin her term in the branch of the county jail where she had been held pending and during her trial. Here another extraordinary thing happened.

One Sunday afternoon some months after the conviction of Mrs Botkin, Judge Cook of the superior court, who had sat on the case, was riding on a street car toward a cemetery, where his wife had recently been buried. On boarding the car he was astonished to see a woman whom he unhesitatingly identified as Mrs Botkin. He was hardly able to believe his senses. Surely, a woman supposed to be serving a sentence of unending imprisonment for murder, would not be out riding on a street car in her best finery. At least, if there was a legal reason for her being at large, she would be accompanied by a guard. Since he saw no official near the woman, Judge Cook began to wonder whether she had escaped, or whether he had made a mistake in identification. He was, however, not long in doubt. As the car passed the branch of the county jail where Mrs Botkin was supposed to be locked away from the world for life, the woman on the car signalled for a stop and left the conveyance, followed at some distance by a man. Judge Cook did not think quickly enough to leave the car and was carried out of sight before he could make sure that the woman had entered the jail. But the jurist soon made his investigations and discovered further proof of the fascinations of the lethal lady.

It developed that she had woven her mysteries about two of her jailers and brought them obediently to heel, with the result that she occupied not a cell, but a suite of rooms in the county jail, was provided with special bedding, linen, and clothing, permitted to receive such visitors as she chose, on such terms as she dictated, and was daily supplied with meals from the outside, though she appears not to have had the means for such luxuries. The officials of the branch jail denied emphatically, however, that the Botkin, as the French would have called her, had been permitted outside the walls, a disavowal which the public and Judge Cook received with something more than polite scepticism.

However, the scandal soon was forgotten, and Cordelia Botkin continued in the enjoyment of her suite of jail rooms and the special comforts and provisions. She was awaiting action on her appeal, and nothing could be done. Finally, after she had reposed in expectation for five years and more, the supreme court of California found that the trial judge had instructed the jury to the effect that circumstantial evidence was in fact superior to direct evidence, since there was likelihood of the latter having been fabricated. This was construed by the appeals bench as an expression as to the weight of the evidence by the judge, and thus a prejudice to the defendant, before the jury. A retrial was accordingly ordered. It terminated on August 2, 1904, in the reconviction of the guilty woman.

She was again returned to the branch jail and her commodious quarters, while a second appeal was carried to the supreme court, which was not decided against her until the fall of 1908, almost ten years after her original conviction. Meantime, however, the earthquake and fire, which devastated San Francisco, had swept away, among other elder glories, the main county jail. As a result, the branch jail became crowded, and Mrs Botkin was eventually forced to give up her comforts. She then requested on her own responsibility that she be taken to San Quentin Prison, and this transfer was made in May of 1906. A little less than four years later she died in the old grey prison house of 'softening of the brain, due to melancholy,' as you may read from the record written by some average incompetent prison medico.

The inner marvel of this unusual case has still to be revealed. It is to be found in the personality, behaviour, and strange powers of the killer herself.

When Cordelia Botkin sat in Golden Gate Park that afternoon and caught the eye of the young and recreant newspaper man and war correspondent, she was already a woman to whom the apparition of the fortieth year was an imminent spectre. She was, in fact, arrived at an unblushing thirty-eight, and time had laid upon her the unkind stigmata of full-blown maturity.

She had been a wife since 1872, in which year she had married at Kansas City a man bearing the name of Welcome A. Botkin, she having been born Cordelia Brown of Brownsville, Nebraska, a town which had taken its name from her pioneering father. Botkin was for long an official of the Missouri Valley Bank in Kansas City, and his wife enjoyed those social distinctions which accrue to a banker's spouse in small towns, such as was the Kansas City of those days. In the later eighties, Botkin, with his wife and their son, had gone to California and settled at Stockton. Whether any earlier romancing on the part of the lady induced this westward trek does not appear, and perhaps it does not matter.

What is significant is that, a woman in the cold and constricting clutch of middle age, she was able to attract a man her junior by at least a decade; to win him from his wife and child and to hold him close for upward of six years, until she was in the inexorable declension of her forty-fourth year. Worse yet—for years afterward, until she was all of fifty-two years old, she was able tc turn men giddily about her capricious will, even in the seclusion of a jail with the mark of Cain on her head and the Borgian adder in her breast.

The Botkin case, aside from its intrinsic interest, is a first-rate warrant of confirmation in the hands of the modern criminologist of the medical school. For her final collapse into brain deterioration and dementia is evidence that she was abnormal and unbalanced at the time of her crime, and the age at which she resorted to murder—forty-four—corresponds exactly with the glandular theory of criminal behaviour, for it is at this precise period in a woman's life that her endocrine system is inevitably in the process of severe disturbance, and hence at this stage that she is most likely to commit acts of aberration and desperation.

Part 3

KILLING FOR CONVENIENCE

LEO GREX

Passion that Passed for Love

'Can I help you?' inquired the pretty girl with a pleasing smile.

The man looked at her. He seemed hesitant and unsure of himself as he stopped at the airport counter. Then, under the girl's scrutiny, he seemed to make up his mind.

'I want to book a passage for my wife on tomorrow's flight,' he said.

'Of course, sir,' she said encouragingly, and then paused. She turned to a page in her flight book, and said, 'I'm sorry, sir. All flights are booked until the 9th, but it's just possible we might get a cancellation.' She peered at the page of figures and times and made a helpful suggestion. 'If you like I'll put your wife's name on a waiting list I have. Then she can be assured of a seat on the first available flight.'

The man nodded. Lucille Levesque worked at the ticket counter at Ancienne Lorette Airport, Quebec. As she reached for her passenger list for the next day, September 7th, 1949, she quickly scanned it and wrote down Rita Guay, the name the man had given her. As she looked up the man asked a question.

'Can you also tell me how I can take out insurance for the trip?' Again he hesitated, like a man not conversant with details and regulations. 'For instance, if something happens on the flight, who will be the beneficiary?'

The bright-eyed French–Canadian girl was used to similar questions from puzzled travellers.

'You of course, Mr Guay, as your wife's husband, naturally. Do you want to fill out an insurance form?'

The man's eyes dropped from the girl's inquiring face. His chin went up and down in a brusque nod.

'In that case I suppose I'd best take out a policy,' he conceded.

He felt for his money and paid the premium on a one-flight policy for insurance valued at ten thousand dollars. The policy was on the traveller's life and was not for the round trip, which would have included the return journey. Whoever Mr Guay was, he seemed to be careful with money. With the insurance policy stamped, and the receipt safe in his pocket, he thanked Lucille Levesque, accepted another of her smiles, and left the airport building. Later he had a 'phone call from her, for she had taken the customer's telephone number.

'I'm pleased to tell you, Mr Guay, that I've had a cancellation for tomorrow,' she said in her pleasant voice. 'I can now accommodate Mrs Guay after all.'

The reply she received was not pleasant, and it was certainly surprising.

'Too late,' snapped the man who had been anxious to book for the flight. 'We'll have to make it the day you originally suggested, September 9th.'

'Very well, Mr Guay,' said the booking clerk, still trying to sound pleasant. 'In that case I'll cancel the cancellation and let September 9th stand. Thank you, sir.'

She rang off and forgot the indecisive man at the airport who had originally booked too late for his wife's flight, while in her home Mrs Guay was packing in preparation for the local flight. Her husband seemingly had other matters to attend to, and it was not until early on the morning of the 9th that he called on a certain Mrs Petri. The couple eyed each other as will people who have been lovers and know what it means for passion and desire to wane like an unfed fire.

The woman couldn't resist a feminine taunt about the past.

'I haven't seen much of you since you fell for that young angel, Joseph,' she observed.

The man scowled. He had no wish to quarrel about Angel Mary. Besides, they had been all through that a good while ago, and each knew where the other stood. He came to the point, as was his way when he wanted something, for he was a selfish man and acquisitive.

'I want you to do something for me, Marie.'

'Any reason?' inquired Marie Petri archly.

'Reason enough. I can't do it myself.'

'What is it, Joseph?'

'I want you to take a parcel to the airport for me. I can't make time myself. It's a religious statuette.'

The glances of the pair clashed in a duel of understanding, and perhaps perception on the part of the woman.

'I'm too sick to go, Joseph,' she said, trying to make it a flat refusal.

But there was more than understanding in the man's grin. There was knowledge.

'You won't be, Marie, if I cancel those promissory notes of yours,' he said nastily. 'They're locked up in the bank, so you be well enough to take the parcel for me, and then you can forget about those notes.'

Marie Petri appeared to make a remarkable recovery from her alleged bout of sickness, for she knew that Joseph Guay held her indeed over a barrel, and she had no alternative but to do what he wanted.

'Very well, Joseph,' she agreed demurely, but there was thought and speculation in her eyes.

It was some time later when she summoned a taxi and told the driver, Paul Pelletier, to go to the airport as she had a parcel. He saw that it was packed for air freight as he put it down on the front seat. He drove to the airport, where his passenger, dressed soberly in black, plumpish and with a turned-up nose, paid off Pelletier and marched off with the package to the weighing counter for freight. The parcel was weighed, the description checked—'a religious statuette'—the freight cost was paid and receipted, and the package placed with other articles going out on that day's flight. The plump woman in black walked away from the weighing counter. She made her way home, still thoughtful.

Some time later Joseph Guay and his dark-complexioned wife Rita arrived at the airport. Mrs Guay hurried through the glass door to the booking clerk, and received one of Lucille

Levesque's bright and engaging smiles of welcome.

'I shall be able to return later today, shan't I?' asked the dark woman with the Spanish look. She seemed anxious to make sure that her return was arranged. Lucille shook her head dubiously.

'I very much doubt it, Mrs Guay.'

The dark woman turned quickly to her husband, who was close behind her, and said in some alarm, 'In that case I shall have to cancel the trip, Joseph, if I can't get back.'

But this time Mr Guay was wearing a smile of his own. Both his words and manner were gently persuasive as Lucille Levesque heard him say to his wife, 'You must make the trip now it is booked and paid for, Rita. After all, if you can't get back, what does it matter? I can join you, and we can have a few days together. Don't you think that would be nice?'

The dark woman smiled in her turn and thought that would be very nice. Both husband and wife turned away from the ticket bureau as the call came for passengers to make their way to the waiting aircraft. Joseph kissed his wife and watched Rita walk to join the queue forming to go into the aircraft waiting on the tarmac. Soon the idling engines were revving up. The 'plane was a Dakota of Canadian Pacific Airlines, and the luggage had already been stowed and secured and the freight manifest cleared. The passengers were climbing into their seats. One group of men who kept together were American millionaires, all directors in a large US copper combine with considerable properties in Canada.

Joseph watched the blur of faces through the small windows as the doors were fastened. He waited for the 'plane to take-off, a curious feeling of mixed emotions possessing him. Occasionally he shifted his stance, but kept gazing at the aircraft as though willing it to become airborne. He stared at his watch.

Five minutes dragged by before the Dakota at last began to taxi down the runway. So it was five minutes late in getting away. Joseph Guay was perspiring as he turned his back on the September sunshine. He left the airport at a smart pace, the quizzical expression on his face rather anticipatory.

He was still on his way home when the Dakota blew up in mid-air. The wrecked aircraft nosed out of control, diving for the thick belt of forest land near Sault-au-Cochon, some forty miles beyond Quebec.

The first newsflash of the disaster reached the city an hour later. Joseph Guay, strangely, seemed rather like a man waiting impatiently for the terrible news. He hurried with his small daughter Lise, who was only five, to the airport. He was among the first of the group of anxious relatives bombarding the airline officials with questions.

He pushed his way forward to where a shocked Lucille Levesque had lost her customary smile, which was now replaced by a look of strain.

'Is the news true?' Joseph Guay inquired anxiously. 'Has there been a mistake—another 'plane—'

He broke off uncertainly.

'I'm sorry,' said Lucille in a dull voice. 'It's only too true.'

At that Joseph Guay appeared to break down. It was quite a histrionic performance. He clutched with groping hands at his small daughter, and surrendered himself to a grief that sounded and seemed inconsolable. He was so overcome that he had to be escorted to the Hôtel Château Frontenac, where he had a room booked for him. In his grief he seemed incapable of taking proper care of either himself or the little girl with him.

Perhaps that is why someone thoughtfully sent for a priest to render what solace and comfort he could to the husband and the wide-eyed child. Joseph was most assuredly not acting like a man who would benefit from the air disaster to the extent of ten thousand dollars.

Reports of the crashed aircraft claimed it had gone down in one of the most inaccessible places in the province, and eventually it took a team of tough backwoodsmen working many hours to reach the wreck and bring out the twenty-three bodies. The tragic disaster was headline news throughout North America, and Canadian Pacific Airlines lost no time in getting experts onto the task of deciding the cause of the fatal accident. They were faced with claims amounting to millions of dollars.

The experts worked day and night without respite and in bad conditions. They started with the power units, for ground witnesses of the disaster claimed to have heard the engines running after the sound of the actual explosion in the sky. It seemed there was mystery to be explained. They found no sign of failure in the engines. Moreover, the state of the ground where the nose of the aircraft had ploughed into it suggested the airscrews were still turning at the moment of impact. In fact, the only sign of fire and scorched metal was in the freight compartment. Twisted pieces of metal from various parts of the freight compartment were cut out by oxy-acetylene, and some items of the baggage and freight were examined and chemically tested.

The chemists produced a shock for the airline company. They discovered minute traces of dynamite.

The accident, in short, had been no accident, but deliberate sabotage, which in turn meant multiple murder. But who could be capable of such a ghastly mass murder? It was a crime that had shocked the whole of Canada.

The mystery of what had happened to the Dakota, and why, was in due course handed over to the police. Detectives who had battled their way to the scene of the wreckage began their investigation by checking every consignment of freight against its listing on the company manifest. They also checked every passenger's background. They covered all freight except a single package consigned to New York and listed as a religious statuette. It had been boxed and wrapped in a brown paper parcel, and its weight was twenty-six pounds. An appeal to the woman who had delivered the package to the freight counter to come forward was broadcast. It was known she had been dressed in black.

Ten days after the disaster she had not been traced.

But on the tenth day Paul Pelletier came forward with a story about picking up a passenger for the airport. This passenger had been dressed in black. He gave the police the address of the house where he had collected her. It was found to be the home of Marie Petri, but when the Quebec detectives called it was to learn that Mrs Petri was in hospital. She was recovering from the effects of a large dose of sleeping pills she had taken, which could have been an attempt to commit suicide.

When she was able to talk to the officers at her bedside she looked scared and very subdued. When they asked questions she told them the story of being asked to take the religious figurine to the airport. The police probing continued until she told them about the promissory notes that were to be cancelled. The probing detectives learned that for a period of years Marie Petri had been the mistress of Joseph Albert Guay, a Quebec jeweller who was thirty-two years old. He had been latterly attracted to the charms of a younger and undeniably lovely girl named Marie-Ange Robitaille, who had a preference for turning her French christian names into their English equivalents of Mary Angel. To Joseph Guay she had been just Angel.

Yet such are the inexplicable relationships between lovers and ex-lovers, that even when Guay was enraptured with his new love, the plump Marie Petri remained on passing good terms with him, despite the hint of blackmail in the matter of the bank-held promissory notes.

Suddenly the plump woman who had dallied with suicide broke down. She was plainly on the edge of an emotional collapse, and the police were not willing to plunge her into its depths. They waited until she had calmed down, when she said miserably, 'I didn't know his wife would be on that 'plane.'

The Quebec detectives exchanged significant glances. They sensed they were close to something even more startling, so on the point of relaxing they kept up their stream of questions, and learned that a few weeks before Guay had rung up his one-time mistress with a strange request. He had wanted her to purchase for him ten pounds of dynamite, and offered a glib explanation. He wanted the dynamite sticks for a Mrs Cote who was anxious to have some rocks blown out of the ground of a property she had in the country. Marie Petri had accordingly ordered twenty half-pound sticks of dynamite. Mrs Parent, a friend of Marie Petri, had collected the dynamite for her, and Marie Petri had taken it to the restaurant where she worked. Guay had come in and taken it away.

Later the police decided they knew the source of the explosive that had wrecked the Dakota over Sault-au-Cochon, but they remained curious as to why the informant had taken that overdose of sleeping pills.

She remained silent after explaining that Guay had shown her a newspaper relating the search for the mysterious woman in black who had left an alleged statuette at the Ancienne Lorette Airport.

Then she said, 'He told me I wouldn't get away with any tale about a statuette,' and she went on to the listening detectives, 'He said I wouldn't be hanged after turning this trick—at least not by the neck. But by the feet—to make me suffer longer. He told me the best thing I could do for myself would be to swallow some sleeping pills and turn on the gas. He even told me I had better write a note saying I'd blown up the 'plane because I was jealous of him.'

The detectives stared at the woman.

'That is what you did, Mrs Petri?' inquired the detective asking the questions.

'Oh, yes,' she said in a husky whisper. 'I certainly tried—because—because . . .'

But when the tears came she couldn't continue.

When she finally left hospital the reporters and photographers were waiting in an eager group for her story. Cameras clicked as she looked strangely birdlike in her black coat and sleek black skull-cap. She was quickly dubbed 'Madame Le Corbeau' by the French-language newspapers. The English-language journals followed suit, and in their columns she became known as 'Mrs Raven'. Once she realized how the publicity was treating her, she began demanding high prices for Press photographs. However, it was not long before the reporters and photographers were off on another scent for fresh copy.

The police had continued their inquiries and learned that Madame Le Corbeau had a crippled brother named Genereux Ruest, who was particularly adept at repairing fine mechanisms, such as clocks. This brother was paralysed from the waist down and had never walked. He propelled himself around in an invalid chair. Like his sister, he too had a story to tell. He told the police the Guay had come to see him about a week before the explosion aboard the Dakota. He had asked the cripple to make a time mechanism for him, rather like an alarm clock, that would detonate some dynamite.

According to the jeweller he wished to destroy some deep-rooted tree stumps. He had produced a clock face for the cripple to use as a time gauge. Ruest had fixed the mechanism as Guay had requested.

At this stage the police realized they had a case, for the mystery of what had happened to the destroyed 'plane could now be spelled out. Guay was arrested. The news was a sensation, and the cripple's contrivance supplied the Press with yet another label, for the mystery had now become 'The Love-Bomb Murder', and it was not to relinquish that title for many years.

Joseph Guay had sent more than twenty people to a terrible death just to be certain that he would be rid of the wife who stood between him and marriage to the woman who had inflamed his passion, the woman he called his Angel. When he appeared for the time in a Quebec court, in October 1949, the public seats were packed, and crowds stood and waited in the streets outside.

Indeed, so great was the crush that it became an ordeal for the Provincial Police to bring the prisoner safely through the throngs to the court building. They looked like men expecting trouble, for one young man of eighteen, whose father had died in the disaster, had made headlines by publicly announcing that he was intending to take summary vengeance on the multiple murderer. He was arrested in order to prevent him attempting to carry out his threat.

The excited crowds thronging through the hilly town chanted their repeated hate against the prisoner.

'The dead must be avenged!' they cried in time to the chanting.

When Guay appeared there was a mass surge forward, but luckily the ranks of police held steady, or there could well have been a riot.

Guay had been charged with murder, and Marie Petri had been charged with attempted suicide, which was enough to hold her on while the full legal position was worked out by busy lawyers.

When the magistrates' hearing opened a new sensation was provided when an acquaintance of the prisoner came forward to tell the court of a curious conversation he had had, together with an offer of five hundred dollars. This witness's name was Lucien Carreau. Like most persons involved in this incredible case of mystery and violence he was a French–Canadian; indeed, the whole case had a strange and remote quality that stamped it as un-English. It was a typical *crime passionnel*, but with a difference. That difference was to make it unique.

In evidence Carreau told the court how one day Guay had come to him and explained how he was having a bad time with his wife. The two men were in Carreau's car at the time and he was driving through Lower Quebec. From a pocket Guay removed a bottle of cherry brandy and a small bag. He offered them to his friend, explaining that cherry brandy was Rita's favourite liqueur. In the bag was poison. He wanted his friend to put the poison in the cherry brandy, and later to offer Rita a couple of drinks from the bottle.

The crowd in the well of the court gasped. The story was horribly consistent with others heard by the police and reported in the Press. It seemed that Joseph Guay was always on the lookout for a scapegoat to do his dirty work for him. In this case Carreau had turned to his companion and looked at him in amazement.

'Are you crazy?' he asked. 'I wouldn't get myself involved in such a racket.'

But Guay had persisted. He had offered a considerable bribe for his friend to join him in murder. However, Lucien Carreau had no outstanding promissory notes. His resistance to bribery could not be weakened. At the end of the car drive Guay still had his cherry brandy and his bag of poison.

There had been a minor sequel. When news of the Dakota crash had been broadcast, with pictures in the papers, Guay had again approached Carreau. This time the bribe was five times larger, as he wanted to buy his friend's silence. He was a man with a strange sense of relative values, probably because he placed an unreal one on his overwhelming passion for a younger woman with a face that drove him demented—he became obsessed with her. When he called on Carreau a second time with the increased bribe, his friend was becoming thoroughly scared by this business in which he had so nearly become involved through no wish of his own, and in which the other was still endeavouring to enmesh him.

'You can't buy me off, Joseph,' he had said bleakly.

Into court came another native of Quebec, Leopold Giroux, who had sold the sticks of dynamite to Mrs Petri. He was followed by Mrs Hector Parent, who had called for the parcel in order to oblige her friend Marie. The court of magistrates eventually decided that Guay had a case to answer, and he was formally committed for trial on the capital charge.

In the intervening months public interest in the case did not lag. 'The Love-Bomb Murder' continued to receive a wide cover-age, as did any word about Mary Angel, who was portrayed as a veritable heart-throb and pictured as a *femme fatale*. She had not been called to give evidence in the magistrates' hearing, so she was seen as a mystery woman to most newspaper readers.

But Mary Angel was to provide her own measure of sensation when she gave evidence at Guay's trial, which opened in March 1950 before Judge Sévigny, with a snow blizzard sweeping Quebec. The day it opened the old Palace of Justice was crowded to the doors and the people turned away huddled together in the biting cold. But they would not leave.

The gum-chewing jeweller appeared and was escorted into the dock. He was now seen as a morose figure with an indrawn gaze and restless hands. His suit was creased and crumpled and his black bow-tie drooped like a broken wing. The crowds that had expected an early sensation were not disappointed, for the paralysed cripple, Genereux Ruest, had disappeared, and Judge Sévigny was asked by the prosecution to issue a court order for the witness to be found and held in custody. He was at last found forty miles away, and duly appeared and told his story of the request from Guay and of the mechanism he had contrived. The defence promptly asserted that it was impossible to make such a contrivance, but Noel Dorion, representing the Crown, called Professor Lucien Gravel of Laval University to explain that such a mechanism was quite possible.

Handed an alarm clock, he demonstrated how the mechanism could detonate a home-made bomb, as used in the Dakota disaster. It took him ten minutes to remove the minute hand of the alarm clock and connect a fuse and dry-cell battery. The hour hand was placed close to a screwed-down terminal. When they made contact the fuse was blown. Professor Gravel was asked how much dynamite, used in this way, would destroy a Dakota.

'Ten pounds of dynamite detonated by such a mechanism,' he replied, 'would be enough to wreck the interior of the 'plane and knock everyone aboard unconscious.'

Carreau then made a reappearance and related to the court how, after the disaster, the prisoner had described the death of his wife as a good riddance and had mentioned holding an insurance policy on his dead wife's life. By this time everyone was straining to get a glimpse of nineteen-year-old Mary Angel Robitaille, who was a cigarette-seller in the Monte Carlo Night Club, where she had met Guay. The most curious *ménage à trois* had evolved when the jeweller and the cigarette girl became lovers. Until then Marie Petri, who had worked in a restaurant, had satisfied the demands of Guay's extra-marital passion. But after meeting the girl in the night club the philanderer's standards had changed. He thought of himself as passionately in love. He was responsible for Marie Petri having the commodious apartment where she lived, and he told her bluntly he wanted to let another woman occupy a room. After an argument she had given way, and just occasionally he had returned to enjoy the charms of the older woman.

However, when Mary Angel appeared she was not quite the novelty that had been expected; in photographic parlance, she had been over-exposed to Press and public alike. Sixteen when she first met Guay, they had become lovers when he said his wife failed to understand him. She had accompanied him to a guest-house in Dorchester Street, Montreal, but Rita Guay had discovered the liaison and demanded that the girl's father do something about it. However, it wasn't the father who acted, but the daughter. Mary Angel moved into the room in Marie Petri's apartment, and changed her name to Nicole Cote. Marie Petri moved out, and the girl became a prisoner of her demanding lover.

She told the court, 'He wanted to get a separation from his wife, but said things were tough because he could find no grounds. He said he was going to have her watched to see if she was going around with anyone. At last common sense took the place of love, and I tried to get away from him.'

She borrowed twenty pounds, intending to reach Montreal, telephone her parents, and go back to them.

'I actually got on the train,' she explained, 'and a Negro attendant was making up my bed when Albert came running up.'

He took her luggage, dragged her from the train and shoved her into a parked car. He removed her footwear and they drove back to her prison room. After what she called a terrible scene she told him she still wanted to leave him. He flung her gloves into the stove. In the morning he tried to make amends with kisses. But his violence was savage, she recalled.

'He bit you?' asked Judge Sévigny.

'In a way,' she replied almost inaudibly. 'The marks remained for a week afterwards. He said it was so that I should not go out.'

Guay was now seen as a loathsome sadist.

After a see-saw existence they patched up their differences and Mary Angel got another night-club job, but again Guay stormed into her life, this time holding a gun.

'I was so scared,' she told the court, 'that I again went away with him to the Seven Isles. We went by 'plane.'

But his innate cruelty and sadism again manifested itself. They quarrelled and he struck her a heavy blow and left her out all night during a violent storm. By this time the court might well have asked if Guay was mad. The next piece of testimony makes one wonder, for after the girl had 'phoned her parents to ask them to send her money Guay had given her a letter. It was headed: 'To be thrown away after reading.' It was a wild protestation of his love in which he promised that he would soon be free of marriage.

It could be that the 'plane trip to the Seven Isles had sparked a fiendish plot in his mind, and he was certainly unbalanced. He told the girl that he wouldn't be able to see her until she was twenty-one, and asked her to wait for him, but by then he had something else to think about. Murder.

The defence put Mary Angel through a meat-grinder, and the grinding became very close-meshed when Mr Gerald Levesque asked her point-blank, 'Was that the first time you had relations with men—with Guay?'

'No,' whispered a very subdued witness.

But her morals, or lack of them, could not materially change the case as it affected the prisoner, and the jury seemed restless and ready to have the case concluded. They were absent only twenty minutes before returning with a verdict of guilty. The crowd seemed stunned, but Judge Sévigny told them, 'You have given a good verdict.' To the prisoner he said, 'For hatred of your wife, and as the result of your passion for your young mistress, you have perpetrated a diabolical, infamous crime.'

It was March 14th that Joseph Albert Guay, who preferred his mistress to call him by his second name, heard the sentence of death delivered, but he did not meet the hangman until January 10th, 1951.

He was only one of three who were executed for the wrecking of the Dakota. Marie Petri and her crippled brother had both been arrested and charged with complicity in the crime. By then the police had uncovered fresh evidence to satisfy a jury that they knew they were abetting a murderer. Ruest died on the scaffold where his sister's former lover had stood eighteen months before. A year later Madame Le Corbeau felt the hangman's noose tighten around her plump neck and suddenly realized that lust and love sometimes assume shapes of terror.

Death at Her Elbow

As a writer of mystery fiction, I have learned that there is a basic formula for the classic murder. The victim must be likeable, someone whose death occasions honest mourning. The murderer must be seeking to gain something—money, power, a woman, vengeance—something which for one terrible moment of his being turns him into judge, jury, and executioner.

There must be evidence of the crime. Not an eye-witness, but circumstantial evidence which, if pieced together properly, will be the instrument of justice. And the detective who enters the case must be capable of understanding the evidence.

It sounds easy, wrapping that formula up in a story, but it isn't. Not in fiction, anyway. But in real life a case will suddenly explode, whirl a handful of people in a gruesome dance of death for a brief moment, and then, when all is quiet again, show that it fits every requirement for the classic murder.

That's what happened one incredible midsummer week in 1934 at Harvey's Lake, a quiet resort spot near Wilkes-Barre, Pennsylvania. It started with some children happily drifting on the lake in an old row-boat.

The boat was almost on top of the body when the children first saw it. It was the body of a lovely young girl dressed in a tight one-piece bathing-suit and a white bathing-cap. It rocked a little in the tiny wavelets of the lake, but apart from that was very still. Frighteningly still.

The body was quickly taken from the water by a life-guard, and Doctors T.J. Wenner and Harry Brown performed an autopsy, and then grimly shook their heads. There were several head wounds, they said, which indicated that the girl had been struck down by the traditional blunt instrument. A blackjack, perhaps. And why would anyone want to wield that blackjack? The answer might be right there on the medical report sheet. The girl was pregnant.

This was no accidental drowning; it was murder. So County Detective Chief Richard Powell entered the case. He was one of the best qualified men in the state for the job, but even he found himself stymied at the outset by the question of the girl's identity. Every summer resident at the lake was shown the body; all shook their heads.

At this time word reached Powell's ear of a missing girl named Freda McKechnie, who lived in Edwardsville, a suburb of Wilkes-Barre. It was a long shot, but Powell grabbed it with both hands. He went to the McKechnie home, explained his mission, and described the murder victim to Mrs and Mrs McKechnie.

They were sick with apprehension, and then they hesitated. Yes, the description fitted Freda—but pregnancy? They knew nothing about that at all, they told Powell. All they knew was that Freda had gone out for a drive with the boy next door, had quarrelled with him, and had left him to come home alone. He had come back, but the girl had mysteriously disappeared.

The boy next door? A fine, decent boy, the son of long-time neighbours. They would trust Bobby Edwards with their daughter any time.

The discussion was suddenly cut short at this point by startling news. Word came to Powell from the lake that the girl's clothes had been found. He left the identification of the body to the McKechnies, and raced to the spot where the garments had been discovered.

They had been thrown carelessly in a bush a quarter mile from the lake, and Powell studied the scene carefully. It was the discovery of heavy tyre tracks in a cleared space nearby which helped Powell piece the first fragments of the picture together.

The girl had driven with someone to the lake. She had undressed in the car. She had walked to the beach unwarily, unthinkingly, with death at her elbow. She had been struck down on the beach, and her body was thrown in the water. And then the murderer had gone back to the car, had tossed the girl's clothing out, and had driven away.

It was here in the investigation that the McKechnies brokenly identified the victim as their daughter, Freda. And it was here that the thought of Bobby Edwards, the 'boy next door', grew larger and larger in Powell's mind.

Bobby Edwards, he learned, was the kind of boy who is the centre of the crowd at the local ice-cream parlour. Good-looking, athletic, pleasant, he was admired by the boys who knew him, adored by the girls.

In a 1929 high-school year-book, one of Powell's men came across a class prophecy, copied it, and handed it to Powell without comment. The prophet had written:

'Smiles for the ladies,
Never tears,
Bobby's conquests
Will last for years.'

Powell read it and frowned. It wasn't much as poetry, but it threw an interesting light on Bobby. Interesting enough, at least, to lead Powell and some of his men on an abrupt visit to the Edwards's home, even though it was long past midnight.

Face to face with Bobby, Powell saw a clean-cut boy, respectful in manner, obviously willing to help in any way he could, and deeply upset by the tragedy that had come so close to him.

Under Powell's questioning, he told his story over and over again. He had gone for a ride with Freda and a friend of hers, Rosetta Culver. It had started to rain, and Bobby had driven back to town and left Rosetta at her door. On the way to Freda's home, Bobby and Freda had an argument, and Freda demanded that he stop and let her out.

Powell checked and found that every detail involving Rosetta Culver was scrupulously accurate. Then he checked further, and found that, on the previous noon, when the McKechnies were distraught over Freda's disappearance, Bobby had worriedly paid them a visit. Two lines spoken during that visit intrigued Powell.

Mrs McKechnie had asked Bobby why he and Freda had quarrelled in the car. 'Well,' Bobby explained, 'Freda told me: "I'm getting out here because I don't want you to take me home. You know my mother does not want me to go with you."'

Mrs McKechnie had looked incredulous at this. 'That's sheer nonsense!' she gasped, wondering what had come over Freda. 'I've known you, Bobby, since you were a little boy, and always have looked on you as one of my sons.'

Powell had one idea now—to make Bobby tell his story over and over until some small discrepancy showed, and then to drive a wedge in there. But the story didn't vary from telling to telling. It was just logical enough to make sense. It was just weak enough, Powell knew from long experience, to make it look real and natural. The man who contrives an alibi too perfectly often makes it look artificial, and the skilled detective has a way of knowing when this is the case.

Powell abruptly changed his tactics. 'Now, Bobby,' he said, 'tell me what you were doing the week-end before your date with Freda.'

'I wasn't in town. I spent the week-end at East Aurora, New York. At the home of a girl named Margaret Crain,' Bobby said wearily.

'Who is this Margaret Crain?' Powell asked amiably, and Bobby went on to explain that she was a girl he had met at college, and that she was now a music-teacher. Something about Bobby's manner changed as he spoke about the girl. The weariness seemed to dissolve. He was all eager interest.

Powell saw this. He asked abruptly: 'Are you in love with her?'

'Yes!' Bobby said defiantly.

Powell deftly drew the discussion to a comparison between Freda and Margaret, and Bobby explained heatedly that he and Freda disagreed about a lot of things.

This was the spot for his trump card, and Powell played it ruthlessly. 'Pregnancy, too?' he demanded.

The words hit Bobby as hard as Powell hoped they would. He was responsible, all right, but he had tried to do the right thing. He was willing to get married. He was willing to do anything for Freda. They had talked about that in the car. They had even set a date—

It was while he was writhing through the agony of these explanations that word was brought in that the tyres of the boy's car perfectly matched tyre impressions at the scene of the murder. Bobby gave up. He would talk. He would tell everything.

He and Freda had been swimming around the float, he explained, and Freda's head had struck the edge. She went under and disappeared, and Bobby, in a panic, had fled for home.

It was a nice story, and he told it well, but all Powell did was to investigate the float, and point out that the water-logged, spongy wood could never have caused the blow that crushed the life from Freda McKechnie.

Bobby had his back against the wall now, and was fighting desperately.

'All right!' he cried. 'I was trying to help her into a boat when she slipped, and her head hit the chain hook, and she fell down. Then I listened to her heart-beats, and there weren't any. I knew she was dead.'

Powell looked mildly amused, and Bobby's temper started to rise. Like a Shakespearean ham who wasn't impressing his audience, he started to overplay his part. He dramatically demonstrated how he had dropped the body into the lake. 'It was supposed to look like a drowning,' he said. 'I was sure it would!'

Powell laughed aloud, and Bobby turned on him furiously.

'All right,' he shouted, 'I hit her with a blackjack so she wouldn't suffer!'

As far as Powell was concerned, it was all over now except for one thing—the motive for murder could be established beyond all doubt. He turned his attention to Margaret Crain in East Aurora, and she staunchly defended Bobby.

'He couldn't do such a thing!' she told the investigator, and, as proof of their mutual feelings, she turned over a bundle of 172 letters written to her by Bobby.

They were scorching, unprintable letters which gave Powell the last link in the chain, the evidence of a fanatic passion in Bobby Edwards for Margaret Crain. A passion which would have been cheated if Freda McKechnie had been left alive to press her claim on him.

The trial lasted one week, and up to the moment that Bobby Edwards was found guilty and sentenced to death, the pattern of the classic murder case was laid in place, bit by bit.

It is likely that the only observer in the court-room to realise this at the time was a quiet, greying man named Theodore Dreiser. Ten years before he had written a novel called *An American Tragedy*. It was about a boy who clumsily drowned his pregnant girl friend because of his love for another woman.

ERIC AMBLER

Doctor Finch and Miss Tregoff

West Covina is a residential suburb in the eastern section of the county of Los Angeles, California. Bisecting this wilderness of long streets, dusty palm trees, small houses, kidney-shaped swimming pools, dichondra lawns, and sprinkler systems, is the San Bernardino freeway. You may drive to the downtown business area of Los Angeles in thirty minutes. Economically, West Covina is plump; not portly, as is Brentwood, nor bloated, as is Beverly Hills; just respectably plump.

About a mile from the freeway is the South Hills Country Club. On the arid slopes beyond are houses belonging to some of the more prosperous members of the community. Until 1960, the home of Dr Raymond Bernard Finch on Lark Hill Drive was one of them. It is in the modern Californian 'ranch house' style and stands on the flattened top of a scrub-covered eminence with a commanding view over the Country Club car park. A steep, curving driveway leads down to the road. There is a heated swimming pool and a four-car garage. Early in 1959 Dr Finch is said to have refused an offer of $100,000 for the place. He would have done better to have accepted.

Shortly before midnight on Saturday, July 18 of that year, the West Covina police were called to the house. They found there a terrified and incoherent Swedish maid, and, at the foot of some narrow steps leading down from the side of the driveway, the dead body of Mrs Barbara Jean Finch, the doctor's wife. She was lying on the edge of a lawn belonging to the adjoining house where her husband's father lived. She

69

had been shot in the back.

At 10.30 the following morning, and three hundred miles away in Las Vegas, Nevada, police officers entered an apartment a few blocks away from the Desert Inn Hotel and found Dr Finch asleep in bed. They wakened him, told him to dress and then placed him under arrest. At headquarters, they booked him on suspicion of murder, and waited for the West Covina police to come and get him.

Dr Finch, the son of a retired optometrist, was a graduate of the College of Medical Evangelists at Loma Linda, California, a surgeon, and part owner of the busy West Covina Medical Center.* I spoke with him during the trial. He was forty-two then, lean and tanned. The eyes were alert and intelligent; the close-cropped, greying hair made no attempt to conceal the bald patch on the crown of his head. He was a good tennis player and looked it. His manner was forthright. 'Call me Bernie,' he would say. The accompanying smile was muscular and confident.

He and Barbara Finch were married in 1951, both for the second time. She had formerly been his secretary and their extramural relationship had furnished evidence for both divorces. Both, too, had had children by their first marriages. Barbara's daughter, Patti, had gone with her when she had married the doctor.

Barbara Finch was eight years his junior and an attractive woman. She shared his enthusiasm for tennis and they were active and popular members of the Los Angeles Tennis Club. The birth of their son Raymond in 1953 might have been expected to cement their relationship satisfactorily. It did not. By 1957, he was complaining of her coldness, she of his infidelities. That year they decided that, although they would continue to occupy the same house, they would, as far as their emotional lives were concerned, 'go their separate ways.'

Dr Finch's way took him promptly to a small furnished apartment in Monterey Park, another suburb five miles nearer town. He leased it, for $70 a month, in the name of George Evans. There was a 'Mrs Evans,' too; young and

---

*A sort of private clinic run by doctors in partnership.

auburn-haired. They used to meet at the apartment every few days and spend two or three hours in one another's company. Sometimes it would be in the morning, sometimes the afternoon, depending on the doctor's professional commitments for the day.

Mrs Evans' real name was Mrs Carole Tregoff Pappa.

She was twenty then. A Pasadena girl, she had for a while been a photographic model. Model agency 'cheesecake' photographs taken at that time showed her posing in 'Baby Doll' nighties for a scent advertiser. She was startlingly pretty. At eighteen she had married James J. Pappa, a twenty-one-year-old cement mason and amateur 'body building devotee.'* It had been he who had decided that she should give up modelling. Dutifully accepting his decision, she had taken a job as a receptionist. It had not lasted long. A month or so later she had gone to work at the West Covina Medical Center. She had become Dr Finch's secretary.

In 1958, Mr and Mrs George Evans leased a more expensive apartment for their meetings, and furnished it themselves. In January 1959, Carole Tregoff divorced James Pappa. In the same month, Mrs Finch went to a lawyer, and discussed the possibility of divorcing the doctor.

At that point in the story it looked as if events were proceeding in a commonplace way towards a commonplace conclusion. Then, the character of the relationship between the doctor and his wife changed. The indifference, or passive dislike, of the 'separate ways' understanding was suddenly replaced by a bitter hostility.

There is little doubt of the reason for it. The community property laws of the State of California call for an equitable division, in case of divorce, of all assets acquired by either or both partners during the marriage. However, when the divorce is granted for adultery, extreme cruelty, or desertion, the court has discretion to grant the innocent party the lion's share of the property. California judges have in general regarded it as mandatory to do so.

*He worked hard at his hobby. But for his lack-lustre smile he could have had a future in the 'you-can-have-a-body-like-mine' advertisements.

Rightly or wrongly—presumably she was acting on her lawyer's advice—Mrs Finch was taking advantage of this situation to claim the *whole* of the community property, including all the doctor's assets in the West Covina Medical Center, and the eight corporations which composed it, then estimated to be worth $750,000. In addition she was asking for $18,000 legal expenses, plus alimony of $1640 a month, plus child support of $250 a month.

If she succeeded in even 80% of her claim, and there was little reason to suppose that she would not, the doctor would be virtually penniless.

She *had* to be persuaded to accept a less punitive property settlement agreement.

However, his arguments and appeals failed to impress her. As the weeks went by, his attempts at persuasion became more urgent.

In February, a nineteen-year-old Swedish exchange student, Marie Ann Lindholm, had been employed as a maid in the Lark Hill Drive home. One Sunday, Mrs Finch showed her a blood-stained sheet and said that the doctor had tried to kill her in bed. There was a bandage on her head. Apparently, the doctor had relented, stitched up the wound and dressed it; but he had threatened to 'hire people in Las Vegas' to kill her if she reported the incident to the police.

After two days in bed recuperating, Mrs Finch moved out and took refuge in the apartment of a woman friend in the Hollywood Hills. She was, she told this friend, afraid of her husband. But not afraid enough, apparently, to change her mind about the community property claim. She went back to her lawyer, a Mr Forno, and on May 18 signed the divorce papers. Three days later, Mr Forno obtained a restraining order enjoining the doctor to refrain from molesting his wife, touching any of the community property or withdrawing bank funds beyond those needed for normal business and living expenses.

He was too late to secure all the bank funds. Two days previously the doctor had given the Medical Center business manager a cheque for $3000, drawn on his wife's account and apparently signed by her, and told him to cash it. The bank, after questioning the cheque, had paid over the money. However, in the light of what happened later, it is doubtful if an earlier restraining order would have been of much help. Dr Finch was in no mood to exercise restraint.

By now he was registered at a West Covina motel. Mrs Finch had moved back to Lark Hill Drive, so as to be with the two children. But he was a frequent visitor. During the weeks that followed, her friends at the tennis club and elsewhere heard tales of persecution.

To one of those friends, a television actor named Mark Stevens, she reported that the doctor would not only pick up pieces of 'bric-a-brac' and hit her with them, but that on one occasion he had 'sat on her chest' from nine o'clock in the evening until one in the morning—surely a record for this method of coercion. Mr Stevens, incensed at such ungentlemanly behaviour, offered her a revolver for her protection and a course of instruction in its use. Mrs Finch, saying that she was scared to death of guns, declined. Mr Stevens then got the jack handle from the back of her car and urged her to 'wallop' the doctor with that. She thought enough of this suggestion to keep the jack handle under her bed.

To another friend she confided that the doctor had threatened to push her over a cliff in a car which would then explode. When, in June, the doctor proposed through his lawyer a reconciliation to halt the divorce proceedings, she was sure that it was a trick. If he could get back into the house, it would be that much easier for him to kill her.

Nevertheless, an attempt at reconciliation was made and the two were interviewed together by a court marriage counsellor. The doctor claimed that he had given up his 'girl friend' and begged for another chance. Mrs Finch modified her position only slightly. The outcome was a further restraining order directing that 'all payments of income from the defendant's medical practice' were to be turned over to Mrs Finch 'to be expended solely' by her 'for the joint benefit, including payment of living expenses for both.'

This was not at all what the doctor wanted, and he never made any attempt to comply with the order. Moreover, Mrs

Finch soon had her doubts of his sincerity confirmed. A few days after the reconciliation plea, he came to the house, hit her with a revolver and again threatened to kill her. The Swedish maid called the police. Dr Finch left before they arrived.

Mrs Finch reported the incident to her lawyer. At one point, she said, the doctor had tried to force her to get into his car. She added that if the doctor came to the house again, she intended to run for protection to her father-in-law's house, next door. On July 7 she signed a deposition to the effect that the doctor had failed to obey the order requiring him to turn over all his income to her. A subpoena was then issued instructing him to appear on a charge of contempt of court.

This document was not served upon him until a week later; but it is unlikely that the delay was of any consequence. In Las Vegas, there had already been set in motion a train of events which, at that stage, no ordinary legal process could conceivably have brought to a halt.

Miss Tregoff—she had resumed her maiden name—had left Los Angeles in May and gone to Las Vegas, where she was staying with old family friends. She had taken this step, she later explained, in order to 'get out of the triangle.'

She merely elongated it.

It was a trying time for the doctor. In addition to his exacting work as a surgeon at the Medical Center and the emotionally gruelling business of hurling bric-a-brac at his wife, he now had a lot of extra mileage to cover. With no good news for him to bring to them, even the Las Vegas meetings lacked the relieving gaiety he needed. As the weeks went by, and the tight-lipped reports and gloomy discussions of ways and means became repetitive, new elements of fantasy began to seep into his conferences with Miss Tregoff.

The family friends with whom she was staying had a twenty-one-year-old grandson named Donald Williams. A law student at the University of Nevada, he had been a childhood friend of hers. In June she asked him if he knew of any men in Las Vegas who were involved in crime.

He told her that a boy he went to college with had a friend from Minneapolis who was 'in the rackets.' Miss Tregoff said that she would like to meet him. Young Williams already knew of her relationship with Dr Finch, and that the doctor was being divorced. When she explained that she was interested in getting some man who would take Mrs Finch out and provide evidence to be used against her in the divorce action, he understood perfectly. One statement she made, however, did make him a trifle uneasy. Miss Tregoff said that she 'would be quite happy when Mrs Finch would be out of the picture permanently.' It made him 'develop an idea' that there might be violence involved in the plan. But he shrugged off his misgivings and agreed to arrange the meeting.

The go-between was a disagreeable delinquent named Richard Keachie. Later he was indicted in Las Vegas for violations of the Mann Act and the rooming-house ordinances* and for being a fugitive from justice. He disappears from the scene. Left in the foreground, with a polite leer on his face and a bottle of bourbon at his elbow, is the man from Minneapolis to whom he introduced her, John Patrick Cody.

He was born in Minneapolis in 1930. His police record, dating from 1946 when he was doing time in the State Reformatory at Red Wing, included nineteen arrests. They covered charges of drunkenness and disorderly conduct (5), suspicion of robbery (2), assault and battery (3), careless driving and other traffic offences of a more or less serious nature (9), and an A.W.O.L. charge from the Marine Corps. The record of convictions told a story of short-term sentences, fines and placings-on-probation. In 1958, however, his public nuisance value had increased, and he had been sentenced to a year in the Minneapolis Workhouse on a charge of passing a bad cheque. Three weeks later, he had escaped from the Workhouse and made his way south to Las Vegas.

What the record did not show was that Cody belonged to that rare and remarkable subdivision of the human species—the amoral realists with no illusions about their own frailties or anyone else's, and no sense of guilt. The odd thing about such men is that, having no pretensions to being less odious than they are, they sometimes achieve a kind of honesty.

His own description of his normal mode of existence was

*He was a pimp.

that he lived by his wits. Specifically, he worked as a gamblers' shill, or decoy, when he had to, but preferred to pay his way by sponging off women. He was a heavy drinker with a pale, puffy complexion and empty eyes. His hair was sleek, however, and his clothes startlingly natty. He wore dark Italianate suits, and white satin neckties. He had his name embroidered on his shirt cuffs. A slack, lop-sided smirk completed the ensemble.

After the initial introduction, when young Williams and Keachie were present, Cody and Miss Tregoff had a number of meetings alone.

According to him, it was on July 1 that Miss Tregoff broached the subject of his killing Mrs Finch. His response was to quote a price of $2000 for the job. She countered with an offer of one thousand. He pointed out that he would need a hundred dollars to buy a weapon, another hundred for a car to get to the Finch house and at least two hundred more for travel and incidental expenses. After further haggling, they agreed on $1400—$350 down and the balance when he had done the job. Then, she drew maps for him showing how to get to the Finch house and the Hollywood apartment of Mrs Finch's woman friend. Asked how he would do the killing, he said that he would make it look as if it had been done during a robbery. A date was decided—the Fourth of July*—so that everyone else concerned could prepare an alibi. The next day, she gave him $330 and an air ticket, and he was ready to go.

At this point, it appears, his finer feelings got the better of him; or possibly he thought that, if he seemed to be temporising, there might be more than fourteen hundred dollars to be gleaned from the situation. He asked Miss Tregoff if she was sure that she wanted to go through with it. 'When I get on that plane,' he reminded her sternly, 'you can't recall me.' But Miss Tregoff was unmoved. 'Good,' she replied, and wished him luck.

If Mrs Finch had indeed been murdered during the Fourth of July week-end, both Dr Finch and Miss Tregoff would have had excellent alibis. She had taken a job as a cocktail waitress in the Sands Hotel in Las Vegas and was working there. He was down in La Jolla, a hundred and twenty miles south of Los

*A Bank Holiday week-end.

Angeles, ostentatiously forgetting his troubles by playing in a tennis tournament. He was in the doubles competition, with a clergyman as his partner.

Cody's Fourth of July week-end was earthier. Upon leaving Miss Tregoff, he cashed in the air ticket, drove down to Los Angeles and spent the holiday with a girl friend in Hollywood. He did not go near West Covina. All he killed was a bottle or two of bourbon.

On the Sunday, he returned to Las Vegas and reported to Miss Tregoff. 'She asked me if I had done the job. I said, "Yes" and she asked me how I had done it. I said: "With a shotgun." She then handed me an envelope with six or seven hundred dollar bills in it. She was smiling. She was very happy. It was the first time I had seen the girl happy.'

The happiness was short-lived. On Monday, the doctor talked to his wife on the telephone. She was very much alive. He called Las Vegas.

Confronted by Miss Tregoff, Cody professed incredulous amazement and insisted that he had done the killing. She was sceptical, but the doctor, who arrived shortly afterwards, was unexpectedly helpful. With remarkable faith in his henchman's probity he concluded that Mrs Finch's woman friend must have been killed by mistake.

'He said a tragic error had been made,' Cody recalled. 'He told me to go back and do it right. He wanted to know how much it was going to cost to get me to go back and do it. I said I needed a weapon. He said he had a shotgun in his car that I could use, but I said no. I would get my own weapon. I agreed to go back and kill her. He told me to let her know what she was getting it for, to tell her, "This is for Bernie."'

Even Cody found this a little troubling. They were sitting on a hotel patio when this conversation took place. Dr Finch, who had been drinking something called an 'Orange Squeeze,' was quite sober. Cody, hitting the bourbon as usual, was just sober enough to make a maudlin appeal to the doctor's common sense.

'I said, "Doctor, are you in love with Carole?" and he said, "Yes, very much." I said, "I can see the handwriting on the wall. Killing your wife for money alone (*sic*) isn't worth it. You

ought to let her have every penny . . . you can take Carole to a
new town and start up a new business, or up on a mountain-top
and live off the wild. If the girl loves you, she's going to stick
with you." But he said no, he wanted it done, that Mrs Finch
had him in a bottleneck.'

There was also some rather sinister jocularity.

'The doctor told me about his clinic. He said after this is all
over, if I was ever on the lam or hiding-out, he could put me
in his clinic. I said, "That is sort of silly, after I have killed
your wife, to put myself at your mercy. . . . I'd just as soon
stay out of your clinic." And we laughed about it. But,' Cody
added grimly, 'I meant it.'

After the doctor had gone, Cody downed another drink and
gave Miss Tregoff some fatherly advice. '"You're twenty-two
years old," I told her, "and you don't know what you're getting
into. Murder is a pretty big beef."'

Brushing aside this understatement, Miss Tregoff replied
that he might back out, but that 'if you don't do it the doctor
will, and if he doesn't, *I* will.'

Some hours later Cody woke up on a plane going to Los
Angeles. He had a hangover and eighty or ninety dollars more
in his pocket than he thought he had had.

He spent another few idle days in Hollywood. Then,
deciding that there was nothing to be gained from further
encounters with Dr Finch—and possibly some front teeth to
be lost—he left discreetly for Wisconsin.

It was a sensible decision. The doctor had by now leased
an apartment in Las Vegas for Miss Tregoff—his 'fiancée' as
he described her to the apartment house manager—and was
driving up there more often. There were tactical as well as
sentimental reasons for this. The doctor was at this time trying
to evade service of the subpoena on the contempt charge. Until
July 14 he was successful.

He was at the Medical Center when the document was
served on him. It required him to appear in court nine days
later on July 23. On Friday the 17th he left his car at a Los
Angeles airport and flew up to Las Vegas.

On Saturday the 18th, he and Miss Tregoff drove down
in her car from Las Vegas to West Covina. They went,

according to subsequent statements of Miss Tregoff's, in order to confront Mrs Finch with the fact of their relationship (of which Mrs Finch had been all too obviously aware for over a year) and to try to talk her into an out-of-court property settlement agreement.

They reached Lark Hill Drive shortly after ten in the evening and parked the car at the Country Club.

According to Miss Tregoff, the doctor went up to the driveway of his house, and then called down to her to come up and bring a flashlight with her.

She did so; but instead of taking just the flashlight, she 'became confused' and took up an attaché case of the doctor's which she knew to contain a flashlight.

The attaché case was found near the garage the following day. It contained, in addition to a flashlight, two lengths of rope, an ampoule of seconal, a bottle of seconal tablets, two hypodermic syringes with needles, a pair of surgeon's gloves, a sheet of rubber bandage, a wide bandage, a wide elastic bandage, and a carving knife with a six-inch blade. All this was later to be described as a 'murder kit.'

When the doctor and Miss Tregoff reached the garage, they saw that Mrs Finch's car was not there, and concluded that she was out. In fact, she had gone to the tennis club early that afternoon and had dined out afterwards at a restaurant with friends.

They decided to wait for her. They did not go into the house. Miss Lindholm, the maid, and Patti, the doctor's twelve-year-old stepdaughter, were watching the Miss Universe Contest on television and remained unaware of them. Miss Tregoff and the doctor passed the time by playing with the dog, an elderly Samoyed named Frosty.

Mrs Finch returned shortly after eleven o'clock.

Miss Tregoff says that as Mrs Finch drove into the garage the doctor walked up and said that they wanted to talk to her. Mrs Finch replied that she did not want to do any talking.

Miss Tregoff said: 'She got out of the car and bent down. Her back was to me, but then I noticed she had a gun pointed towards me. Dr Finch reached behind his wife into the car, threw something at me which hit me in the stomach and yelled at me to get out of there. The object he threw was a leather case.'

Miss Tregoff says that, as she ran across the lawn, she tripped over a sprinkler head and heard Mrs Finch scream.

'I heard another sound from the garage and it sounded like Dr Finch was in trouble. I started back in quite cautiously. Then I saw Barbara on the right side of the car. She took off down the driveway. She had a gun in her hand. I ran back around the lawn. I was scared. I was afraid of being shot at. I guess I stayed there until about 5 a.m. while all kinds of police came around. I seemed to be paralysed.'

In the end, she left her hiding place, behind a large bougainvillaea, and made her way down the hill to the car park. Her car was still there. She drove back to Las Vegas.

Miss Lindholm's account of what happened is very different. She never saw Miss Tregoff and did not know that she was there.

Just after eleven the television was switched off and Patti went to bed. Miss Lindholm went to her room. She heard Mrs Finch's car drive in. A few seconds later, she heard Mrs Finch scream for help.

Miss Lindholm had some difficulty in expressing herself in English, and her accounts of the events of the next few minutes varied; but the general pattern was clear.

She ran out, thinking that Mrs French might have fallen into the swimming pool, or had some other accident. Patti ran out with her; but, when they heard the doctor's angry voice, Miss Lindholm sent the child back to the house and went on alone. When she reached the garage, she turned on the lights. She saw Mrs Finch lying on the floor. She was bleeding from a cut on the forehead. Dr Finch was standing over her.

As Miss Lindholm started towards Mrs Finch, the doctor grabbed the girl 'by the face and chin' and banged her head against the wall. A broken area of plaster on the wall seemed to bear out this part of her story. She was not clear what happened immediately after that. She was not sure whether or not she lost consciousness, nor whether she remained on her feet. She did remember clearly that the doctor ordered her into the car and that he had a gun in his hand. In one account, she said that he fired a shot to enforce his orders.

At all events, she climbed into the rear seat of Mrs Finch's convertible. At the same time, the doctor was ordering his wife to get into the front seat. As she got to her feet he told her to give him the car keys. Then he shouted at her: 'So help me, I will kill you if you don't do as I say.'

Apparently, Mrs Finch made as if to obey, then suddenly turned and ran out of the garage. A week or so earlier, it will be remembered, she had told her lawyer that if the doctor came to the house again, she would run for protection to the house of his parents. That was the direction in which she ran now. The doctor ran after her.

Miss Lindholm said he had a gun in his hand. Miss Tregoff said that it was Mrs Finch who had the gun.

There is no doubt, however, about the rest of Miss Lindholm's story. She got out of the car and ran to the house. Patti unlocked the door and let her in. At just about that time, they heard a distant shot. Miss Lindholm called the police.

Mrs Finch's body had only one shoe on. The other shoe, together with some pieces of earrings, was found by the police on the shoulder of the driveway above. In addition to having been shot in the back with a 0.38 bullet, Mrs Finch had two skull fractures and a number of bruises and abrasions which could have been the result of her being hit with a gun. A torn surgical glove was lying on the floor of the garage.

No gun was found. No one saw Miss Tregoff hiding in the bougainvillaea. Dr Finch had left.

At the time the police arrived at the house, the doctor was, in fact, on South Citrus Avenue, a few minutes' walk away, stealing a Ford car from a driveway. He abandoned it two miles away in La Puente, and then stole a Cadillac, in which he drove up to Las Vegas. It was about 6.30 a.m. when he reached Miss Tregoff's apartment. She had not yet returned. The manager let him in with a pass key.

Then, the doctor went to bed. He had had a tiring day.

Miss Tregoff says that it was on the way back to Las Vegas and over the car radio that she learned of Mrs Finch's death. When she awakened the doctor and told him, he 'seemed quite shocked.' 'I asked him if he had killed his wife and he said no.'

Relieved to hear this, Miss Tregoff went off to work at the Sands Hotel, where she was a cocktail waitress on the morning shift. Some hours later, after the doctor's arrest, she was taken to Las Vegas police headquarters, questioned, and then held as a material witness. She made a number of statements. Eleven days later, after she had given evidence at the preliminary hearing of the case against Dr Finch in the municipal court, she was arrested on a charge of 'aiding and abetting' him in the murder of Mrs Finch.

An indiscreet conversation between two Las Vegas prostitutes led the police to question Keachie. In August, Cody was picked up by the police in Milwaukee.

The Los Angeles County Court building looks like the new head office of a prosperous building society. There are escalators inside as well as lifts. Courtroom No.12 is spacious, well-lighted, and efficiently air-conditioned. There is no dock. Defendants sit beside their lawyers at a long table facing the judge's rostrum. Also at this table are the prosecution lawyers. The witness 'stand' is a throne-like chair placed beside the judge's desk and furnished with a microphone so that the whole court can hear plainly what is said. The jury sits to the left of the judge. The press box is on the right. A wooden barrier with swing gates separates all this from the main body of the court where the public sits. Over three hundred spectators can be accommodated.

American courtroom scenes in films and books had prepared me for most of the differences of lay-out and procedure. What I had not been prepared for was the informality of Western justice.

Each defendant was in the charge of a uniformed sheriff (in Miss Tregoff's case, an attractive girl-sheriff) and they were brought into court via the public corridor. Once seated at their table to await the arrival of the judge, they were immediately surrounded by press photographers, television cameramen and reporters, who only moved out when the bailiff announced the judge's entrance. During the frequent and lengthy recesses, the photographers and reporters would move in again. Photography in court was forbidden only during the actual hearing; but during the recesses lawyers and witnesses could pose for pictures re-enacting the proceedings. As the trial progressed a circus atmosphere developed that even the regular crime reporters began to find disconcerting. One Los Angeles paper was running a series of 'impressions' written by Hollywood actresses—a different one each day.* The sight of those ladies, pad and pencil in hand, dark glasses removed and skirts hitched up becomingly, being photographed while they interviewed the eagerly co-operative defendants, made one wonder if this really could be a murder trial, if perhaps the whole thing had not been engineered by one of the studio publicity departments to promote a new picture.

The bearing of the defendants themselves did nothing to correct that impression. They appeared relaxed and unselfconscious, even a little bored. The smiles they exchanged now and again were fondly rueful. They behaved a little like a pair of newlyweds separated for the first time by different bridge tables.

The Deputy District Attorney in charge of the prosecution made no noticeable contribution to the dignity of the proceedings. He was a lanky, soft-spoken, middle-aged man with the apologetic air of an amateur actor cast as Marc Antony in a charity performance of *Julius Caesar*, and worried about the draping of his toga. He smiled too often, as if to inform us that he appreciated the joke, too. He was, no doubt, a most capable lawyer. Unfortunately, he had a habit of mislaying his documents and exhibits. Photograph in hand he would advance on a witness. 'I show you this photograph of a Cadillac car,' he would begin sternly, 'and ask if you can identify. . . .' At that moment he would himself catch sight of the photograph, realise that it showed a house or a bullet wound, and break off. 'Excuse me, Your Honour,' he would say to the judge, and then pick his way unhurriedly through the contents of a big soap-flakes carton in which he kept his records of the case. If this failed him, he would cross to the courtroom

---

*Miss Jayne Meadows was heard to say, after her interview with Dr Finch, that he was 'fascinating.' Miss Patricia Owens, after her interview, thought that Miss Tregoff 'was being very sensible about the whole thing.' That, at least, was good to know.

filing cabinet, containing the already labelled exhibits, and try there. Usually, he found what he wanted in the end, but the delays were boring and gave the prosecution's case an indecisive air.

Mr Grant Cooper (for Dr Finch) and Mr Egan (for Miss Tregoff) were more impressive; Mr Cooper in particular.

His cross-examination of the Swedish maid was in the best tradition. The young woman was harassed and confused. It would have been easy for him to have confused her still further. Instead, he handled her quietly and gently, obviously earning the liking and respect of the jury as he did so. He threw just enough doubt on her recollection of events to make room for the defence's accidental death story which was to come later.

The stumbling block, however, was Mr Cody. If he were believed, the doctor and Miss Tregoff were conspirators with a very determined intent to murder. Accident would be out of the question. Cody's evidence had to be discredited.

With his record, it should have been easy. It was not. He could admit to the basest motives and behaviour without a trace of embarrassment. He was the defence lawyer's nightmare. It is hard to discredit the evidence of a man who insists so cheerfully on his own perfidy, his total *lack* of credit.

Cooper did his best. For example, he brought out the fact that the witness was an escapee from a bad cheque sentence, and that, in the period of a year, he had worked a total of four days at two jobs.

Mr Cooper: 'What did you do?'

Cody: 'I loafed.'

Mr Cooper: 'How did you support yourself?'

Cody: 'By my wit.'

Mr Cooper (later in reference to one of Cody's girl friends): 'Did she support you?'

Cody: 'Yes.'

Mr Cooper: 'Did she support you in Hollywood or did you live by your wits?'

Cody: 'Both.'

Mr Cooper: 'How about Las Vegas?'

Cody: 'I got a job as a shill at the Fremont Hotel—for two days.'

Mr Cooper: 'Was that very hard work?'

Cody: 'Oh, no. I was forced to quit. I had to get a police card. They would find out where I was and take me back to Minneapolis.'

Cooper became impatient with his frankness. Concerning the transaction with Dr Finch and Miss Tregoff he asked: 'You felt that, regardless of what the agreement had been, you had swindled Dr Finch and Carole?'

Cody: 'Well I don't know if I would call it swindled.'

Mr Cooper (sarcastically): 'Cheated?'

Cody (accepting the distinction): 'Yes.'

Mr Cooper tried another gambit. 'You wanted to co-operate with the law enforcement officers. Was that out of the goodness of your heart?'

Cody: 'No, on the advice of my lawyer.'

Laughter in court. Mr Cooper turned in his hand.

Mr Egan also tried. He adopted the classical mode of attack. After a build-up based on the witness's lamentable record, he delivered what he hoped would be the *coup-de-grâce*.

'You've testified you've been hired to murder someone for money. Is that right?'

Cody: 'Yes, sir.'

Mr Egan: 'Would you lie for money?'

Mr Egan was silent. Cody thought about the question. Obviously he wanted to give a helpful, reasonable reply. Finally, he nodded. 'It looks like I have,' he said thoughtfully.

His meaning was plain. He meant that he had lied to get money out of Dr Finch and Miss Tregoff. There really was nothing to be done with the man.

With the departure of Cody (he returned to a cell in Minneapolis), the trial left the front pages for a bit. Asian flu and bronchitis claimed one of the male jurors, who was replaced by a female alternative—seven women and five men were the arbiters now. Important witnesses were also ill. Miss Tregoff's attorneys scored a minor victory when they eliminated some of her self-incriminating statements from the record. There were scenes of jubilation and kisses were lavishly bestowed. But everyone knew that there were real charges for the pair to answer and that the only man who could answer them was Dr Finch.

As the moment approached when we would hear Grant Cooper outline the argument for the defence, the tension rose. The queues waiting to occupy the seats reserved for the public lengthened. There was pushing and shoving. And not only in the corridor outside the courtroom. The press box became crammed. A San Francisco paper sent in a columnist noted for the trenchant advice he gave to his readers about the joys of mixed bathing in the nude. It was even rumoured, on the basis of the appearance in the press room of a tall, thin man with a bright blue suit and a long ginger beard, that the beatnik paper *Underhound* was covering the trial. Actresses with reporter's notebooks were two-a-penny.

On February 3, a month after the trial had begun, Cooper rose to address the jury.

The defence was that Dr Finch had lied steadily to Mrs Finch about his relationship with Miss Tregoff and that, until he had been served with the divorce papers in May, had believed that he had lied successfully.

When he learned that he had not, all his efforts had been bent to preventing a divorce, which would, he had feared, damage both his business prospects and his professional standing.

He had had two courses open to him. He could stall by pretending to want a reconciliation, or he could try to get evidence that his wife had been going with other men and was not, in fact, the innocent party she claimed to be.

He had tried to do both. When the reconciliation idea had not worked, he had employed private detectives to follow her. They had proved useless. They would follow her for a couple of hours and then lose her. And they had proved expensive. He had asked Miss Tregoff if there were not someone in Las Vegas who could do the work.

Dr Finch was also prepared to admit to discreditable behaviour. When Cody, whom he had hired to follow his wife, had suggested that, if it proved impossible to get other evidence against Mrs Finch, he himself should seduce her in order to provide it, the doctor had agreed dubiously that he could try. That had been all that Cody had been paid to do.

As for the alleged assaults on her, Dr Finch's case was that his wife had been a neurotic woman, who had imagined things and spread stories of his violence solely in order to substantiate her charges of cruelty in the divorce case. As for her being scared to death of guns, she had been able to hit a beer can at twenty feet with the very revolver that had killed her. In happier days, they had used it to practise target shooting on a hillside behind the house.

All in all, some very questionable behaviour; but murder, no.

On the day that the doctor was to give his evidence the corridor outside the courtroom became packed to suffocation. For once, the air-conditioning seemed ineffective. One elderly lady, who fainted in the queue, came to as she was being borne away and piped a despairing 'Hold my place.' Nobody did. Inside, things were scarcely better. Five visiting South Americans somehow managed to get into the press box. All credentials had to be checked before the interlopers could be identified and ejected. A columnist famed for her appearance on the 'What's My Line?' television programme was mobbed by autograph hunters. A woman juror got into a violent argument with one of the court sheriffs who refused to leave his post to get her book autographed. One cameraman was standing on the judge's desk to get a wider angle on the scene. The court was a little late in getting down to business; but in the end order was restored and the great moment came.

Dr Finch took the stand with the air of an experienced pilot taking over for an instrument landing in dense fog—tense but steady, nerves well under control. He asked at once if he could dispense with the microphone and rely upon the strength of his own voice to carry. 'If you can't hear me,' he instructed Cooper, 'hold up your hand.'

After Cooper had taken him through his account of the events leading up to the night of July 18, the doctor described what had happened at the house.

He had approached his wife in the garage saying that he wanted to talk to her. She had pulled out the gun. He had closed with her in order to take it away. She had fought with him. He had to hit her with the gun—hence the skull fractures. When he had put the gun down (presumably to deal with the maid) she had snatched it back and started running down the driveway.

He did not know where Miss Tregoff was. He thought that his wife had seen her. He ran after his wife. When he caught up with her, she had the gun in her two hands (as she had always held it in target practice) and was pointing it—not at him but in a direction that could have meant that she had seen Miss Tregoff and was going to shoot her.

He grappled with her and there was a second struggle. As he again wrenched the gun away from her and started to throw it into the bushes, she started to run.

At that moment—he did not know how or why, or even if the gun had been cocked—the gun went off.

When he reached his wife, who was lying on the ground, he did not realise that she had been shot.

He said to her: 'What happened, Barbara? Where are you hurt?'

She said that she had been 'shot in the chest.'

'I told her not to move. I said, "I've got to get an ambulance for you and get you to the hospital." Barbara said, "Wait." She said, "I'm sorry, I should have listened." I said, "Barbara, don't talk about it now. I've got to get you to a hospital."'

At this point Dr French began to weep as he told the story.

'She said, "Don't leave me" and then she paused and said, "Take care of the kids."'

Dr Finch's voice broke and he had difficulty continuing.

'I checked her pulse right away. There was no pulsation. I turned up her chin. There was no respiration. She was dead.' And then he repeated it. 'She was *dead*. I said "Barb," but she couldn't answer.'

Dr Finch was not the only weeping now. Some of the jurors were weeping with him.

But not all of them.

Cooper made the doctor act out the second struggle over

the gun to show how it happened; but the demonstration did not really help.

Mrs Finch had been shot in the back and not at very close quarters. The doctor said that the gun had gone off as he had flung it away into the bushes. Could it have been defective? There is no way of knowing. The bushes had been searched and searched again. The gun had not been found, there or anywhere else.

The cross-examination of Dr Finch seemed curiously ineffectual. The first struggle in the garage was barely touched upon. Yet the doctor's own account of it contained some clear contradictions. If, as he claimed, his wife had had the gun and he had merely been trying to get it away from her, why had he not done just that? Why, when he had had the gun in his hand, had he *then* battered her about the head with it, and with sufficient force to fracture her skull in two places? And how had this woman (who must at least have been dazed by the blows) then managed to snatch up the gun, and run so fast down the driveway that he had only caught up with her when she had stopped and appeared to be aiming the gun?

The doctor's behaviour after the shooting seemed equally strange. Miss Tregoff said that she had hidden behind the bougainvillaea and remained there. Did her lover not try to find her? Had he not even called to her? The grounds surrounding the house were not that extensive—little more than an acre. Did he think that she had run away and left him to it? There had been an easy way for him to find out. Her car, in which they had driven down from Las Vegas, was in the Country Club car park at the foot of the hill. He had had to pass the Club in order to get to Citrus Avenue, where he had stolen the Ford. Had he not looked to see if her car was still there? We know it was because she drove back to Las Vegas in it later. Therefore, she had had the keys. Rather than run the risk of stealing a car, would it not have been easier to run back up the hill and find her? Or were the approaching police car sirens already audible?

Miss Tregoff's account was no less extraordinary. From her hiding place she had heard screams, a shot, police cars and policemen. If, as she said, Mrs Finch had had the gun, she must have feared that the doctor had been shot. Yet she claimed not to have known what had happened until she heard it over the radio as she was driving back to Las Vegas.

It really was too much to swallow.

The admitted facts were that they had made their separate ways back to Las Vegas. Even allowing for the conventional panic after the accidental killing ('I didn't know *what* I was doing!') the rest of the evidence looked remarkably like a pathetic and ill-considered attempt to improvise an alibi for Miss Tregoff.

When her evidence came to be heard it added nothing to what the jury already knew. She just stuck to her story and that was that.

Superior Judge Walter R. Evans summed up accurately and fairly.

The jury deliberated for eight days and then announced that they were unable to agree upon a verdict. Some of the jurors were indiscreet enough to discuss the matter with the press later. They had been together for almost ten weeks and racial dissensions (the jury was not all-white) had, it appeared, led to ugly scenes in the jury room. The possibility of their agreeing about anything had been remote.

On June 28 a new trial was ordered.

It began, before Superior Judge LeRoy Dawson and a jury of eleven women and one man, on July 20. For the prosecution, this time, was Assistant District Attorney Crail. Mr Cooper again defended Dr Finch.

On October 19 the case went to the jury.

Twenty-four hours later, when it had become apparent that this jury, too, was unable to agree, Judge Dawson called them back into court and admonished them in startling terms.

He said that in his opinion they ought not to believe the evidence of Dr Finch and Miss Tregoff.

Cooper immediately protested. As the judge continued, Cooper interrupted constantly, and was twice told to be silent. Finally, he was cited for contempt of court.*

Brushing aside further protests, Judge Dawson now told the jury: 'The explanation given by the defendant, Dr Finch, as to the circumstances surrounding the firing of the fatal shot

---

*At the end of this trial he was fined $500. Later, the State of California set aside the conviction and reprimanded the judge.

to me does not sound reasonable. In none of its aspects does it appear to me to have been anything but an attempt to justify what is shown by the evidence, in my opinion, to be a wilful and deliberate taking of human life. . . . To my mind the testimony given by the witness John Cody regarding the purpose for which he was employed was more believable than the testimony of the two defendants on the subject.'

But it was no good. After deliberating for a total of twenty days, the jury announced that they were unable to agree upon a verdict.

Dismissing them, Judge Dawson commented that, 'the failure of this jury to reach a verdict in this case raises a very disquieting question in the minds of all of us who are interested in the maintenance and function of the jury system.'

A third trial was ordered. It began on January 4, 1961, before Superior Judge David Coleman and a jury of ten men and two women. This time, Dr Finch was defended not by Mr Cooper in person, but by one of his associates.

The case went to the jury on March 23. Five days later they asked for the judge's guidance. Would there, they wanted to know, be any legal conflict in verdicts of guilty of first degree murder against one defendant, guilty of second degree murder against the other, and guilty of conspiracy against both?

The judge said that there would not.

The jury then brought in those verdicts: Dr Finch guilty of murder in the first degree, Miss Tregoff guilty of murder in the second degree, both guilty of conspiracy.

On the following week the jury reconvened to determine the sentences. After a further twelve hours of deliberation, they asked the judge if they could return a verdict of life imprisonment without the possibility of parole. He told them that the law did not permit the qualification.

Forty minutes later the jury determined sentences of life imprisonment for both defendants.

After dismissing motions by the defence for a new trial and modification of Miss Tregoff's sentence, Judge Coleman said: 'The jury's verdict speaks for itself. This was a brutal murder.

There is no miscarriage of justice. The proof of their guilt is overwhelming.'

Both may apply for parole after serving seven years of their sentences.

Meanwhile, the doctor has had time for reflection. If Mrs Finch had lived to go through with the divorce suit he would have been stripped of most of his assets. As it was, he had to pay for his defence. The services of the best lawyers are never cheap. One day in September, 1959, at the jail, the doctor signed an agreement which was then lodged with the Country Recorder.

In it, the doctor agreed to pay Mr Cooper a retainer of $25,000, plus $350 a day for each day of the trial in Superior Court. In order to cover these fees, the doctor assigned to Mr Cooper his assets in the West Covina Medical Center and its corporations, plus the deeds of his house, plus his cars and a twenty-two foot speedboat. Mr Cooper was empowered to sell what was necessary to pay his fees and expenses and hand back what remained afterwards. This fee arrangement covered the preparation of a motion for a new trial if that became necessary; but not the conduct of the case in any appelate court. If Mr Cooper were called upon to render further services to his client, fresh financial arrangements would have to be made. No doubt they were.

Perhaps Cody's mountain-top idea had not been so foolish after all.

Part 4

KILLING FOR JEALOUSY

COLIN WILSON

The Buck Ruxton Case

The remarkable deductive abilities of Sherlock Holmes showed themselves in many fields. He was able to reconstitute a man's personality and history from the scratches on his pocket watch. He was able to deduce the background of a criminal from a cigarette butt left in the ashtray. The man upon whom Conan Doyle based Holmes was a Scotsman, Dr Joseph Bell, a surgeon at the Edinburgh Infirmary, who used to impress his students by guessing the profession and background of his patients—a callous inside the forefinger indicated a slater, a pair of trousers worn shiny inside the knees revealed that the man was a cobbler.

But neither Holmes nor Watson ever had direct experience of that ultimate science of deduction: forensic detection. Doyle knew better than to shock his Victorian readers with the grisly details of true murder cases. Yet there have been cases in the annals of medical detection that Holmes might have been proud to have been involved in. One of these I am now going to describe.

The 'medical detective' whose work was so vital to the prosecution was Dr John Glaister, Regius Professor of Forensic Medicine at the University of Glasgow.

September 29th, 1935 was a cool autumn day; a young lady from Edinburgh had paused in her afternoon walk to lean on the parapet of a bridge across a pretty stream called the Gardenholme Linn. It was an attractive spot; the stream, shaded by trees and ferns, ran in a narrow rocky bed, forming small pools and waterfalls. But as she stared at this delightful scene, she noticed something that made her stomach turn over. Below the bridge, resting on the boulders, there was some kind of a bundle wrapped in a piece of cloth. It had burst open, and something that looked like a human arm was sticking out.

The girl hurried back to her hotel in Moffat, two miles away, and told her brother what she had seen. He went back with her, clambered down under the bridge, and quickly realised that she was correct. It *was* a part of a human arm; and the parcel it was sticking out from looked as if it contained several more pieces. They hurried back to the police station.

The police soon located four bundles. And it immediately became clear that they were dealing with a case of double murder. For one of the bundles contained a human head, and a few feet away, under the bridge, there was another head. The other parcels contained severed pieces of arms and legs, and chunks of flesh.

The next morning, the remains were examined by two local doctors in the morgue; then Professor Glaister arrived, together with a colleague, Dr Gilbert Millar.

They were confronted by a problem that would have made Sherlock Holmes rub his hands. This killing was not the work of some frightened amateur. It had been carefully thought out and executed by a man who knew exactly what he was doing. He had made only one major miscalculation. He had dropped the parcels into a swollen, flooded stream, and assumed that they would be carried away into the River Annan, a few hundred yards downstream. Once in the Annan, they might have ended up in the Solway Firth. But the Linn was full of boulders, and some of the parcels had caught against them. Then the rain stopped, and there were a few days of Indian Summer; the stream dwindled to a trickle among the rocks, and the incriminating parcels were left high and dry.

Even so, the murderer had taken care in covering his tracks. He had not only dismembered the bodies; he had also removed skin from the heads, to make the faces unrecognisable, and had cut off the fingertips from some of the hands, to prevent fingerprint identification. Glaister and Millar found themselves confronted by a gruesome pile of decomposing flesh, a few stray pieces of two bodies of unknown age, unknown sex, unknown identity. It was difficult to know where to begin.

The first step was to make sure that no further decomposition took place. The remains were sent to the Anatomy Department at the University of Edinburgh. There they were treated with ether, to destroy the maggots, then left in a weak formalin solution, to 'pickle' them. This also had the advantage of removing the worst of the smell. As the weeks went by, a few other pieces of body turned up from the Linn area—one even found by the side of the road. Glaister and Millar found themselves confronted with a human jigsaw puzzle with seventy pieces. But the puzzle was far from complete; one 'body' consisted only of head and limbs.

Now it is true that there have been plenty of examples of dismembered bodies in British criminal history. But in most of the famous cases, there was no problem of identification. In 1875, Henry Wainwright, a London businessman, murdered his mistress, Harriet Lane, and buried her dismembered body in his warehouse in East London. But he was caught when he tried to remove the remains to another hiding place. In 1910, the notorious Doctor Crippen murdered his wife Belle Elmore, and buried her body in the basement of his house. Sir Bernard Spilsbury's examination and reconstruction of the body was another masterpiece of medical detection; but there was never the slightest doubt about the identity of the body—Crippen was caught running away to America. In 1924, Patrick Mahon murdered his mistress, who was pregnant, and scattered bits of her dismembered body from the windows of trains; but his wife's suspicions led the police to a bungalow in Sussex, where they found the remaining parts of the unwanted mistress. And in the following year, a poultry farmer named Norman Thorne killed his mistress and buried her pieces under a chicken run; but he ended by showing the police where to look for them.

Of course, there *had* been the occasional case where the body was difficult to identify. In March, 1725, a night-watchman found a severed head on the Thames mud, near Lambeth Bridge. The Parish officers ordered the head to be set on a stake in a churchyard at Westminster, and it was finally recognised as the husband of a woman called Catherine Hayes. She was convicted, together with two of her lovers, of her husband's murder, and burned alive. The preservation of a head also caused the downfall of James Greenacre, who in 1836 murdered and dismembered a woman he had promised to marry; the head was found in the Regent Canal in Stepney, and kept in spirits; it was identified by her brother. (The motive here seems to have been robbery.) And in 1917, a torso found wrapped in a sheet in Regent Square, Bloomsbury, was quickly identified by means of a laundry mark, and a Frenchman named Louis Voison was hanged for the murder of his mistress. (This was probably a miscarriage of justice; it is almost certain that she was murdered by another mistress, in a jealous fit, and Voison merely helped dispose of the body.)

In all these cases, the problem of identification was fairly simple. But Glaister and his colleagues were confronted by a case in which there had been a systematic attempt to destroy all means of identification.

The first step was certainly the easiest—to sort out the pieces into two separate bodies. Fortunately, one of the victims was more than six inches shorter than the other. So it was not difficult to separate the smaller from the larger body. When this was done, Glaister and his team found they had one almost complete body—the taller one—and one body without a trunk. They also found one relic that at first caused them much bafflement: an enormous single eye—a 'Cyclops eye'—which certainly did not belong to either of the bodies. A Cyclops eye is a physical malformation that occurs in some human beings and animals; the two eyes have run together into one, like Siamese twins. The doctors dissected it, but they never found out where it came from—or even what animal it belonged to. It remains one of those minor mysteries connected with the case.

And what could Glaister say about the remains of the two bodies? His first guess was that one of them was a man—the smaller of the two. The other was certainly a woman, for the remains included a pelvis. This looked like a crime of passion. A jealous husband who found his wife in bed with her lover, who killed them both in a fit of rage, then set out to cover up all trace of the crime . . .

And what could they deduce about the murderer? Well, it was almost certain that he was a medical man, or had had some medical training. For there was one feature that distinguished this case from nearly all other cases of dismemberment. The killer had used a knife, not a saw. Unless you have some knowledge of anatomy, a human body is a difficult thing to dismember with a knife. It is easier to use a saw. This man had separated the limbs neatly at the joints, which argued that he was either a butcher or a doctor.

He had carefully removed most of the skin from both the heads. But he seemed to have been interupted in the case of the smaller of the two, for he had left some of the hair, although it had been cut short. Teeth had been removed from both heads, obviously to prevent a dentist from identifying them by means of his dental records. For some strange reason, the killer had even removed part of the foot of the taller body. He had obviously spent a lot of time making sure it should not be identified. It looked hopeless. Even if the police could find a case of a missing man and woman, they would find it difficult to prove that these were their remains.

But Glaister was in luck. The hands that were found under the bridge had no fingertips—and therefore no fingerprints. But in later bundles, the police found the hands of the other body—plus fingertips. After being soaked in hot water, it was possible to get fingerprints from them. It seemed incredible, but the murderer had made an elementary error, and made it possible to identify one of his victims beyond all doubt.

Glaister and his team—which included Dr James Brash, another brilliant anatomist—now settled down to the gruesome work of examining the small pieces of flesh that had

been found in the bundles. Many of these were unrecognisable. There were two breasts present, which is what
had been expected. Then the team made a discovery that
cast an entirely new light on the case. Another piece of flesh
also looked like a female breast. Under a microscope, there
could be no doubt whatever: this was mammary tissue. So the
bodies were those of two women, not a man and a woman. A
closer examination of other pieces of flesh revealed that this
was undoubtedly so, for there were also parts of the external
genital organs of two women.

The next major question was the age of the two bodies.
There are several methods of determining this. Our skulls
have 'joining lines' which are called sutures. While we are
still growing, these remain unclosed. When we cease to grow,
they very gradually seal themselves up; this is usually around
the age of forty. One of the two skulls—the smaller of the
two—had unclosed sutures. On the other, the sutures were
almost fully closed. This indicated clearly that one of the
victims was around forty, and the other was certainly under
thirty. X-rays of the jawbone of the younger woman showed
that the wisdom teeth had still not pushed their way through.
This meant that she was probably in her early twenties. The
joints of the bones also gave a reliable indication of age. The
cartillage—the soft material of which bones are originally
made— gradually changes into 'caps', called 'epiphyses',
and age can be estimated from how far this change has
taken place. The epiphyses of the two bodies confirmed
that one was of a girl of twenty or so, the other of a woman
approaching middle age.

As to the cause of death, this was fairly clear, in spite
of the condition of the two bodies. The taller woman had
five stab wounds in the chest, several broken bones, and
many bruises. The hyoid bone was fractured, suggesting
that she had been throttled into unconsciousness before
the other injuries were inflicted. The swollen and bruised
tongue confirmed this inference. A murderer who strangled
his victim, then beat and stabbed her, was obviously in
the grip of violent rage—the kind of rage often inspired
by jealousy. . . . Since the trunk of the other body was

missing, there was no way of telling whether she had also been stabbed; but the evidence was against it. Glaister concluded she had been battered to death with a blunt instrument. It hardly needed a Sherlock Holmes to infer that she had been killed as an afterthought, probably to keep her silent. The fact that the murderer had taken less trouble to conceal her identity pointed to the same conclusion.

But if he was really anxious to conceal the identity of the bodies, there was one major point he had overlooked. The older woman had an unusually long face; in life, her appearance must have been distinctly 'horsey'. He would have done well to make sure it was never found.

And so even if there had been no other clues, the facts uncovered by Glaister's team would have provided the police with all the necessary leads. In fact, the police were already working on another set of clues. The head of the younger woman had been wrapped in a pair of child's rompers. One of the bundles had been wrapped in a blouse with a patch under the arm. Some of the remains had been wrapped in newspaper before being tied in sheets. Some of these newspapers had dates in August, but the most recent was a *Sunday Graphic* of September 15, 1935, which indicated clearly that the murder had taken place on or after that date. Moreover, this *Sunday Graphic* was a special local edition, printed especially for the Morecambe and Lancaster area . . .

In Lancaster at this time, the police were investigating the murder of a woman called Mrs Smalley, and in the course of their investigations, they questioned the servant of a Persian doctor named Ruxton. Ruxton's real name was Bukhtyar Hakim, and he was born in Bombay; he had been practising medicine in Lancaster since 1930. Ruxton was upset by the questions about Mrs Smalley—a lady from Morecambe whose body had been found a year earlier; on September 24, five days before the bodies were found in the Linn, Ruxton went to the Lancaster police to complain about the questioning of his servant. The doctor was a short, rather goodlooking man of thirty six, with a wildly excitable manner; he talked volubly and waved his hands. It was not the first time the Lancaster police had met this excitable foreigner. Two years before, Mrs Ruxton had come to the police station to complain of her husband's brutality. Ruxton was brought to the police station, where he waved his arms, foamed at the mouth, and screamed that his wife had been unfaithful and he would kill her if it continued. Then, quite abruptly, he calmed down, and gave his wife money to go to see her sister in Edinburgh. Later that day, after she had packed her bag, she changed her mind and decided to stay. Obviously, the relations between this couple were somewhat stormy.

So when Ruxton came to complain about the questioning of his servant, the police were not surprised when he added that his wife had left him again—the second time in a year. He said she had gone off to Scotland a fortnight before. She had apparently taken the maid, a twenty year old girl named Mary Rogerson, with her.

Mary Rogerson was a Morecambe girl, and her parents were not at all happy about her disappearance. She was strongly attached to her family; every time she had a day off, she spent it with them. She once spent a fortnight's holiday on a farm with Ruxton's three young children, but then she wrote every day. Now they had heard nothing from her for nearly two weeks, and they were worried. They were even more worried when Ruxton called on them—the day after he had been to see the police—and told them that Mary had got herself pregnant with the laundry boy, and that his wife had taken her away for an abortion. The Rogersons were flabbergasted. Mary just wasn't that type. She was rather a quiet girl, not particularly pretty—she had a cast in one eye—who was strongly attached to the three Ruxton children. (Their ages ranged from four to seven.) She was as unlikely to get herself pregnant by a laundry boy as to rob a bank. Yet Ruxton assured them that Mary *was* pregnant; he implied he had examined her himself. The father, upset and suspicious, told Ruxton that he was going to the police. Ruxton looked alarmed. 'Don't do that', he told them, 'I'll bring her over on Sunday'. They agreed to wait that long. But Ruxton didn't bring her over on Sunday. Three days later, in spite of Ruxton's pleas, Mary Rogerson's stepmother reported to the police that Mary was missing. One week later, she gave the police a description of her stepdaughter, which was circulated to the newspapers and to other police forces. That evening—October 9—Ruxton again appeared at the Lancaster police station, in his usual state of feverish excitement. The police would have to help him find his wife, he said. It was being suggested that she had been murdered and thrown in the Linn, and it was ruining his practice. He burst into tears. 'Can't you have it published in the papers that there is no connection between the two?' The Chief Constable made soothing noises, and drew up some kind of noncommital statement to be issued to the press. This seemed to satisfy Ruxton, who went away.

But in fact, he had been the chief suspect in the Linn case since earlier that day. The Chief Constable of Dumfriesshire had seen an article in the Glasgow *Daily Record* describing the disappearance of Mary Rogerson. He immediately decided to contact the Lancaster police, and Mary's parents. The Scottish police arrived in Morecambe, bringing with them the blouse and the children's rompers. As soon as Mrs Rogerson saw the blouse, she knew her stepdaughter was dead. She recognised it as one she had bought in a jumble sale and patched under the arm; she had given it to Mary the previous Christmas. She was unable to identify the rompers, but she suggested someone who might know—a woman with whom Mary and the Ruxton children had spent a holiday earlier that year, a Mrs Holme. Mrs Holme dispelled the last vestiges of doubt about the bodies; she identified the rompers as a pair she had given to Mary for the children. She was able to be positive because she recognised the knot which she herself had tied in the elastic.

The Lancaster police were now certain they had their man; but they acted with caution. Ruxton had no less than three charladies who worked at the house: Mrs Smith, Mrs Oxley and Mrs Curwen. The police talked to Mrs Oxley, who usually arrived at the Ruxton house—at 2

Dalton Square—at seven in the morning. On the morning of Sunday, September 15—the day Mrs Ruxton and her maid had disappeared—Ruxton had arrived at her house at 6.30, and told her husband that she needn't go to the house that day, because Mrs Ruxton had gone to Edinburgh, and he intended to take the children to Morecambe. She went to the house the following day, and found it in a state of chaos. The stair carpets had been removed, and the bath was full of yellow stains. In the backyard there was a pile of some material that seemed to have been burned with petrol.

But the clinching evidence came from one of Ruxton's patients, a Mrs Hampshire. She told how Ruxton had called on her on Sunday afternoon. He had apparently taken his three children over to Morecambe—five miles away—to stay at the house of a dentist called Anderson, Ruxton's closest friend. His wife had gone to Blackpool, Ruxton explained, and Mary Rogerson had gone for a holiday. The decorators were coming to his house the next day, and he had to remove the carpets. Unfortunately, he had cut his hand badly on a tin of peaches, and he needed some help. . . . Mrs Hampshire and her husband obligingly returned with him to 2 Dalton Square, and helped 'prepare' the place for the decorators. There was an untouched meal—for two persons—in the lounge, and an uncooked Sunday joint. The carpets had been taken up from the stairs and the landings, and one of them was stained with blood. The bath was stained yellow. Mrs Hampshire scrubbed at it with scouring powder, but there was still a great deal of stain left in it. Her husband scrubbed the stairs. Ruxton left them there while he went off to Morecambe again. Here he suggested that his children should stay the night with the dentist and his wife. The Anderson's agreed, and Mrs Anderson and the children returned with Ruxton to collect their night clothes. On the way, they stopped at the home of Mary Rogerson's parents, where Ruxton left a message to say that Mary had gone to Scotland for a few weeks. Back at Dalton Square, Ruxton told the Hampshires—who were still busily scrubbing—that they could have the carpets, and also a blue suit which he had been wearing at the time he cut his hand; it was badly bloodstained. Once again, he went off, leaving the Hampshires to their cleaning. They stayed until 9.30, and then locked up and went home. They noticed that the doors of Ruxton's bedroom and Isabella Ruxton's bedroom were locked.

What would the Hampshires have seen if they could have found the keys and looked into the locked rooms? In all probability, they would have found Isabella Ruxton's body already hacked into pieces, and perhaps already parcelled up. They would probably have found Mary Rogerson, naked but so far untouched. Her body would be dismembered in the bath that night—for when Mrs Oxley came the next morning, the bath was again stained yellow.

So Ruxton had actually given the bloodstained carpets to the Hampshires. These carpets were outside in the yard. Ruxton's original intention had probably been to burn them; but it had rained heavily. The carpets were so wet that the Hampshires decided to take them home later. But they took the suit. And early the next morning, Ruxton called on Mrs Hampshire again, and told her he wanted to send the suit to be cleaned. Ruxton looked ill and unshaven, and he was wearing an old raincoat—although he was normally careful of his appearance. Mrs Hampshire promised she would send the suit to be cleaned. Ruxton insisted that she cut out the tag with his name on it, and burn it in his presence. When this was done, he seemed satisfied and went away.

Mrs Oxley, the charlady, further added that when the newspapers published the story of the finding of the remains in the Linn, Ruxton seemed very pleased with himself. He read the account to her, and said: 'So you see, Mrs Oxley, it is a man and a woman. It is not our two'.

All this made it fairly clear that Ruxton was the man the police were looking for. And Ruxton himself realised how close the chase was getting. On the day Mrs Rogerson identified the blouse as Mary's, Ruxton went off the Edinburgh to see his wife's sister. He asked her if Isabella was staying with her. The sister—Mrs Nelson—countered by asking him if he had done anything to her. (She had read of the finding of the bodies in the Linn.) Ruxton said of course not—he loved her too much.

When he got back to Lancaster in the early hours of the morning—October 10—he was met by a detective. Ruxton must have thought for a moment that he was about to be arrested; but the detective only wanted to ask him a few questions. Ruxton told him that he had been to Edinburgh, looking for his wife. And he added that a man called Bobbie Edmondson probably knew where she was. Edmondson, said Ruxton, was having an affair with his wife. A few weeks earlier, Bobbie Edmondson and Isabella Ruxton had gone to a hotel in Edinburgh, and stayed there together.

Oddly enough, this was true—but not in the way Ruxton suggested. Robert Edmondson was an assistant solicitor in the Town Hall, opposite the Ruxton's house. His whole family—including his parents and sister—were friendly with the Ruxtons, and he had often been a guest in their home. A week before Mrs Ruxton's disappearance, the whole Edmondson family went to Edinburgh with Mrs Ruxton. They all stayed in a hotel, in four separate rooms. Ruxton did not tell the detective that the whole Edmondson family had gone to Edinburgh; and he told a lie when he added that Edmondson and Mrs Ruxton had booked into the hotel under the name of Mr and Mrs Ruxton.

Later that day, Ruxton called on Mrs Hampshire, and asked what had happened to the blue suit; she said it was upstairs. 'Then burn it', said Ruxton. He asked about the carpets, and was told that one of them was too badly stained to be cleaned. 'Then burn that too'. He went off saying he intended to make a statement to the police. In fact, he called at the police station, and complained about the gossip; he also gave a description of his wife, which was written down. The following day he spent writing out a long account of his movements for the police, and paid more visits to the police station; it was on this occasion that he asked the Chief Constable, Captain Vann, to issue a statement to press saying there was no connection between Mrs Ruxton and the bodies in the Linn.

The next day, Saturday October 12, was his last day of freedom. He called on several people, asking them to support his account of various facts. But most of the 'facts' he wanted them to confirm were false. He asked Mrs Oxley to say that she had spent a couple of hours cleaning his house on the Sunday morning of Mrs Ruxton's disappearance; Mrs Oxley replied that she couldn't say it, since it was not true. He also asked an odd job man to swear that he had come to the house on the Saturday evening before the disappearance, and that Mary Rogerson had opened the door to him; the odd job man pointed out that this was untrue. (The exact point of this request is not clear, for there can be no doubt that Mary Rogerson died in the early hours of Sunday morning; but Ruxton was becoming confused by this time.)

That evening, October 12, Ruxton was asked to call at the police office. Both the Scottish and English police were present. Ruxton was questioned all night; and at 7.20 the next morning, he was charged with the murder of Mary Rogerson. He indignantly denied it. In the face of overwhelming circumstantial evidence, Ruxton continued to deny that he was guilty of either of the murders. His story—and and story of the Defense—was that the bodies found in the Linn were not those of Isabella Ruxton and Mary Rogerson. They had disappeared, and it was not the business of the defense to say where they were now. But Ruxton was innocent of their deaths. This meant, of course, that the whole weight of the prosecution depended on the medical evidence. If the jury could be convinced that the bodies in the Linn were Mrs Ruxton and Mary Rogerson, then Ruxton was condemned; if not, he was free.

Judges are normally unhappy about sentencing a man to death on purely circumstantial evidence; but in this case, it must be admitted that the evidence was overwhelming and irrefutable. No murderer has ever taken more trouble than Ruxton to spin the net around himself. At the trial, ninety nine per cent of the evidence was for the Prosecution; Ruxton himself was the only witness for the Defense. It is the kind of case that makes the layman feel that our legal system is an elaborate game. Ruxton's counsel, Norman Birkett, must have known that his client didn't stand the remotest chance. Every witness who appeared drove another nail into his coffin. The opening speech for the crown by J.C.Jackson made Ruxton's guilt so obvious that the jury could have filed out there and then. He pointed out that two years before the murders, Ruxton had threatened to murder his wife in front of policemen. He was convinced his wife had been unfaithful. Again, in 1935, he 'behaved like a madman', accusing his wife of infidelity—again to a policeman—and threatening to kill her. The week before the murder, Mrs Ruxton went to Edinburgh with Edmondson family, and Ruxton hired a car (his wife had taken his car) and followed them. He was convinced his wife had spent the night in Bobbie Edmondson's bed. The following Saturday, Mrs Ruxton drove to Blackpool to visit her two sisters; she spent the evening with them and drove back to Lancaster around midnight. It did not take much imagination to guess what happened next. Ruxton had worked himself into a frenzy of jealousy; throughout the evening he was probably conjuring up visions of his wife being possessed on the sands at Blackpool, or in the back of his own car. . . . The fact that there was a meal set out in the dining room implies that he had expected her back in time for supper; when she came back after midnight, he was half insane with rage and jealousy. He probably beat her in an attempt to make her confess her infidelity, then throttled and stabbed her. Mary Rogerson probably heard the screams and came to the bedroom—or perhaps Ruxton went to her room and killed her. In the previous year he had told a policeman that there were *two* people in the house he felt like killing. Why two? Because he believed that Mary Rogerson was Mrs Ruxton's confidant and accomplice, who knew exactly what was going on . . .?

At 6.30 the next morning he was at the house of the charlady, telling her that she needn't come that day. At ten to nine, the woman who delivered newspapers rang the doorbell of Ruxton's house but got no reply; she went back at nine, and this time Ruxton opened the door. He told her his wife had gone to Scotland with the maid. When the girl with the milk came, Ruxton let her in; his hand was bandaged and he told her he had 'jammed' it—presumably in a door. Later he told other people he'd cut it while opening a tin of peaches. At 10.30, Ruxton was at a local garage—not his usual one—and bought two large cans of petrol; then he went to his own garage and had another four gallons put in the tank of his car. Why use two garages, unless to cover up His tracks? The petrol in the cans was used to burn something in his yard that day—bloodstained clothing and carpets. When he had taken up the carpets from the stairs, he asked Mrs Hampshire, one of his patients, to help him get the house ready 'for the decorators'. (Two days later, he called on a decorator, and tried to persuade him that he had promised to come and start work the previous day; the decorator flatly denied this.) Mrs Hampshire noticed the bloodstained bath, bloodstained carpets, and fragments of straw—the bodies were partly packed in straw. He took the children to his friends the Andersons, and asked the Andersons to look after them overnight. And that night, he made his first trip to dispose of the bodies. He certainly went *somewhere*, for the charlady who called at 7.10 the next morning could get no reply to her knocks. At 9, he was again at Mrs Hampshire's house, looking tired and dissheveled, asking her about the bloodstained suit and carpets. Later that day, he told Mrs Hampshire that his wife had left him with another man, and gone to London. The next day, Tuesday, he put his own car in the garage for a service, although it didn't need one, and hired a larger car. He had evidently decided that if he was not to make several more journeys, he needed a larger boot. Later the same day, this hired car knocked down a cyclist in Kendal and drove on without stopping. The cyclist got the car's number and reported it; Ruxton was stopped half an hour later; he had one of his children with him. He made an incoherent statement about having been to Carlisle, and afterwards changed it and said he had been to Seattle, the place where his family had spent their holiday. It seems that Ruxton had dumped more parts of the body somewhere, but it could not have been in the Linn this time—Moffat was at least three hours from Lancaster. But Lake Windermere was well within his range. . . . (No parts of bodies were ever found in Windermere; but then, there is no reason why a well-weighted parcel should ever come to the surface.)

And so the evidence went on piling up. On the morning of Wednesday the 18th, Ruxton made several trips up and down to his bedroom, telling the charlady he was going to see a specialist about his hand. (But why a specialist for a flesh wound?) When he left, the charlady entered the bedroom—now at last open—and noticed the foul smell— later Ruxton told her to spray it with *eau de Cologne*. And later that day, with the last part of the body disposed of, he turned his attention to other problems—pacifying the Rogersons about Mary's disappearance, scraping the wall in his backyard with an axe. (He even told the charlady he was doing it to remove bloodstains.) Never, at any point during the trial, was there the faintest hope of convincing the jury of Ruxton's innocence. But when the doctors entered the box—Professor Glaister, Dr Millar, Professor Sidney Smith (who returned from abroad in time to add his own comments to the case for the prosecution)—all hope of a recommendation to mercy vanished: those gruesome photographs of severed feet (neatly fitted into the shoes of the dead women) hands without fingertips, heads without eyes or ears, were enough to convince the most humane jury that they were dealing with a monster. And Ruxton's own performance in the witness box was pathetic. Whenever possible, he simply contradicted the statements of witnesses —witnesses who had no reason to lie, unless the whole town of Lancaster was in a conspiracy against him. Where he had explanations, they were feeble: it was his children who had scattered straw over the house that Sunday morning . . . The defending counsel summarised the matter when he said: '. . . if you are satisfied that the identity of those remains in the ravine at Moffat had been satisfactorily proved to be the remains of Mrs Ruxton and Mary Rogerson, then your task is well–nigh completed. Members of the jury, with all the powers I have, I deny it . . .' But there was not a person there who didn't realise that he was whistling in the dark. The jury took only one hour to decide unanimously that Ruxton was guilty. Three months later, an appeal was dismissed, and Ruxton was hanged at Strangeways Jail, Manchester, on May 12, 1936.

The question remains: should Ruxton have been hanged? He was guilty, but guilty of what? Of an unpremeditated murder, committed in a state of mindless, frenzied jealousy. If he had walked into the Lancaster Police Station in the early hours of that Sunday morning, and said: 'I have just murdered my wife, and I think I may have killed the maid as well ..', there would have been a 50/50 chance of a life sentence, or perhaps of confinement in Broadmoor. It may be argued that his subsequent actions show cunning; but they also show a kind of insanity—the kind of insanity of Lady Macbeth trying to wash imaginary bloodstains off her hands. A psychiatrist examining Ruxton's activities after the murders would say that he showed no sense of reality. The house was full of bloodstains, so that even if he could have made the bodies vanish into thin air, his chances of escaping were still a hundred to one. He showed apparent cunning in mutilating the bodies—pulling out teeth, even amputating a bunion from his wife's foot—yet forgot that the length of his wife's face was unmistakable identification—as Glaister showed when he superimposed a photograph of Mrs Ruxton on to the skull. He might have convinced the police that one of the bodies was that of a man—or at least, left some doubt in their minds—if he had not included three breasts and two lots of female genitals in the parcels—items that could have been burnt in his stove in ten minutes.

If Ruxton had had any sense, he would have pleaded guilty; then his Defense might have stood a chance of saving him from the gallows. For the only real chance of saving Ruxton would have been to tell the whole story of his 'marriage'. This can be read between the lines of the account of his trial, but it is overwhelmed by the other evidence. Now Ruxton has been dead for many years, we can afford to examine his side of the story dispassionately.

Ruxton was born in 1899 in Bombay; he qualified in 1922, and served in the Indian Medical Corps. When he came to England in the mid-1920s, he was a Captain. He spoke French better than English. He was good looking, clever, extravagantly affectionate and extravagantly emotional. As a human being, he certainly lacked self-discipline. We should also bear in mind that he grew up in India at the time of the Raj—that is, at the height of the British empire's power there. The British gave the native Indians a strong inferiority complex; anyone who has read E.M. Forster's *Passage to India* will understand this.

Isabella Kerr was a Scot, two years Ruxton's junior. She was not pretty, but she had a great deal of vivacity and charm. She was also intelligent and efficient enough to have held several jobs as manageress in restaurants. She had married at the age of 19—a Dutchman called Van Ess; but the marriage broke up. Not long after, she met the handsome Captain Hakim, who was studying at Edinburgh to become a surgeon. The attraction that sprang up between them was deep and powerful. For her, he was the mysterious and romantic foreigner—this was the era of Rudolph Valentino—totally unlike the phlegmatic Dutchman from whom she was separated; he was also a qualified doctor. For him, she was the cool, detached Englishwoman, balanced, level-headed, but very sexually desirable. She represented a kind of dream. There can be no doubt that she was far from sexually cold. They hurled themselves into a passionate physical relation, intoxicated with each other. When Ruxton went to study in London, she gave up her job as a manageress and followed him. Possibly there was some masochistic element in her; they had violent quarrels, followed by violent lovemaking sessions. 'We were the kind of people who could not live with each other and could not live without each other', Ruxton said in court. She tried living without him, leaving him to return to Edinburgh; but she returned to London after a few months. They never married, although she told relatives they were married. Her previous marriage had been dissolved. This again suggests a masochists element in her makeup: at that time, to 'live in sin' meant a great deal more than nowadays, particularly to a respectably brought-up Scotswoman.

Ruxton found her infinitely desirable, physically. The list of exhibits at the trial includes a great many silk garments: a silk nightdress, silk corsets, silk underskirts, silk blouses, fawn silk stockings. There are also a pair of silver evening shoes and a green silk coatee. Ruxton liked to see her beautifully dressed—and undressed; and, as a Persian, he wanted his lady dressed in silk.

Was she actually unfaithful to him? There is no evidence of it. In a small town like Lancaster in the mid-30s, it would have been all over the town if the doctor's wife had been misbehaving herself. But she was lively and vivacious, and she may have flirted with men like Robert Edmondson. And Ruxton, with his eastern ideas of a woman's position in the home, would find it hard to realise that in England there may be an abyss of difference between flirting with a man and going to bed with him. He found his wife so maddeningly desirable that he could believe that every man in Lancaster wanted to undress her. Hence the violent quarrels that sometimes ended with her being beaten black and blue, and which led her to leave him on at least two occasions. After one of these quarrels, she tried to gas herself. Yet they remained together, and she continued to produce babies—three who lived, and one still-born. Ruxton adored his children, and seems to have been an excellent father. Their colour would have made it clear to him that he was the father. Yet, with his inferiority complex, he would still find it difficult to believe that she would not prefer an English lover. He was convinced that Edmondson was her lover—and the night in the Edinburgh hotel certainly gave them the opportunity to sleep together—yet he continued to be polite, even friendly, towards him. Again, the inferiority complex.

After that trip to Edinburgh, he was convinced that she was unfaithful to him. She was stupid enough to lie to him about it, claiming she had spent the night at her sister's house. So when she went to Blackpool, he was almost certainly convinced that she was with her lover. And who knows what happened when she finally returned home after midnight: In their quarrels, she was certainly not tongue-tied. (Ruxton said that she sometimes came into his surgery smiling, and asked, 'I'm wondering how I can pick a quarrel with you?') Perhaps she admitted that she had been unfaithful. Or perhaps Ruxton simply drove himself to a new height of screaming, manic fury. He hit her; he choked her; he stabbed her; he went on battering the body with some heavy instrument. It was the final transport of his strange, sado-masochistic love for her. The maid interupted, and he struck her with the blunt instrument too; although the original fury had probably by now evaporated; he was killing her to prevent her rushing out and giving the alarm.

The children were still asleep, in spite of the shrieks and groans. (They slept in Mrs Ruxton's bedroom—the murder probably took place in his bedroom.) Now Ruxton was left alone with the bodies, and it must have seemed to him as if he was waking up. The woman he had loved for ten years was dead. The pattern of his rages involved a swing from one extreme to another—hysterical anger, followed by tearful contrition. And usually he could undo any damage he'd done. Now there was no way back. He probably thought of suicide, then decided against it because of the children. Finally, he made the decision to hack up the bodies and dispose of them piecemeal. No doubt he at first considered the possibility of weighting the bodies and dropping them in the sea or in a lake; but that would require a boat. Since the place was already covered with blood, he might as well go ahead with the dismemberment scheme. But he was not a cool, level headed man; he was accustomed to indulging his violent fits of emotion. How did he feel when he hacked off his wife's head, then pulled out the teeth with pliers, then levered out the eyes? Dismembering Mary Rogerson was probably just an unpleasant job; but Isabella was the mother of his children, the woman he adored. To mutilate her body must have seemed like a form of self destruction.

By daylight, he must have been physically and emotionally exhausted. But the charlady was due at seven o'clock, and the house was still covered in bloodstains. He had to rush out and tell her not to come. Then he went back and started to tear up the carpets. He kept discovering new bloodstains on the walls and on the floor; obviously, the wallpaper would have to be stripped and the place re-decorated. And all the time he worked, he thought of the children: what would happen to them now? By this time, he must have wished a thousand times that he could bring Isabella back to life and ask her forgiveness; it must have seemed like a nightmare—that her dismembered body now lay in his locked bedroom, while her blood had flowed down the drain. The doorbell rang; for a moment he panics; then he realises it is the girl with the newspapers. His hands and arms are bloodstained; there is no time to wash before he goes downstairs; he decides not to answer it. Then he hears voices in the children's bedroom; in a few minutes, they'll be coming out and asking where their mother is. Will they notice the bloodstains on the carpet? No—they're too innocent. They'll believe whatever he tells them. . . . And the thought of their innocence wrenches his heart and makes him want to burst into tears of self-pity. But this is no time for self-pity. Someone is ringing the doorbell again. . . .

Everything was against Ruxton; all his lies found him out. Even his assertion that Mary Rogerson had been pregnant was disproved when the charlady found some used sanitary towels in her bedroom. Fate was against Ruxton. After the murder, every decision he took went wrong, from the dismembering of the bodies to the decision to plead Not Guilty—which meant that the prosecution had the easy task of proving that he was a murderer, a liar and a monster. If he had pleaded Guilty, it would have given the Defense a chance to play for sympathy, to plead that he had already suffered torments as a result of that burst of jealous frenzy.

It seems, in fact, as if Ruxton had *wanted* to be sentenced to death; everything he did after the murder of his wife shows a powerful subconscious desire to join her. 'We were the kind of people who could not live with each other and could not live without each other'. It sounds enough like Shakespeare's 'one that loved not wisely but too well' to make us wonder if he had read *Othello*.

RUPERT FURNEAUX

Jealous Woman with a Gun

More lethal bullets are fired in the United States in a day than in Britain in a decade, although the British are catching up rather too fast. When the British housewife or deceived mistress reaches for a weapon, her hand seldom alights on anything more destructive than a piece of crockery. But in the United States firearms seem to lurk in every woman's bottom drawer. This chapter tells the stories of three women, an American, a French girl and an English woman who, at the moment of emotional crisis, happened to have a gun in their hands, and how the males of their race dealt with them. Sisters they may have been under the skin but their fates were very different.

The *crime passionel* is supposed to be an exclusively French institution, but the stories of Nan Patterson and Ruth Ellis suggest that murder in jealousy is as international as the crack of a shot.

Shot number one was fired early on a glorious June morning in 1904 in the ebullient city of New York, that city of 'intoxicating women and intoxicated men', as my late uncle, the famous 'F.E. Smith' once described it. It is 8.50 a.m. and a hansom cab comes bowling down Broadway, then, as now, the 'Great White Way' of show business, swinging from side to side for its driver, Albert Michaels, is suffering from what he was later to describe as a 'shattering hangover', one so overwhelming that he was not able 'to take any profound interest' in what was happening inside his cab.

Into Michael's befuddled mind came the sound of a shot

and the girl, whom he vaguely remembered hailing his cab with a young man, called to him to drive to the nearest drug store. 'Hurry, hurry', she exclaimed. It was not for the driver to reason why and he pulled his cab to the side-walk where a small but eager crowd of New Yorkers had been attracted by the sound of the shot. Frequent as is the crack of gunfire in America's leading city, its citizens never grow blasé.

The crowd of Broadway hangers-on were quickly shouldered aside by one of the 'finest' as New Yorkers called their policemen in those slap-happy days before the hard-faced 'Dragnet' cop and the 'prowl-car' became the emblem of American law enforcement. Officer O'Bannion, as Irish as most of his comrades, took in the situation at a glance, one he had often seen before and would frequently see again.

A dying man lay slumped across the knees of a beautiful girl, his bleeding head clasped in her lap, her pretty face streaming with tears as she sat wringing her hands and crying, 'Caesar, Caesar, why did you do this?'—Confirmation, or apparent corroboration that the man had taken his own life was provided by the discovery of a .32 revolver, still reeking from its discharge, in his pocket.

Officer O'Bannion was satisfied at once. 'Poor chap committed suicide,' he told his superiors. But not all New York cops are or were Irish, and some of them have nasty suspicious minds. To the boys of the Homicide Squad one off-key note in the shooting stuck out a mile.

The gun with which Caesar Young had been shot lay in his left jacket pocket, yet he was a right-handed man. If he shot himself in the head, it meant that he had had the presence of mind to free his fair companion from blame by carefully placing the gun in his own pocket. But he had put it in the wrong pocket, or Nan Patterson had.

Everything the police learned from their enquiries confirmed their belief that Nan had shot the lover who had jilted her. The dead man was Caesar, or Frank, Young, a gambler, of English parentage. He had planned to sail for Europe that morning at 9.0 o'clock. At 7.30 he had left home, telling his wife he needed a shave, and promising to be on board with her before the liner sailed. Now he lay dead in the cab in which he had been riding, unshaven and hatless, with his show-girl mistress, Nan Patterson, with whom he had been associating for two years. Yet, only the night before he had hit her in the face and sworn never to see her again. As he walked out of her life, she had shouted threats, declaring he would not sail on the morrow.

That night Nan's brother had purchased the .32 revolver, now found in the dead man's pocket.

Nan was charged with the first-degree murder of Caesar Young. With an unwise lack of caution in such tricky matters, the District Attorney's office declared it 'an open and shut case', and the city's newspapers with their usual abandon, named Nan a 'murderess' and regaled their readers with lurid descriptions of the delights of Sing Sing's electric chair, in which undoubtedly she would fry.

But it is very hard indeed to execute a pretty girl in America. Even in a woman-run world, men have the last word in such important matters. The sanctity by which American womanhood is held by men is confirmed by the oft-proven fact that, while many male killers escape the death penalty, they never do when their victim is a pretty woman. Even to convict a pretty girl is difficult. That was particularly true in New York in the early nineteen hundreds, the hey-day of the shyster lawyer, the tear-jerker, the jury spell-binder. In the old Felony Court building on Lower Broadway, Howe, Hummel and William Fallon reigned supreme, wresting acquittals from all male juries by all sorts of devious devices. On one famous occasion the partnership of Howe and Hummel freed a butcher charged with hacking several inoffensive women to death with an axe, by bringing into court a timid little woman and her nine brats. 'Will you send this man to the chair, or return him to his loving family?' Hummel demanded of the jury, waving his hand in the direction of the grief-stricken family, whereupon ten handkerchiefs, purchased for the occasion, mopped twenty streaming eyes.

Nan's Attorney, Abe Levy, swore to do as well for his beautiful client. Despite the apparently damning evidence against her, her threats against her lover's life, the purchase of the murder weapon and the fact that it was found in the wrong pocket, Abe Levy felt confident of the result. Nan, as she walked into court was the cynosure of all eyes, especially those of the twelve male jurors, Abe noted. A gorgeous brunette with a lovely figure enhanced by the 'Floradora' style of the period, Nan swept to her seat at her attorney's side.

District Attorney Rand presented the case for the State of New York. The dead man, the murdered man, the exemplary husband and father, he declared could not have shot himself. The direction of the bullet, the wound it had made, the powder burns on the skin, the heavy trigger action, proved he could not have fired the shot. Nan, he denounced, as a conspirator, a parasite, a kept woman and a murderess.

If not brief, Abe Levy's reply was to the point. To simple men like himself and the jurors, all this talk of bullet trajectories, wounds and powder burns was outside the realms of reality. How could anyone say, he demanded to know, that the gun had been fired six inches or six feet from Caesar Young's head? It was just as likely, more likely, that Caesar, remorseful and unhappy, had taken his own life, than that Nan had shot him. Repentant of his treatment of Nan, Caesar had implored her forgiveness; but the discarded mistress, her love scorned, had refused to take him back. In desperation, Caesar Young had shot himself. It was as easy as that, declared Abe Levy.

But it was not quite as simple as that, as Levy well knew. In his opening speech the District Attorney pin-pointed Nan's cry in the cab, 'Caesar, Caesar, why did you do this?' That wasn't the cry of a love-sick girl, declared Mr Rand. It was the quick thinking of a Broad-way-toughened show-girl. An allegation which called for the defence's reply.

'Do you believe,' Abe asked the jury, banging his hands on the rail of their box, 'do you believe that this empty, frivolous, if you like, pleasure loving girl could conceive the plot that would permit her at one second to kill and in the next to cover this act by a subtle invention? Is there a possibility that within two seconds after the shot she could have been so consummate an actress as to have been able deliberately to pretend the horror which showed itself in her face at that moment? The greatest actress on Broadway could not have shown such ability,' declared Abe Levy.

Mr Rand accepted the challenge. 'It does not require the greatness of histrionic talent to pretend that something has happened which has not,' he told the jury in his turn.

Some of the men on the jury were either doubtful of Nan's guilt, or they were captivated by her charms, for they failed to reach a verdict. At her inevitable second trial Nan went on the witness stand herself. Life without Frank wasn't worth living, she declared.

Again, Mr Rand demanded that the jury send Nan to the electric chair. Nan, he told them, had lost her lover. 'She saw red,' Mr Rand declared, 'the murder in her heart flamed; there was a crack of the pistol-shot, a puff of smoke, her lover was dead, the wages of sin were paid.'

For fourteen hours the jury deliberated. Eleven declared her Guilty, but the twelfth man held out for acquittal, because, he said, he was sorry for Nan. At last they could only tell the judge that they had failed to agree.

Nan was too exhausted by her ordeal to stand trial again, declared Abe Levy. The State of New York withdrew the charge. A few days later Nan starred in a Broadway show, for her part in which she was paid $1,000 a week. New Yorkers still discuss the case after a lapse of fifty years. If there are any who do not share the jury's doubts as to who shot Caesar Young, it must be because they never saw Nan Patterson in the flesh.

FRENCH VERSION

The crime of passion is losing its glamour in the eyes of Frenchmen, we are told by M. Marc Ancel, Judge of the Supreme Court of France. For a hundred years, he said in 1956, French juries had taken pity upon deceived husbands and discarded mistresses. But French women, he says, who have qualified as jurors since 1945, are less sympathetic of killings alleged to have been done in jealousy. Let us see how this view is borne out in the case of Pauline Dubuisson. The shots that landed her in the dock, charged with premeditated murder, were fired in Paris on March 17, 1951.

At first glance it looked a typical case of the old, old story, lover shot dead, ex-mistress dying in a gas filled room, on the floor by her side an automatic pistol. When the room had been cleared of gas and the girl revived by oxygen, the detectives turned to examine the man, whom they learned was Felix Bailey, a young medical student. He had come from Lille and had been friendly with Pauline Dubuisson, who appeared to have shot him. The detectives, being Frenchmen, shrugged their shoulders. Jealousy was clearly the motive, they thought. But when they looked closer at Felix Bailey, suspicion of something far more serious crept into their minds; Bailey had been shot three times, twice in the forehead, and once through the back of the neck, facts which were quite out of keeping with a lovers' quarrel.

Bit by bit, the Paris police pieced together the story of the love affair that had ended in death. Felix's murder had been fully premeditated, the element in French law which makes murder capital, it seemed. It was not a passionate crime of jealousy, punishable by a few months' imprisonment.

The clues came fast and thick. A few weeks before, Pauline had bought a gun. She travelled to Paris and tried to see Felix, but he refused to admit her. That morning she had returned; for an hour she watched the apartment. Then seeing another student leave, she had knocked at the door. Taken unawares, Felix let her in. 'It was an accident,' Pauline told the police. She had taken the gun out of her bag to frighten Felix; in the struggle for its possession, it had fired, a statement that did not fit the facts. 'You shot him in the fury of a woman scorned,' the police told her. 'Then, to make certain he was dead, you shot him again in the back of the neck.' 'I shot him because I was jealous,' she declared. Felix had become engaged to be married, she said. He had betrayed their love.

Tiny doubts began to creep into the detectives' minds. Pauline, an outstandingly beautiful girl, did not look a tigress robbed of her cub. Quiet and demure, with large melting eyes, she seemed a sweet girl, innocent and appealing. She may have 'premeditated' the murder of her ex-lover, the detectives thought inasmuch as she had bought a gun, but nonetheless it could be a case of inflamed jealousy, the mad frenzy of a woman scorned, a young girl seduced and flung aside. But that picture quickly collapsed when they looked into Pauline Dubuisson's private life.

Searching her room in Lille, the detectives came across Pauline's diary, the 'Orgy Book' as it was to be described at her trial. It dispelled all doubts of her character. She was no innocent girl. She had been the seducer, not Felix. Her love affairs with men started when she was fourteen, her first man a German soldier. During the Occupation she had indulged in nude orgies with German officers and had been expelled from school for describing them too fully. To escape deportation to a forced labour-camp, she had acquired a Nazi protector, a doctor for whom she had, in her own words, made a 'tasty mistress'. After the war, to evade the wrath of her more virtuous fellow citizens, she fled to Lyons where she trained to become a doctor. There she passed her exams with flying colours, and at the same time had her pick of the students. Felix Bailey fell into her net. Every man wanted to love and protect her. She played hard to get, but she was the easiest push-over on the campus.

When Felix fell in love with her, she flaunted her affairs. When she wanted him she took him, when she tired of him she flung him aside. Distracted in the agony of his jealousy, Felix tore himself away. He went to Paris, where he became engaged to be married. To Pauline, he was the one who had got away, the man to be recaptured at all costs. She faked suicide; from Felix her death agonies drew no response. She went to Paris and shot him dead.

'That was premeditated murder,' declared the Public Prosecutor. Once again Pauline attempted suicide, she cut her wrists in her cell and her trial was held up until she recovered. At last on November 15, 1953, she was brought into court. Her counsel called her a pathetic creature. The Public Prosecutor named her a monster, a female hyena, a depraved woman, and he demanded that Pauline's fate should be the guillotine. The spectators in the court leaned forward eagerly. Pauline stood in the dock, pale, demure, sweetly-innocent. It seemed hardly possible that this was the girl who had had hundreds of affairs with men and minutely described them in her diary.

Pauline admitted her guilt. She and Felix had not fought for the gun. It was not a murder of jealousy. She had bought the gun intending to shoot Felix. To make sure he was dead she had put a final bullet into the back of his neck. Then she had staged a suicide to make the killing look a lovers' quarrel. She pleaded guilty to a fully premeditated murder for which the statutory sentence was death.

But that was more than the jury of six men and one woman could bring themselves to decide. They found Pauline guilty of simple murder, and she was sentenced to life imprisonment only. The spell Pauline had cast over innumerable men was too strong. She was made for love, not death.

ENGLISH VERSION

In this century, up to 1956, the English have executed fifteen women. Most of these female murderers killed by poison or for gain. Ruth Ellis was hanged because she was a jealous woman who happened to have a gun in her hand. The crime of passion, the unwritten law which excuses in some degree murder committed in the frenzy of emotion, is not officially recognised in England but, usually, a reprieve mitigates the harshness of the legal axiom that an eye shall be extracted for an eye and a life taken for a life.

The hanging of women who kill in emotional frenzy is not an English custom. The execution of Ruth Ellis in 1955 set a new degree of ruthlessness; other nations drew back in horror at the barbarity of the English.

But it was a Welsh Home Secretary who denied Ruth a reprieve. This is the story that was laid on Major Gwilym Lloyd George's desk.

Ruth was born in Rhyl in 1927 and brought up in Manchester. During the war she was a munitions worker, a waitress and a dance band crooner. In 1944 she had a son by an American soldier who, she said, was killed the same year. In 1950 she married a dentist, by whom she had a daughter, but the marriage was dissolved. In 1953 she met David Blakely, a racing motorist, a Public School boy and the son of a Sheffield doctor, aged twenty-nine.

The girl from the wrong side of the tracks and the man born with a silver spoon in his mouth, began a tempestuous love affair which ended two years later in the man being shot down in the street, and the girl having her neck broken by the public hangman.

Some people hold that love is only chemistry. If that is true, the Great Alchemist must have laughed at the mating of Ruth and David for their passion, the merging of their bodies into one, produced not life, but death. Love and hate were the fruits of their desire. The merging of their chromosomes gave birth to jealousy. And jealousy consumed them.

Soon after Ruth and David met in June 1953, she became hostess at a club in Knightsbridge, and she went to live in the flat above the club. After two weeks David came to live with her, although Ruth was still married and David engaged to a girl in Huddersfield. He slept at the flat every night from Monday to Friday, going home to his mother's house at Penn each weekend. 'At this time I was not very much in love with David', Ruth said at her trial. In December she had an abortion; David offered to marry her, but she preferred to get herself out of trouble. Ruth says she refused to take the affair with David seriously as long as he was engaged to another girl. She told him that their friendship was not good for business, and he did not like it at all.

In June, 1954, David went to race his car at Le Mans, and while he was away Ruth went to bed with another member of her club. When David returned he was suspicious, but the affair continued. He urged Ruth to marry him and he broke his engagement. 'I thought he was devoted to me, and I became more affectionate,' says Ruth. But she didn't trust David. He stayed away one night and the next night she found love-bites over his back. When she asked him about them, he told her that someone had bitten him while he was playing darts. She ordered him from the flat. Next day he telephoned and asked to be back. He came to the

Club, falling on his knees, crying, 'Please marry me'. Ruth suggested, 'I don't think your mother or family would agree to that', but she let her divorce go through undefended so that she could marry him.

According to Ruth, she supported David financially, paying for the flat herself, and settling his drink and cigarette bills at the Club. She didn't mind because she knew he was spending £10 a week on the development of a racing car. She decided to end the affair, because due to her association with one particular man, her earnings at the Club, where she was on a commission basis, were deteriorating. David was drinking heavily: he became violent and he hit her with his fists and hands. The scenes became unbearable, and in December Ruth moved into another man's flat. David arrived on Christmas night and there was a scene. She went to an hotel with him, and moved into a flat he had taken in Egerton Gardens in Kensington. 'I was in love with David', Ruth says and she made no further effort to part from him, but within a few weeks she became suspicious that he was sleeping with other women. When she accused him he hit her, giving her bruises, a black eye and a sprained ankle. She had to go to hospital to have the injuries attended to. While she was there David sent her flowers with a card saying, 'Sorry, darling. I love you, David'. They made up the quarrel, but Ruth's jealousy continued.

David gave her cause. She learned that he had a girl in the country. Her reaction? She persuaded another man to drive her there. She stayed all night outside the house and saw David leaving in the morning. Ruth surprised him as he got into his car, which he had hidden behind a public house. 'It was my turn to be jealous now,' she said, and she told him that all was over between them. But she took David back because she still loved him, she said.

In March, she was pregnant again. David hit her in a quarrel and she had a miscarriage. When he learned that she had been going to have a baby, he was sorry; sometimes he said he wanted a child, at others he remarked, 'I can just about afford seven shillings a week'. In April, they talked again of marriage, and he gave her a photograph of himself, inscribed, 'To Ruth with all my love, from David'.

On April 6 David went to Hampstead where a garage owner was building his racing car. Ruth became suspicious that other purposes were being served, and she got a friend to drive her there. She rang the bell of the flat but there was no reply. From it came the sound of female giggles. David's car was outside and she broke a window. The police arrived, called by David from the flat.

Next day she went to the flat again. She thought that something was going on. She hid in a doorway opposite, from where she observed a party was being held in the flat. About 9.30 p.m. David came out with a woman. She was dark and attractive. Ruth heard David say, 'Let me put my arm round you'. They went off in his car. David was up to his tricks again, she knew. She went home to her flat. 'I had a peculiar idea I wanted to kill him', Ruth said at her trial. Next day she telephoned David at Hampstead. The garage owner who answered the phone, asked at her trial, 'Was it obvious that she was in a considerable state of emotional disturbance?' replied, 'I did not get that impression'.

On Easter Monday, April 10, 1955, Ruth went again to Hampstead. Waylaying him in the street, she shot David Blakely six times with a revolver, five times at point-blank range as he and a car salesman named Bertram Clive Gunnell, came out of the *Magdala* public house. At the trial Gunnell said, 'I came out first, carrying a bottle. I went round to the car but the door was locked, so I had to wait for Blakely. I heard two bangs and a shout of "Clive," I went round the back of the car and saw David lying on the ground. Mrs Ellis was firing a gun into his back. I ran to Blakely and heard Mrs Ellis say, "Now call the police". One bullet had been fired into David's left shoulder from a distance of less than three inches.'

When Detective Inspector Davies saw Ruth that night, he was impressed by her composure. There were no signs of passion. She told him that Blakely saw her outside the public house but turned away. She took the gun from her bag and shot him. She shot him as he was running. As he lay on the ground, she shot him again.

At her trial Ruth said, 'I did not know why I shot him. I was very upset,' and in reply to Prosecuting Counsel's one question she said, 'It is obvious. When I fired the revolver at close range I intended to kill him.'

That Ruth Ellis killed David Blakely, and that she intended to do so, there could be no doubt. The only question at her trial was whether she had provocation. There was no question of her sanity; she knew what she was doing was wrong and against the law.

But, said her counsel, Mr Melford Stevenson, Q.C., on her behalf, malice was absent. He asked the jury to return a verdict, not of wilful murder, but of manslaughter. He told the ten men and two women, 'She is charged with murder, and one of the ingredients of that offence is what lawyers call malice. The law of England provides that if a women has been subject to such emotional disturbance as to unseat her judgement, then it is up to you to say that the offence of which she is guilty is not murder, but manslaughter'.

He said that Ruth had found herself in the emotional prison, guarded by Blakely, from which she could not escape. He had treated her brutally; he went off with other women, but he ultimately came back to her and she always forgave him. 'There is no question in this of any unwritten law,' Mr Stevenson told the jury. 'You may take the view that this young woman was driven by the suffering she had endured at the hands of this young man to do that which she did.' It was in these circumstances, driven by a frenzy which for a time unseated her judgment, that she committed the crime.

A psychiatrist, Dr Duncan Whittaker, said that a woman was more prone to hysterical reaction than a man in the case of infidelity, and in such circumstances could lose her critical faculties and try to solve the problem at a more primitive level. 'The situation was intolerable to her,' declared Dr Whittaker. 'She both hated and loved him.' Over the weekend there was a build-up of emotional tension, and she was impelled to violent action to relieve that suppressed emotion.

In the witness-box, Ruth said she had found the Smith and Wesson revolver in her suitcase. It had been given her by an

American service man for a bad debt. On April 10, she took it with her and went to Hampstead by taxi.

The Judge, Mr Justice Havers, overruled defence counsel's submission that the charge could be reduced to manslaughter by provocation. 'The jealous fury of a woman scorned is no excuse for murder. That is the law of England,' he instructed the jury. There was an intention to kill, he said. He reminded the jury that Ruth Ellis had said directly after the crime, 'I thought I had missed him, so I fired again'. To prosecution counsel's one question she had answered, 'I intended to kill him'. She fired the shots at Blakely deliberately. Finally he warned the jury, 'I have felt constrained to rule in this case there is not sufficient evidence, even on the view of the evidence most favourable to Mrs Ellis, to reduce this killing from murder to manslaughter. It is my duty to direct you that the evidence of this case does not support a verdict of manslaughter on the grounds of provocation'.

Inevitably, Ruth Ellis was found guilty of the wilful murder of David Blakely. According to law, jealousy was no defence, even if she knew her lover was committing misconduct with another woman, so that she could not control herself.

That was the law of England in 1955. Since 1957, the new Homicide Act has extended the scope of provocation, which can now be induced by words alone. In 1955 for provocation to reduce murder to manslaughter, the threat or fear of extreme violence was required, or the provocation received had to be 'gross'. In the case of adultery, the actual sight of a spouse caught in the act was necessary, but such provocation was allowed only to married people. It did not extend to lovers and mistresses. Mere confession of adultery was not sufficient to reduce the crime from murder to manslaughter.

Sufficient time had elapsed between deciding to go to Hampstead, and reaching there, for Ruth's anger to cool.

Ruth Ellis refused to appeal, so the question raised by her counsel, a new point of law, that a woman thwarted in love is more irresponsible than a man, could not be argued.

Major Lloyd George, the Home Secretary, found himself unable to intervene, and Ruth was hanged at Holloway Gaol, while a thousand people knelt and prayed outside. As nine o'clock struck, a street musician played, 'Be Thou with me when I die'. All over the world people criticised the barbarity of the English.

In *The People*, January and February, 1956, the claim was made that Ruth Ellis was given the gun and driven to Hampstead by a man. Forty-eight hours before her execution, she had told a prison officer that the man had promised to educate her ten-year-old son if she kept silent. She shielded this man because she thought her son's future would be assured. If this story is true, it means that Ruth Ellis's crime was not entirely wilful. She may have been incited to commit murder.

The execution of Ruth Ellis shocked the people of England. Not since the execution in 1922 of Edith Thompson had such a wave of anger and incredulity swept the nation. It was one of the factors that led to the majority vote in the House of Commons in 1956 to abolish hanging, which was rejected by the House of Lords.

Because Ruth Ellis was hanged in 1955, other women who now kill in emotional frenzy may be sent only to prison. If Ruth hadn't had the gun handy, she would probably have done no more than slap David's face.

The significance of the case lies in the way the English people treated Ruth Ellis. She killed in emotional frenzy. She was hanged for calmly premeditated murder. The other deaths described in this chapter suggest that she might have been treated more leniently in America or France. But, then, the English have to live up to their reputation as the most ruthless race on earth.

Part 5

KILLING FOR LUST

NORMAN LUCAS

Conman, Casanova, Killer

There was no reply when the young chambermaid knocked on the door of room No. 4 at the Pembridge Court Hotel, Notting Hill, London. The girl hesitated a few seconds, then opened the door quietly and peeped inside. The curtains were drawn across the windows, but in the shaded morning light she was able to see the outline of a figure under the coverings of one of the two beds. Not wishing to disturb a visitor who evidently wanted to sleep late, she closed the door and went about her duties in other rooms.

By two o'clock that afternoon of Friday, 21st June, 1946, there was some concern about the non-appearance of the occupant of room No. 4, and Mrs Alice Wyatt, who assisted her father-in-law in the management of the hotel, decided to investigate. She drew back the curtains and moved the bed-clothes a little from the shoulders of the figure in the bed. To her horror she saw the badly bruised and blood-flecked face of a woman who was quite plainly dead.

The room had been let on Sunday 16th June to a couple who registered as Lt-Colonel and Mrs N. G. C. Heath and gave their address as Black Hill Cottage, Romsey. The woman in the bed was not the girl who had called herself 'Mrs Heath'—and the mysterious 'Colonel' had disappeared.

Mrs Wyatt telephoned the police and the first officers to arrive at the hotel—Detective Inspector Shelley Symes and

133

Sergeant Frederick Averill, both stationed at Notting Hill, and Detective Sergeant William Cramb, of Scotland Yard's photographic department—were left in no doubt that the woman had been murdered in a hideously ferocious and sadistic manner. When they pulled back the bedclothes they saw the weals of seventeen whiplashes across her naked body. The nipples had been practically bitten from her breasts and there were extensive genital injuries. Her ankles had been tied together with a man's handkerchief and there were marks on both wrists indicating that they too had been tied, probably behind her back. An attempt had been made to wash away the blood resulting from the injuries to her face, but some remained in her nostrils and eyelashes.

The second bed in the room had been roughly covered with the bedclothes, as if they had been pulled up hurriedly, and there were extensive blood stains under the coverings, suggesting that the victim had been attacked on one bed and had then been moved to the other. On the pillowcase of the second bed the detectives found criss-cross interlacing marks in blood that matched the whip marks on the woman's body.

Dr Keith Simpson, the pathologist, estimated the time of death at about midnight or the early hours of that morning. The woman, he said, had died from suffocation, possibly by having her face pressed into the pillow. All her injuries had been caused before death.

The victim of this barbarous attack was a woman named Margery Aimee Brownell Gardner, a creature of mystery who was well known in the so-called 'Chelsea set' of that period but was apparently without relatives or close friends. Sh was known to be married, but separated from her husband, and it is perhaps indicative of the lonely road she walked that she was not officially identified until five days after her death—and then by a solicitor from Sheffield who had not seen her for nearly a year.

Even her age was uncertain, but she was thought to be thirty-two. Certainly she was a strikingly handsome woman, with her finely chiselled Grecian nose, well-shaped mouth and arched eyebrows. She scorned the curly 'permed' styles fashionable just after the war and wore her long dark hair drawn smoothly back into a bun on the nape of her neck. Her unusually long, slender fingers were often adorned with heavy rings and she loved to wear earrings and wide, ornate bracelets. She was an artist of some considerable talent and when she was not working as a film extra, earned a living as a freelance commercial illustrator.

Detectives also established that she was sexually promiscuous with a masochistic streak which made her a popular partner for certain types of deviates.

On the evening before her death, 20th June, Margery Gardner had spent some time at the Panama Club, Cromwell Place, South Kensington, where she had shared a table with a tall, fair-haired man. She exchanged a few friendly words with an acquaintance, Miss Winifred Humphrey, and was noticed by the club's receptionist, Solomon Joseph, as she and her companion left soon after midnight. Outside the club the couple hailed a taxi. The driver, Harold Harter, took them to Pembridge Gardens and saw them strolling—the man with his arm round Mrs Gardner's waist—towards the gate of the Pembridge Court Hotel.

All these people were able to give detectives a good description of the man—and it was clear that he was the visitor who had booked room No. 4 at the hotel.

From the police point of view this was merely corroborative evidence, for they were already sure they knew the identity of the murderer. Although he had in the past used a number of aliases, on this occasion he had obligingly signed the register in his true name—Neville George Cleveley Heath.

At this point Scotland Yard officers were faced with a terrible dilemma. Heath had to be found, and found quickly. All the evidence pointed to him as the killer, a man of such violent propensities that it was reasonable to assume him to be a sexual maniac. The surest way of finding him would be to publish his picture in the national newspapers. But if as a result of the publication of such photographs, Heath had been caught and put on trial for Mrs Gardner's murder, his defenders would be able to argue that he had been identified by witnesses as the companion of the murdered woman only because they had seen his picture in the papers. The police knew that in those circumstances any defence lawyer would destroy the identification evidence of Winifred Humphrey, taxi-driver Harter and Mr Joseph of the Panama Club.

The Yard officers had to make a tremendously difficult decision. If they authorised the publication of Heath's picture, would they see a sadistic murderer acquitted to kill again? Should they run this risk, or trust that the normal machinery of the law would catch up with him before he claimed another victim?

A compromise decision was made. Fleet Street newspapers were forbidden to print photographs of the hunted man, but were permitted to give his name and description and state that he was 'wanted for questioning', and pictures of Heath were sent to every police station in the country.

These measures were not enough. Twelve days after the first murder Heath killed an innocent girl whose life might well have been saved. There was a great deal of criticism of the police ban on the publication of his picture after the killing of Mrs Gardner, but many years later the decision was defended by Sir Ronald Howe, Assistant Commissioner (Crime) at Scotland Yard at the time of the murder, in an article in the American magazine *Saturday Evening Post*.

'In the light of after events, this may seem a difficult decision to take,' he wrote, 'but at the time I did not find it difficult, nor do I now think I was wrong. All we knew about Heath was that he had a criminal record for larceny, housebreaking and false pretences. There was no reason to believe he would kill again. He was not yet convicted of murder, nor is there, as far as I know, any previous record of a murderer of Heath's type committing another murder within a few days of his first crime.'

It is true that until the Gardner murder Heath, then aged twenty-nine, had no official record of violence or sexual crimes. It was not until his trial—in evidence introduced by his own counsel in an attempt to prove him insane—that mention was made of Heath's savage attack on a woman at the Strand Palace Hotel, London, earlier that same year. In that case the victim recovered from her injuries and, for reasons undisclosed, no charges were brought.

After the murder trial a number of stories were circulated which purported to show that Heath had been violent from an early age. He was said to have beaten an eight-year-old girl so severely that she needed hospital treatment, and that he had attempted to rape and choke a girl of fifteen. There were suggestions that he might have been involved in the murder of a young WAAF during the war and there was another story of a nurse who had been found dead in his burned-out car. The truth or otherwise of these rumours must remain a matter for speculation because nothing appeared on police records. Heath was known only as a man who had been in a good deal of trouble during his service career and as a civilian had faced a number of charges for fraud and theft, having twice been sent to borstal and several times fined or placed on probation. He was not entitled to call himself 'Lt-Colonel', or to use any of the other elevated service titles he assumed from time to time, having only reached the rank of captain.

As soon as his name and description appeared in the newspapers, a mass of information—all useless—flooded into police stations all over the country. Heath had been seen at an airport in Scotland, boarding a ship at Southampton, walking in the streets of Chichester . . . he was still in London, he had reached France, he was in places hundreds of miles apart at the same time. . . .

In fact, he left the Pembridge Court Hotel early in the morning of the murder, after having bathed, shaved and dressed, and took a taxi to the Grosvenor Hotel at Victoria. He asked for breakfast, but was told he was too early, so settled for some coffee before catching a train to Brighton from Victoria station. At a hotel facing the sea he ate a good breakfast of bacon and eggs, toast and marmalade, then took a stroll round the town before returning to the station and boarding a train for Worthing. Here he had a few drinks at a public house before telephoning a girl friend.

Pretty, dark-haired Yvonne Symonds had first met Heath only six days previously, at a dance in Chelsea on Saturday 15th June, but such was the man's overwhelming fascination that she had already agreed to marry him and regarded herself as unofficially engaged. There is no doubt that Neville Heath was unusually attractive to women—and understandably so. Well educated and intelligent, he had a man-of-the-world assurance and an air of distinction which was enhanced by the titles he assumed. Six feet tall, with muscular shoulders and slim hips, he had blond, crinkly hair and clear blue eyes. He might have been the prototype for any of the heroes of the popular romantic novels of that period.

So far as Miss Symonds was concerned, he certainly pursued the 'sweep-'em-off-their-feet' technique so often described in romantic fiction. After the dance, at which he was persistently attentive, he took her to the Panama Club for drinks before escorting her to the Overseas Club where she was staying. Early next morning he telephoned her, and during the course of a full and happy day he proposed marriage. On the understanding that they were unofficially engaged, the nineteen-year-old girl agreed to spend that night with him—and she was his companion when they booked into room No. 4 at the Pembridge Court Hotel as Lt-Colonel and Mrs Heath.

He treated her with tenderness and she returned quite happily to Worthing the following day. During the course of that week he telephoned her several times and told her he was anxious to meet her parents, so she was delighted when he rang on the following Friday morning and told her he was in Worthing. They lunched together and Heath booked a room for himself at the Ocean Hotel. The next day, Saturday, they met again in the morning and lunched together, after which Miss Symonds introduced her handsome 'fiancé' to her parents.

That evening Heath took her to the Blue Peter Club at Angmering and it was while they were dining that he asked her if she had read anything about the murder of Margery Gardner in London. Miss Symonds had been too concerned with her own romantic affairs to take any interest in sordid murder cases, and she was shocked when Heath told her that the woman had been killed in the very room that he and she had occupied such a short time previously.

Heath then told her an extraordinary story. He said he had lent his key to room No. 4 at the Pembridge Court Hotel to

Mrs Gardner and a man friend and that he himself had slept in North London that night. In the morning, he said, he had been telephoned by Superintendent Thomas Barratt, of Scotland Yard, and the inspector had later taken him to Pembridge Court to see Mrs Gardner's body. Heath told Miss Symonds that it was 'a gruesome sight' and that a poker had been 'stuck up' the woman's body. He offered the opinion that the murder had been the work of a sexual maniac.

The story was entirely untrue. Heath had been in Worthing lunching with Miss Symonds before Mrs Gardner's body was discovered, Superintendent Barratt was not called to the hotel until four o'clock in the afternoon, so far from accompanying Heath to see the body, Barratt was taking all steps to ensure that Heath was found as soon as possible.

There was no poker in room No. 4 and it was later deduced, although never definitely established, that the victim's genital injuries had been caused by the steel-tipped whip which had also been used to lash the body.

Yvonne Symonds was naturally concerned about Heath's involvement in this tragic affair, but it did not occur to her to doubt his story and the couple parted on affectionate terms after he had escorted her home later that night.

It was not until the following morning, when she read in the Sunday newspapers that the police were looking for Heath, that the first awful doubts began to creep into her mind. She telephoned Heath and told him that her parents were rather worried by the news in the papers.

'Yes,' he said, 'I was afraid they would be.'

He was jauntily reassuring, however. He said he had hired a car and was going up to London to sort things out, and promised to telephone her that evening.

Fortunately for this unhappy girl she did not see Neville Heath again until he stood in the dock on a charge of murder.

On Monday 24th June the following letter, postmarked Worthing, 5.45 p.m., 23rd June 1946, addressed to Superintendent Barratt, arrived at Scotland Yard:

'Sir,

'I feel it to be my duty to inform you of certain facts in connection with the death of Mrs Gardner at Notting Hill Gate. I booked in at the hotel last Sunday, but not with Mrs Gardner, whom I met for the first time during the week. I had drinks with her on Friday evening, and whilst I was with her she met an acquaintance with whom she was obliged to sleep. The reasons, as I understand them, were mainly financial. It was then that Mrs Gardner asked if she could use my hotel room until two o'clock and intimated that if I returned after that, I might spend the remainder of the night with her. I gave her my keys and told her to leave the hotel door open. It must have been almost 3 a.m. when I returned to the hotel and found her in the condition of which you are aware. I realised that I was in an invidious position, and rather than notify the police, I packed my belongings and left. Since then I have been in several minds whether to come forward or not, but in view of the circumstances I have been afraid to. I can give you a description of the man. He was aged approximately 30, dark hair (black) with small moustache. Height about 5′ 9″, slim build. His name was Jack and I gathered that he was a friend of Mrs Gardner of some long standing. The personal column of the Daily Telegraph will find me, but at the moment I have assumed another name. I should like to come forward and help, but I cannot face the music of a fraud charge which will obviously be preferred against me if I should do so. I have the instrument with which Mrs Gardner was beaten and am forwarding this to you to-day. You will find my fingerprints on it, but you should find others as well.

'N. G. C. Heath.'

The instrument to which Heath referred was not sent to Scotland Yard and when eventually it was found it had been cleaned of all fingerprints.

Soon after posting this letter Heath left Worthing, arriving later the same evening at the Tollard Royal Hotel on the West Cliff at Bournemouth. It is perhaps indicative of his own unreal picture of himself that he registered in the name of Rupert Brooke, the romantically handsome and tragic poet who died on active service in the First World War. He could not resist adding the embellishment 'Group Captain' to the name.

Heath was given room No. 71, but four days later he asked for a room with a gas fire and was moved to room No. 81. It was later suggested that he wanted a gas fire because he intended to commit suicide, but he showed no sign of depression during his stay at the hotel. The handsome and charming 'Group Captain' soon became popular with the other guests and joined freely in their social activities. He was also on friendly terms with the staff, making a point of engaging them in conversation. Apart from using an assumed name, he made no attempt to disguise himself.

On the afternoon of Wednesday 3rd July he was strolling along the promenade when he saw two girls, one of whom he had previously met at a dance. She introduced him—'Group Captain Brooke, staying at the Tollar Royal' to her companion, Miss Doreen Marshall. There seems to have been an immediate mutual attraction between Heath and Miss Marshall because within a short while she had accepted his invitation to tea at his hotel. It was a very 'proper' arrangement—tea in one of the public rooms of an hotel, with the good-looking young man showing just the right degree of flattering interest, so that the girl had no reason to decline his further invitation to dinner that evening.

Doreen Marshall was a pretty, soft-featured, wavy-haired brunette, aged twenty-one, recently demobilised from the WRNS. Because she had been ill with influenza and measles, she had been sent by her father, Mr Charles Marshall, of Woodhall Drive, Pinner, to recuperate at the four-star Norfolk Hotel, Bournemouth. By the time she met Heath she had been staying alone at the hotel for five days and probably welcomed the idea of an evening out in the company of such an apparently suitable young man.

After tea she went back to the Norfolk to bath and change, then returned to the Tollard Royal by taxi in time for dinner. Other guests noticed the attractive couple chatting happily during the meal and in the public lounge afterwards. At about

11.20 p.m. they were joined by some other guests, including Mrs Gladys Phillips, on holiday from Cardiff.

Mrs Phillips thought that 'Group Captain Brooke' had been drinking rather a lot and noticed that Miss Marshall looked pale and tired, so she was not surprised when the girl asked Mr Phillips to call a taxi to take her back to her hotel. Mr Phillips arranged this with the night porter before he and his wife went upstairs to their room. When the cab arrived, however, Heath told the night porter, Fred Wilkinson, that they did not need it because Miss Marshall had decided to walk.

'I shall be back in half an hour,' said Heath, but Miss Marshall corrected him with 'No, in quarter of an hour.'

Nobody knows what time Heath did, in fact, return to the hotel because instead of entering by the front door he went round to the back and climbed a ladder, left by workmen, to enter his second-floor room through the window. At 4.30 a.m. the night porter peeped into Heath's room and saw him soundly asleep. The next day Heath told Mr Ivor Relf, joint manager of the hotel, of his unconventional method of entry, saying that he had done it 'as a joke' to confuse the night porter.

At eight o'clock that morning Fred Wilkinson went to room No. 81 with the daily papers and found Heath still asleep. He roused the visitor, who seemed his normal cheerful self. No one, in fact, noticed any difference in Heath's demeanour that day. He mixed as usual with the other guests and made his customary amiable remarks to members of the hotel staff.

On the morning of Friday 5th July the manager of the Norfolk Hotel telephoned Mr Relf at the Tollard Royal to say that a young lady guest was missing from his hotel and that she was believed to have dined at the Tollard on the Wednesday evening. Mr Relf mentioned this to Heath and asked if his guest had been a Miss Marshall from Pinner.

'Oh, no,' replied Heath. 'I have known the lady for a long while and she certainly does not come from Pinner.'

Heath then took the extraordinary course of telephoning the local police station on Saturday 6th July and asking if they had a photograph of the missing girl so that he could say definitely whether or not she was the young lady with whom he had dined. He was told that no picture was at that time available, so offered to telephone again later. This he did, and at 5.30 that evening he went, quite voluntarily, to Bournemouth police station to meet Doreen Marshall's father and sister, who had travelled down from London as soon as they learned that Doreen was missing.

Mr Joshua Casswell,QC, who led the defence for Heath at his subsequent trial, said in his memoirs many years later that he believed this direct approach to the police—like the letter Heath wrote to Superintendent Barratt after the killing of Margery Gardner—was prompted by a desire to be caught. He was convinced that Heath wanted to be hanged.

Certainly he walked straight into the arms of the law. He must have known that every police station in Britain had his description and picture and could hardly have been surprised when Detective Constable Souter, whom he saw when he first entered Bournemouth police station, recognised him and challenged him as Neville Heath.

Heath insisted that his name was Rupert Brooke, but Souter detained him at the police station, and an hour later, when Detective Inspector George Gates arrived, Heath was ready to admit his true identity. That evening he was told that officers of the Metropolitan Police were on their way to interview him in connection with the murder of Margery Gardner, and Heath replied, 'Oh, all right.'

When he was asked about his association with Doreen Marshall, Heath agreed that she was the girl with whom he had spent part of the afternoon and the evening of 3rd July. He said that after leaving his hotel they sat on a seat overlooking the sea and talked for about an hour. They then walked down the slope towards the Pavilion and he accompanied her as far as the pier, where they said 'good night' and he watched her cross the road.

'I asked her if she would come round the following day,' said Heath, 'but she said she would be busy for the next few days and would telephone me on Sunday if she could manage it. I have not seen her to speak to since then although I thought I saw her entering Bobby's [a department store] on Thursday morning.'

While Heath was at the police station he complained of the cold and asked if he could return to the Tollard Royal to collect his jacket. Needless to say, this request was refused. Detective Inspector Gates picked up the jacket, and found in the pockets three significant items. One was the return half of the first-class London-Bournemouth railway ticket issued to Doreen Marshall; the second was a cloakroom ticket for a suitcase deposited at Bournemouth West station; and the third was a single artificial pearl.

Among clothing in the suitcase, which was collected by detectives, was a square blue handkerchief scarf and a blue woollen scarf, both heavily stained with blood, and a steel-tipped riding whip which Heath had NOT sent to Superintendent Tom Barratt.

The importance of the single pearl bead did not become apparent until Monday 8th July, when twenty-seven matching beads were found scattered among the bushes in Branksome Chine—part of the gruesome scene uncovered when a girl out walking with her dog noticed a swarm of flies persistently buzzing around one particular section of the copse. Behind some rhododendrons, and further concealed by the broken branch of a fir tree, lay the shattered body of Doreen Marshall. It was naked except for one shoe, but had been roughly covered with the girl's own clothing. Her powder compact and bloodstained stockings were found several feet away from the body and some time later her pocket knife was uncovered on the beach by Miss Patricia Howe, a holidaymaker.

As in the case of Margery Gardner, there was evidence of a sadistic attack, one nipple having been bitten from the breast, the genitals savagely injured by some rough instrument, and the rest of the front of the body deeply cut several times.

Mr Crichton McGaffey, the pathologist who examined the body, said that these injuries had been inflicted after death, which had resulted from knife cuts to the throat. There were signs that the victim's wrists had been tied together, and one of the exhibits produced at Heath's trial was a knotted handkerchief, soiled with blood and earth, which was found in his hotel bedroom by Divisional Detective Inspector

Reginald Spooner, from Notting Hill police station, who was in charge of enquiries into the killing of Mrs Gardner.

If further evidence against Heath on this second murder was needed it was provided by a crystal fob watch and a dress ring, both belonging to Doreen Marshall, and sold by Heath to two different jewellers in Bournemouth on the day following her disappearance.

He was charged with both murders—though he subsequently stood trial at the Old Bailey only on a charge of killing Margery Gardner—and was visited by Mr Casswell while on remand at Brixton Jail. Asked by Casswell if he wished to give evidence in court, Heath replied, 'Oh hell, why shouldn't I plead guilty?' When it was pointed out that his parents and younger brother would suffer even greater shame and pain if he admitted that he had killed two women in such a manner while he was in his right mind. Heath hesitated for a second, then shrugged and nodded.

'All right,' he said, 'put me down as not guilty, old boy.'

When the handsome young ex-airman stood before Mr Justice Morris at the Central Criminal Court in September 1946, the only real issue to be decided was whether or not he was sane. The facts of the case were never in any real doubt and it was in an attempt to show that Heath was not responsible for his actions that his defence counsel took the unusual step of telling the jury about the second murder, arguing that no man in his right mind would, without attempting to disguise himself, deliberately savage a second victim when he knew that the police of every county in England were looking for him in connection with the first killing.

Mr Casswell invited the jury to 'step back out of the wood of detail' and look at the case from a distance.

'Say to yourselves perhaps what you said when you first heard of the two terrible crimes committed within a fortnight,' he said. 'What did you say? That the man must be mad? Can you have come to any other conclusion? Can you believe that a man who was merely a brutal sensualist, a mere sadist, was capable of those things? Remember those awful injuries of which you have been told. Picture the scene. Was that the work of an ordinary criminal? Surely that man at that time was as mad as a hatter, absolutely insane, a maniac. Can he have been anything else?'

The chief witness for the defence was Dr William de Bargue Hubert, who for five years was the psychotherapist at Wormwood Scrubs, and was part author of a psychological study of the prevention of crime which was presented to the Home Secretary in 1938. This witness, who had also worked at Broadmoor and at Feltham Prison, expressed the opinion that Heath was not an ordinary sexual pervert, but was suffering from moral insanity and was at times quite unaware that he was doing wrong. He believed Heath to be certifiable as morally insane.

Heath himself appeared to object to this classification because during Dr Hubert's evidence he passed this note to Mr Casswell:

'It may be of interest to know that in my discussions with Hubert I have never suggested that I should be excused or that I told him I felt I should be because of insanity. This evidence is Hubert's opinion—not what I have suggested he say on my behalf.'

Heath need not have worried. Dr Hubert—who six months after this trial was found dead from an overdose of drugs—was unconvincing under cross-examination by Mr Anthony Hawke, who led for the prosecution.

'May I take it that at the time Heath murdered Margery Gardner he knew that he was doing something that was wrong?' asked Mr Hawke.

'No,' replied Dr Hubert.

He knew he had bound and tied a young woman lying on a bed?—Yes.

He knew when he inflicted seventeen lashes upon her with a thong that he was inflicting seventeen lashes with a thong?—Yes.

He knew those things, but did not know they were wrong?—He knew the consequences.

When he suffocated that woman, lashed her, having tied her up and made her helpless first, he knew it was wrong?—No.

Would you tell me why?—Because people during sexual behaviour generally consider what they are doing is right and their own business.

Because he could only satisfy his sexual appetite by inflicting cruelty, you say that he thought it was right to inflict it, do you?—Well, he was doing what he wished to do.

The medical witnesses called by the prosecution were positive in their opinions that Heath was sane. Dr Hubert Young, senior medical officer at Wormwood Scrubs, said that the man had a psychopathic personality and was a sadist, but was not insane and was not a moral defective. Dr Hugh Grierson, senior medical officer at Brixton Prison, who had reviewed Heath's history from an early age, said there was no history of mental abnormality or disordered conduct when he was young. His offences in later life had been advantageous to himself and were not of the vicious or senseless kind characteristic of the moral defective, Heath having always taken precautions to cover his traces.

Questioned by Mr Hawke about the meaning of the word psychopath, Dr Grierson said that it was a person who took a short-term view—a person who did what he felt like doing at the moment without any thought of what the consequences might be. He agreed with Mr Hawke that a psychopath was not suffering from a disease of the mind but rather from an abnormality of character and temperament.

Under cross-examination by Mr Casswell, Dr Grierson said that Heath had strongly denied being sexually abnormal and insisted that he had no perverted impulses, but was not willing to talk about his sexual relationships. Dr Grierson did not agree that this denial of his perversions was an indication of insanity.

'I suppose you would agree that this man is a psychopathic personality?' asked Mr Casswell. 'He is a most abnormal individual, is he not?'

Dr Grierson replied 'Yes' to both questions.

The jury of ten men and two women took just an hour to decide that they preferred the opinions of Dr Young and Dr Grierson to those of Dr Hubert. They were unanimous in their verdict that Neville Heath was guilty of the murder of Margery Gardner and that he was not insane at the time he committed the crime.

He refused to appeal and was hanged at Pentonville Prison on 26th October, 1946.

Mr Casswell, in his memoirs, said he did not share the views of those who thought Heath was enjoying the publicity brought by the trial and wanted 'to make a hero's exit'. He believed that Heath was appalled at the crimes he had committed and realised that it would be best for him, and best for the world at large, if his life were to be ended.

Neville George Cleveley Heath was twenty-nine years of age when he spoke his last words—'Come on, boys, let's be going'—to hangman Pierrepoint and his warders, and in spite of all attempts at his trial to show that he had been morally defective from an early age, there is nothing on record to show that he had been in any trouble until he was twenty.

Born in Ilford, Essex, in June 1917, he enjoyed a comfortable middle-class life with his parents and younger brother. Educated at a Catholic preparatory school and later at a minor public school until he was seventeen, he was a satisfactory if not a brilliant pupil and got his General Schools Certificate. The Heaths had by now moved to Wimbledon and Neville took a job in a City office, but found the work boring and after only a few weeks he left to join the Artists' Rifles. He decided that he was going to enjoy service life, but felt that the Air Force offered more excitement and glamour than the Army, and in 1936 he joined the RAF. After initial training at Cranwell, Lincolnshire, he was given a short-term commission and early in 1937 he gained his wings and was gazetted a pilot officer, serving with No. 19 Fighter Squadron and No. 87 Fighter Squadron.

The uniform of a RAF officer added to the attractions of this tall, fair-haired young man, and wherever he went there were dozens of pretty girls competing for his attentions. His vanity demanded that his social life should match the glamorous standard set by his good looks. He liked to take beautiful girls to the 'best' places and needed fast sports cars to bolster his image in their eyes. His pay as a junior officer did not match the standards he set, so he 'borrowed' from the RAF sports fund of which he had charge, and took a car belonging to an NCO. Later he was charged with those offences and with being absent without leave and escaping while under arrest.

For these misdemeanours he was dismissed from the RAF, but it is perhaps typical of Heath that he insisted that the real reason for his dismissal was because he had flown his plane under a bridge. He never wavered from this romanticised version of his exploits, even attempting to convince those who had access to his records and knew the true story.

'Always I have been dogged by this simple piece of folly that led to my dismissal from the RAF when I was a twenty-year-old pilot officer,' he said in a statement published after his trial.

During the following two years Heath had only one honest job—two weeks as a sales assistant in an Oxford Street store in May 1938. For the rest of the time he lived largely on his wits. He went to Nottingham after his dismissal from the RAF and there, posing as Lord Dudley, he obtained credit by fraud at the Victoria Station Hotel and tried to get a car by false pretences. When he was caught he admitted eight other offences, most of them for obtaining money in the name of Lord Dudley.

These were his first official offences and he was placed on probation for two years. He did not take the chance offered to him. He returned to London and continued his career of crime. He broke into the house of a friend at Edgware and stole fifty pounds' worth of jewellery, and used a forged banker's order to obtain clothing worth £27. When he was caught he asked for ten other cases, mostly for obtaining money by fraud, to be taken into consideration. He was still only twenty-one and the magistrates took the lenient course of sending him to borstal for three years.

Luck was on his side because after serving fourteen months at Hollesley Bay Colony he was released on the outbreak of war in September, 1939. He immediately tried to rejoin the RAF, but they did not want him, so he enlisted as a private in the RASC. Within four months he was commissioned as a second lieutenant and in March 1940 was posted to the Middle East with the rank of acting captain.

Heath seemed incapable of taking the chances offered him because within a year he was in trouble over bouncing cheques. It was discovered, too, that he had fraudulently obtained a second pay book and that he had told a false story in order to obtain leave to which he was not entitled. He was courtmartialled and cashiered in July 1941.

Here again, Heath's later story of events bore little relation to the truth. He said that he was bored with 'enforced inactivity' at his station on the Haifa-Baghdad road, where he was supposed to be in charge of prisoners who had been rounded up as pro-Nazis.

'Then I heard of a raiding party made up of the Arab Legion and men of the Beds and Herts Regiment,' he wrote. 'They were going to attack Fort Rutbah and I decided it would be a good idea to go with them. I did, and we had quite a party. Unfortunately the Commander chose that particular night to visit the station . . . he was very cross when he found I wasn't there and that there were some prisoners waiting. The net result was that I was returned as unsuitable. Still, the gin we found at Spinney's in Rutbah was pretty good, and anyway every officer of the RASC who tried to take part in the war at this stage was always classified as unsuitable—but they'd never let one of us leave the wretched organisation.'

Heath was put on to the troopship *Mooltan* to be returned to England, but he jumped ship at Durban and made his way to Johannesburg, calling himself Captain Selway, MC, of the Argyll and Sutherland Highlanders. Again he started passing dud cheques, but he eluded the authorities and no charges were brought. With his usual audacity, he then changed his name to James Robert Cadogan Armstrong and joined the South African Air Force. He enlisted as a private, but was soon commissioned and ultimately reached the rank of captain.

There is no doubt that Heath was a trickster, a thief and a complete rogue, but there is equally no doubt that he was a first-class airman. The South African authorities discovered that he was using a false name and found out all about his past misdemeanours, but valued him so highly that they overlooked the whole sorry business and allowed him to remain in the service and to keep his captain's rank.

Official records show that Heath was engaged on transport and instructional duties during the whole of his period of service with the South African Air Force, but he always insisted that he was on operational duties in Egypt, Tripoli and Algeria and that he took part in the Battle of Alamein.

Soon after his arrival in South Africa, Heath met an attractive girl named Elizabeth Rivers, daughter of a wealthy Johannesburg couple. Neville and Elizabeth were mutually attracted and were married in February 1942. A son, Robert, was born in September 1944.

Before the birth of this child, Heath (or Armstrong, as he still called himself) was seconded to the RAF with the rank of captain and was posted to England. As the pilot of a bomber he was engaged in raids over enemy countries. In October 1944 his aircraft was hit by anti-aircraft gunfire and the crew baled out. According to Heath he saw his plane disintegrate in flames, but there is no Air Ministry record of this.

Later, he wrote: 'I have done things which I am ashamed of, but never in the air. My war record, as a fighter pilot, is a good one, and it may be that some of the experiences of those frenzied years have played a part in bringing me where I am today. Maybe here, but for the grace of God, might stand other pilots who lived as close to death as I did. Maybe they, too, need sympathy, understanding and help in changing their lives from being wartime killers.'

In other documents published after his murder conviction, Heath blamed his moral disintegration on the break-up of his marriage. He returned to South Africa early in 1945 and in October that year his wife divorced him for desertion and was given custody of their son. There is no evidence that he was ever cruel to his wife or that the marriage was anything but happy in the early days, and no reason for the break-up of the marriage is recorded.

Heath commented, 'Eventually my wife divorced me and that was the end. From then on I lost interest in everything. . . . I have never felt the same since it happened

and ever since I have acted in a peculiar way on occasions
. . . . From the day of my divorce I have had a couldn't-care-
less attitude towards life generally. Everything went wrong.'

Everything, in fact, 'went wrong' very quickly. On 4th
December 1945 he appeared before a general court-martial
in South Africa and was convicted on three charges of wearing
military decorations without authority and three of conduct
prejudicial to military discipline.

For the third time in a career of less than twelve years he was
dismissed from the service. At the same time he began passing
dud cheques again. He was deported from South Africa and
returned to London in February 1946.

Flying was undoubtedly an obsession with him because,
in spite of a record which would surely have prejudiced his
chances of success, he enrolled at the London School of
Air Navigation with the idea of getting a commercial pilot's
licence to enable him to apply for a post in civil aviation.

Once again he spoiled his own chances. Keeping the name
Armstrong, he began to wear the uniform of a lieutenant-
colonel of the South African Air Force—complete with an
impressive row of medal ribbons. He was quite brazen in this
masquerade, frequenting the night spots of the West End and
spending a lot of time in Fleet Street drinking-haunts, where
he was speedily recognised for the phony he was. On 5th April
1946, at Wimbledon Magistrates' Court, he was fined £5 for
unlawfully wearing the uniform and a further £5 for wearing
decorations to which he was not entitled.

He was not deterred. Reverting to his true name of Heath,
he was still calling himself 'Lieutenant-Colonel' when he took
Margery Gardner to the Pembridge Court Hotel on the night
of 20th June 1946. . . .

It seems that Neville Heath was a sexually perverse
individual with a psychopathic personality. The megaloma-
niac elements in him were the most dangerous, in that he
was constantly contriving to award himself a more grandiose,
worthy, dignified or superior rank to the one which he
actually occupied. His trouble was that he had to falsify
reality in order to maintain this image of himself. Inevitably
events caught up with him. He was forced to create even

more complex identities to satisfy his ego and maintain his prestige.

He seemed to show little or no capacity to learn from experience. There was profound 'splitting', in that for some time he could sustain the work of a captain in the South African Air Force, but his experiences in the war, or his fantasies of what those experiences might be, brought him face to face with a fear of death which he could neither digest nor metabolise. His moral disintegration is to be ascribed not to the break-up of his marriage but rather the break-up of his marriage and his moral disintegration can both be ascribed to his inability to metabolise, and digest his thoughts about, and fears of, his own death. He externalised the whole business, linked it with what was probably a pre-existent sexual sadism within himself and then proceeded to have unscrupulous sexual relationships with a variety of women. What made him resort to two crimes, the second of which was even more fantastically sadistic than the first, seems to have been the need to exclude a highly pathological part of his inner world, by which he was plagued constantly, into the external world, by enacting it, and then to get himself caught and dealt with.

The affair between the two murders with Yvonne Symonds stemmed from the other side of Heath's character—the desire to show that he could have loving relationships with a woman and get her to love him and promise to marry him, without doing her any grievous harm.

The trouble with Heath was that the two sides of him were never integrated and articulated but remained separate, and therefore the highly pathological, sadistic, murderous side was never mitigated. The relatively benign side of him was probably shocked and horrified at what was perpetrated by the other side. Psychological testing would undoubtedly have revealed the dangerous internal situation, but of course Heath was the kind of person who had to preserve his idealised image of himself—in other words face—at all costs, and it is highly doubtful whether he would have allowed himself to get involved in a meaningful psychotherapeutic endeavour.

MIRIAM ALLEN DEFORD

The Pitiful Monster

Perhaps the kind of world in which he was born and died helped to make of John Christie the monster he became. Here was a man who had murdered at least six women and probably seven—all but one of them sex murders (combined with their giving him what Rupert Furneaux called 'a sense of power')—and yet to many human beings his trial was only a gorgeous, gaudy spectacle; 'ordinary good-living, decent people' flocked to gape at his effigy in Madame Tussaud's Waxworks; and Sean O'Faolain tells us that in Dublin his case was discussed 'with peals of laughter,' and he 'was commonly referred to as Corpus Christie.' When Jack the Ripper carved up his victims, at least his exploits were greeted with horror instead of mirth. We have had two World Wars since then in which to become accustomed and callous to such stories as that of John Reginald Halliday Christie.

When he was hanged in London on July 15, 1953, it was the end of a man who might be considered almost a walking, breathing model of a warped personality of a fortunately rare and grotesque kind. Technically he was not insane—he knew the difference between right and wrong, he was aware of what he did, and he realized it was wrong—in other words, he passed the test of the McNaghten Rule: but psychologically few men have ever been so thoroughly and incurably abnormal. As the judge said, in effect, in his summing up in Christie's trial for the murder of his wife, Christie was indeed a monster. The murders he undoubtedly committed—plus the other murder which he both confessed and denied, and the possible one

154

he 'couldn't remember'—make his case one of the classics of crime. But he was a monster who, when all is known of his unhappy history, may be pitied rather than loathed: which does not mean that it may not have been the best thing for society, and perhaps for himself as well, to have put an end to his miserable life.

Christie was a small, thin, bald, bespectacled man, fifty-five years old, who seldom spoke in a voice above a whisper—it became necessary finally during his trial to install a microphone so that the jury could hear his testimony. He was diffident and anxiously polite. In the slum neighborhood in which he lived he was noted for always raising his hat to feminine acquaintances he met on the street. He loved animals and fondly tended a cat and a dog. Before he walked out of his home for good he saw to it that the dog was painlessly disposed of. (Cats can take care of themselves.) He was of above-average intelligence, with a special gift for mathematics. He was rather puritanical in his tastes, was a teetotaler, and had a horror of public houses and low associations. He was a believing member of the Church of England. So far as he could love another human being, he loved his wife; they never quarreled, and were considered a devoted couple, even though they had been separated several times—once for nine years—and though he was more than once unfaithful to her.

But he also had a record of theft and assault, beside having murdered at least six women (and probably raped them at the moment or immediately after). Death and the dead held a fascination for him against which he was seemingly helpless. He was completely aberrant sexually. He was a necrophiliac, or near to one—a man with a sexual fixation on the dead. It is the most uncommon, and to normal people one of the most repulsive, of all perversions.

The Christie case begins in the dingy kitchen of a slum tenement. Number 10 Rillington Place was in a dreary terrace of one block of run-down houses, leading to a dead-end wall, in Notting Hill, part of the Kensington district of London. Once highly desirable as an address, still fairly respectable when the Christies moved there in 1938, Notting Hill had by then become the sort of neighborhood where policemen preferred to go in pairs. Drab prostitutes on their way downward to the gutter prowled the streets and frequented the public houses; petty criminals abounded; the lack of a marriage certificate was taken for granted; most of the inhabitants who worked at all held unskilled, badly paid jobs.

Number 10 was a three-story house with a front bay window in the ground floor flat where John and Ethel Christie lived, and a back yard which Christie, an ardent gardener, kept blooming in summer with forsythia and roses. The house was lighted by gas, there was no bathtub or shower, and the only toilet was an outdoor lavatory next to what was meant to be a communal washhouse but for years had been used mainly as an overflow storage room. The three flats, one to each story, were not self-contained, and the only way to go in and out was by a hall passing the Christies' front room. The only way the other tenants could use the toilet was by going past the Christies' kitchen window.

A harder place in which to commit murders unnoticed and to conceal the victims' bodies can scarcely be imagined—and yet John Christie managed it very well: in one case, for ten years before discovery. His neighbors were not very observant of one another's activities; they were too well occupied with their own. The house did have a bad reputation, however, since two murders had already occurred in it, in the top-floor flat. The Christies, who were the chief prosecution witnesses against Timothy Evans, the man who was hanged for killing his wife and infant child, continued to live quite as a matter of course in the same place they lived in then, their back wall huddled against the washhouse where a strangled girl and her strangled baby had been found.

But then John Christie knew, if his wife didn't, that already the skeletons of two murdered women lay beneath the garden soil.

The owner of the house at the beginning of 1953 was a Jamaican named Charles Brown. The Christies continued to live in the ground-floor flat, but there was a major fuss every time the landlord tried to collect the rent. (Mrs Christie didn't like 'the blacks'—Commonwealth citizens—who were infiltrating the neighborhood.) Charles Brown must have been relieved when Mrs Christie apparently went away, and when, a little later, her husband quit his job as haulage clerk for the British Road Services, sold his furniture, all but a few sticks needed for his own temporary use, and soon after departed. He left on March 20th (without paying up his back rent), and four days later another West Indian named Beresford Brown (no relation to Charles Brown), tenant of the second—in English parlance the first—floor, went downstairs to look the ground-floor flat over preparatory to moving into it.

Poking around in the kitchen to find a place where he might attach his radio, Brown tapped the walls and heard a hollow sound. He discovered an alcove or cupboard concealed behind plasterboard covered with heavy paper and tore the paper away.

The alcove was already three-quarters full. The first thing Beresford Brown's horrified eyes fell on was the back of a trussed-up woman, partly wrapped in a blanket. Shuddering, he glimpsed behind the decomposed corpse, two others. That was enough; he ran for the police.

It was they, under Chief Detective Inspector Albert Griffin, who pried up some loose floor-boards in the front room. Under them was the body of still another woman.

The three young women stuffed into the cupboard were identified by clothing left on them under the brown blankets in which they had been wrapped and the dust and ashes sprinkled over them. All of them, subsequent autopsies revealed, had been strangled; two of them had also been gassed. All had been attacked sexually either just before or just after death, certainly while they were unconscious. The woman under the floor had been neither gassed nor raped; she had merely been strangled.

The first three were Kathleen Maloney, Rita Nelson, and Hectorina MacLennan. All of them were well known in the neighborhood and of dubious reputation. Though they all had relatives near-by with whom they had more or less kept in touch, and Hectorina at least had a lover who had left his wife to live with her, they were the kind of women who could disappear for a long time before anyone would think of foul play. They would be missed, but it would be taken for granted that they had gone somewhere voluntarily for private reasons of their own.

Rita Nelson, a girl from Northern Ireland, was a slight cut above the others; she was an art student and sometime artists' model who supplemented her earnings by occasional pick-ups. She was the only one of the three with any claim (in life) to prettiness, and she had some talent. In fact, lacking a photograph at first, the police circulated a sketch she had made of the bald, staring-eyed little man in their search for a now vanished Christie.

For Christie, wearing his usual rather good clothes, carrying a borrowed suitcase, and tipping his hat to neighbors as he went, had walked quietly out of the house, ostensibly to join his wife at some point outside of London. The police were pretty sure he was still in the city, and they were right. The newspapers naturally reported the spectacular finds in full, and Christie could hardly have avoided seeing the stories. But though he did not give himself up, he made no particular attempt to deny his identity. He stayed at flophouses where he gave his own name and the Rillington Street address. He did change his hat and coat for others, but if that was an attempt at disguise it was a very feeble one. His own account later was that he 'just wandered around.' He was finally spotted by P.C. Thomas Ledger standing on the Putney Embankment, beside the Thames, idly watching a car being loaded beneath. At first he gave a false name and address, but when the constable charged him with being John Christie he acknowledged it at once and meekly turned over his identification papers. He made willingly a full statement confessing all four murders. The police have seldom had a more cooperative, earnest, acquiescent suspect than Christie.

By this time, the ground floor flat at Number 10 Rillington Place had been gone over inch by inch. The corpse under the floor had also been identified—it was Ethel Christie's. The garden of which her husband had been so fond had been dug up, and in it were found the disarticulated bones of what had apparently been two more women; for a while, so scattered were they that it was not certain whether there were two or three. But there was only one skull. Christie obligingly explained later that his dog had dug up the other skull, and he had taken it that night and dropped it into the cellar of a bombed house not far off.

The two women in the garden were a Viennese girl named Ruth Fuerst, whose mother was living in New York (what an Austrian subject was doing, uninterned, in England in 1943, when Ruth was murdered, has never been explained), and a woman about thirty, named Muriel Eady, with whom Christie had worked in a radio factory in 1944.

Since by English law an accused can be tried for only one murder at a time, Christie was indicted for the killing of his wife. Her murder would be the easiest to prove. There was little to go on in the other cases except his own confession, but in her case he had forged her name on a Christmas card, had changed the date on a letter, had both spoken and written provable lies about her disappearance, and had sold her wedding ring and her wrist-watch to a jeweler.

His trial began in the famous Old Bailey on June 22nd. The judge was Sir Donald Finnemore, a sixty-three-year-old bachelor, president of the National Sunday School Union. The case was considered important enough to be prosecuted by the Attorney General, Sir Lionel Heald, in person—the first instance in his two years in office. He was assisted by John F. Claxton, R.E. Seaton, and Maxwell Turner. Christie was defended—it must have been free of charge, since he had no money—by William Frederick (Derek) Curtis-Bennett, Q.C., son of the noted barrister Sir Henry Curtis-Bennett, with Colin Sleeman as junior counsel.

No attempt was made to deny that Christie had murdered his wife—and the five other women, evidence concerning whom was admitted because it was so relevant. Curtis-Bennett's endeavor was to persuade the jury of nine men and three women that his client was demented at the time of each killing (though not necessarily between times), and that he should be found 'guilty but insane' and committed to Broadmoor, the prison for criminal lunatics. There was at that time in England no penalty for deliberate murder by a sane person except hanging, though on appeal the sentence might be commuted to life imprisonment. (It is ironic to think that under the present law Christie might well have escaped execution, since he shot none of his victims and did not kill them in the course or furtherance of a theft!) He pleaded not guilty.

'I want you to know this man's whole story,' Christie's lawyer told the jury. And hear it they did, in all its bizarre details, before the four-day trial was over.

Christie was born on April 8, 1898, near Halifax, in the West Riding of Yorkshire. The family setup was typical of the late Victorian era. His father, Ernest John Christie, chief designer at a big carpet mill, was domineering, hot-tempered, tyrannical; his mother, a talented musician, was soft and submissive. John (or Reg, as many people called him) was one of six children, four girls and two boys. It was a prosperous middle-class family, conventional, conforming, and altogether ignorant of the needs and problems of a maladjusted child.

Not that John seemed at first to be abnormal. In his early childhood the Christies moved from the isolated house on the moor where he had been born to a suburb of Halifax. He was sent to a Church of England school, Holy Trinity, up to the age of fifteen, and did well there. He was an enthusiastic Boy Scout, who rose to be assistant scoutmaster, and he sang in the choir of All Souls Church. But he was only eight when his first severe psychic shock set the direction of his whole aberrant life.

In 1906 his grandfather died. Whether the old man and the boy had been close or not, nobody knows, but he was certainly the first person near to John to die. The child wanted to evade, to pretend, not to acknowledge that his grandfather was dead. His outraged father ordered him to stand watch over the body, and forced the shrinking boy into the room where the dead man was laid out.

Many sensitive children would be harmed by such an experience, but the normal reaction would be a still more active horror of death. With John Christie the effect was precisely the opposite. Death thereafter fascinated and enthralled him. He fell in love with it. Dormant for many years, that emotional twist was always there, and in the end it overwhelmed him.

From this time on, a discerning eye might have observed and perhaps forestalled the deviations from the norm in the boy's character. But there was no discerning eye to see. When he had night terrors, and screamed in the dark, his father scolded him and his mother soothed him uncomprehendingly. He was beaten often when he got in the way of his father's hot temper. But still he seemed an average boy, if perhaps a 'nervous' one, who played football, led his class in his studies and won prizes in arithmetic and algebra, loved animals and was always protecting them from ill-treatment. He was quick with his hands, too, could repair watches and clocks and make toys, and became a fairly good amateur photographer.

He had no sex instruction whatever from his parents or his teachers. Like most children of that period, what he knew he gathered from the talk of other boys. He was still in school when he was initiated by a precocious girl of about his own age but of vastly more experience, whom he picked up one Sunday evening after church. He was clumsy and unsuccessful. The girl jeered at him and left him, and the next day she made fun of him to his best friend, who promptly told all his other school-mates. For years John writhed under an insulting nickname they gave him. Another complex had been born, to join his fixation on death. It is no wonder that, forty years later, he was described by a psychiatrist as 'sexually immature.'

Yet he married at twenty-two. His bride was Ethel Waddington, a girl of the same age, of slightly lower social class, the daughter of an engineer's foreman. At the time of his marriage, Christie had already been in and out of the Army in World War I. At nineteen, in 1917, he was called up and joined the Royal Engineers as a sapper. He was a good soldier—he always did well under discipline, a significant throw-back to the stern training of his childhood—but a year later, in Flanders, he was injured by blast and mustard gas. He was in and out of military hospitals for a year more before he was invalided out. His disabilities were real; but the best guess is that they were what, later on, medical men learned to call psychosomatic. He was blind (in all probability a hysterical blindness) for five months, and mute for three and a half years. When he became able to speak again, it was in a voice hardly above a whisper, and for the remainder of his life he had great difficulty in talking so that he could be heard.

When a neurotic illness such as his is 'cured,' the still uncured subconscious mind often turns from physical symptoms to empty out its load of guilt, fear, shame, and rebellion through petty criminality. Thus it was with Christie.

He had worked briefly in the same carpet mill as his father, and as an assistant motion picture operator. In 1921, a year after his marriage, he received a temporary appointment as a postman in Halifax. It did not last long. Complaints of missing letters on his beat piled up, and a lot of them were found that had been thrown down a drain—letters that had once contained money. In his home the police found checks and money orders aggregating nearly £175. He was lucky: he received only a three-month sentence.

Two years later he was placed on probation for obtaining food at a boardinghouse under false pretenses. His wife left then, and did not rejoin him for nine years.

In 1923 he left Halifax, and got a job as operator of a cinema in Uxbridge, in Middlesex. Before long he was accused of stealing money and cigarettes from the theater and a boy's bicycle from a schoolyard. It was also brought out that on a visit to Halifax he had broken into his parents' house and stolen some of his mother's jewelry. His bewildered, unhappy parents refused to prosecute, but he got nine months on the other charges. In 1929, after five blameless years working as a hired car driver, he got six months for hitting one Maud Cole, described as his landlady, over the head with a cricket bat. In 1933 he served three months for auto theft. Reconciled with his wife, who visited him in prison, after serving this term he went back to driving, then in 1938 got another movie job, this time as staff foreman in charge of the usherettes at a theater in Notting Hill. It was then that he and his wife moved into the ill-fated house on Rillington Place.

His serious criminal career was still before him. But one of the most curious things about Christie was the way in which he kept getting in and out of trouble, and the numerous times he landed on his feet thanks to the obtuseness of other people. For example, hard up as England was in 1939 for able-bodied male workers ineligible for military duty, it seems hardly likely that anyone with Christie's police record would be appointed as even a temporary police constable! But he was—P.C. WRX112—and he served for four years, earning two commendations for good conduct—another instance of his need for strict discipline to keep him out of mischief. Not altogether out of mischief, however: he was accused of 'immoral consorting' with a policewoman whose husband later named him as co-respondent in a divorce suit. After this he was taken out of uniform and ordered to do industrial war work for the duration. But that was not until 1943—and just about the time he was 'consorting' with the woman constable he was also meeting (while still a policeman), and about to murder, Ruth Fuerst, the first of his victims.

Discharged from the force, Christie went to work as a despatch clerk in a radio factory in Acton, where he met Muriel Eady, who also worked there. She was the second woman he killed. (And after her sudden disappearance he kept on, unsuspected, for two years more in the same factory.)

And in 1947 the General Post Office, which had dismissed him for theft in 1921, actually made him a clerk in the savings bank department! He served there for three years.

His last job was as an £8-a-week haulage clerk for the British Road Services in Hampstead. It was this job which he left voluntarily after his last murder, saying that he was going to a position in Sheffield. He had, of course, no job in Sheffield or anywhere else. He was simply approaching the point where the tangle he had got himself into was too much for him, and his only solution was to run away aimlessly from it.

Christie was his own chief witness at his trial. He was more than willing, a witness pathetically eager to acknowledge everything suggested to him. His suggestibility was obviously pathological; if there had not been some corroborative evidence for most of the killings to which he confessed, it might have been suspected that he would have confessed gladly to any crimes at all of which he might be accused.

Seldom has a man on the witness stand displayed so open a conflict between his conscious and his subconscious mind. 'I must have done' . . . 'I never gave it a thought' . . . 'Sometimes I have got something in my mind and cannot get it out'—such phrases dotted his testimony. His memory seemed genuinely abnormal. Sometimes he stood silent, visibly struggling to dredge up a suppressed memory, a fragment of which would come with agonizing slowness and be delivered in a choking murmur. At such times his slight Yorkshire accent became more marked. Sometimes he smiled weakly and ingratiatingly at his questioner. He wept, he corrugated his bald brow, he twisted his knuckly hands—and he kept on condemning himself. Before he was done, he laid open before the jury the record of seven murders, six of which he had undoubtedly committed, and probably all seven.

He had done something more: he had painted a picture of a man whose distorted personality could find gratification only with a completely unresponsive partner—which meant in the end a partner either unconscious or dead; and who from that perversion had developed one still greater, harking back to that childhood trauma, so that the very atmosphere of and association with death enthralled him, and so that (in so far as he did not submerge all thought of the four corpses in his flat and the two more in the garden) the very consciousness of their proximity fascinated and pleased him.

The two broken skeletons could not tell all their story, but there is no reason to suppose they would not have told much the same one as did the three rotting corpses in the alcove, all of whom had been violated about the time of death. In a tin can on a shelf there was something almost too horrible to describe; Christie was making a little collection of samples of women's pubic hair, swatches cut off and tied together. They were never completely identified, but they were probably taken off after death as grisly souvenirs.

Mumbling and muttering, John Christie on the witness stand wrenched from the depths of his memory the details of his murders.

Ruth Fuerst he met in a 'snack bar' in 1943, while he was still a police constable and while his wife was away on a visit to her family in Sheffield. Ruth came to Rillington Place 'two or three times.' She was by far the most respectable of the girls he killed—she was a student nurse—and he may have been able to carry on a fairly normal affair with her for a short time. In any event, she 'would have liked to be affectionate' and she wanted him 'to go away with her.' He had no such intention; and besides, a telegram arrived announcing his wife's imminent return. So he strangled Ruth—he couldn't remember whether he had gassed her first or not, but he probably had—and buried her under the floor-boards of the kitchen, wrapped naked in her leopard-skin coat. Later when his wife was out, he hid the body in the washhouse and at night buried it in the garden.

Muriel Eady was next. She had a husband, and they had visited the Christies socially. However, as it happened, one day, while his wife was out again, Muriel came alone; she had some sort of bronchial trouble, and Christie, who had studied first aid when he was a policeman, had offered to treat her. He sat her in a deck-chair in front of the gas-stove, and 'treated' her with a mixture of friar's balsam—but only after he had passed coal gas through a tube into the jar 'to make her dopey.' When she was unconscious, he strangled her and then attacked her. Again, he put the dead body in the washhouse, where he kept it until he had a chance to bury it in the garden. Her sudden disappearance became an unsolved mystery, but not even her husband seems to have suspected Christie.

Chronologically, his next murder (if he committed it) was that of Mrs Evans, and the next after that of his wife. But these did not conform to the pattern, so let us postpone them to describe the three which followed the death of Mrs Christie.

Kathleen Maloney, who was a prostitute, accosted him (she was drunk, he said) and followed him home, demanding thirty shillings from him. 'I tried to get rid of her, because she was very repulsive. She tried to hit me with a pan.' So he strangled her, had intercourse with her ('repulsive' as she may have been while she was alive), and then tied her up in a blanket and hid her in the alcove.

Rita Nelson he may have invited to the house to pose for him—in his desk drawer at the office were found numerous nude photographs, most of them obscene, and there were more negatives hidden in the chimney at Rillington Place. But she 'got affectionate,' 'started to take her clothes off,' and 'wanted to stay,' and he didn't want her to. The clip was taken off the tube from the gas-pipe, she was strangled with a stocking, violated, wrapped up, and thrust behind Kathleen into the cupboard.

Hectorina MacLennan, the Scottish servant girl, and her 'boy friend' got into conversation with Christie on the street and told him they had been evicted and were looking for a place to sleep. Christie told them they could stay with him, since, as he said, his wife was living next door while they prepared to leave London. The couple spent three nights at Number 10; Hectorina slept in the deck-chair in which two women had died. 'At that time,' his lawyer reminded him, 'there were in fact two bodies in the cupboard and your wife's body under the floor-boards in the front room?' 'I know that now,' said Christie, 'but I just dismissed it from my mind.'

Hectorina and her companion left with the understanding that if they could not find a room they might come back for the fourth night. Hectorina came alone. The whole dreary story was repeated: 'she insisted on staying,' he tried to push her out, she 'went limp'—and in the end she joined Kathleen and Rita. Later her boy friend came looking for her, and Christie offered to help him search. But nobody found her again until the police fished her corpse out of the alcove, three months later.

The most confusing and controversial of the murders to which Christie confessed was that of Beryl Evans. The detailed investigation made by J. Scott Henderson, Q.C., at the insistence of the Home Secretary, after Christie's conviction, came to the conclusion that Timothy Evans did murder his wife and that Christie was lying or imagining when he confessed to the murder. (Ludovic Kennedy, in *Ten Rillington Place*, disputes and pretty well refutes Scott Henderson's findings.) In any event, Evans was hanged, not for her murder but for that of his baby daughter, and Christie never confessed to that—though he may have committed it. Evans had made contradictory statements, in some of which he confessed to both murders, in others of which he accused Christie. He was abysmally stupid, almost illiterate, and inextricably confused. At his trial, where the Christies were the chief witnesses against him, it was openly suggested that Christie was guilty of Mrs Evans's death, and Christie indignantly denied it.

Probably the real and whole truth will never be known now. It is just barely possible that, incredible as it may seem, there were actually two stranglers, not one, in that squalid house in Notting Hill. Certainly one of Evans's claims, that Christie had killed Beryl while attempting to perform an abortion, was untrue, for her body was exhumed ad there were no signs of any interference with her existing pregnancy. (Rita Nelson had been pregnant too, and there had been no attempt at abortion.)

Christie's story was a wild one of attempted suicide by Mrs Evans (who was on very bad terms with her husband), which he frustrated, and then of her asking him the next day to help her kill herself, whereupon he gassed and strangled her. She had bribed him, he said, by offering to be intimate with him, but though he attempted intercourse both before and after he had strangled her, he was suffering from fibrositis (a doctor was treating him for it, but like his other complaints it was in all probability psychosomatic), and his back was too painful. (All of which throws a perplexing light on Evan's account of Christie's helping him to carry Mrs Evan's body into the then empty flat between his and the Christies', and then helping him take it to the washhouse, where it was found.) Christie himself insisted throughout that he had no knowledge of what happened to the body after Beryl was killed, or of what became of the baby. It may be that Christie did murder Mrs Evans, then persuaded the weak-minded Evans to dispose of the corpse, and that Evans later killed his little daughter and placed her with her mother. (Against this is the fact that he did not dispose of the baby's cradle and other belongings, but left them with Christie. All his stories were tangled and contradictory.)

So Christie may or may not have been guilty of Beryl Evans's murder. If he was not, then that murder presents the most unlikely series of coincidences in criminal history—a practically unbelievable one.

But John Christie was tried, convicted, and executed, not for any of these murders, but for that of his own wife. This killing, as I have said, did not follow his usual pattern. It was the only one that had no sexual connotations—they had not had marital relations for two years past, though they slept in the same bed. His murder of Ethel he described, sobbing and whispering, in full. Some of the details were palpably untrue, but one gets the impression that most of his lies arose from emotional disturbance and deep suppression, rather than from defensive attempts to conceal the truth.

Ethel Christie herself is an interesting psychological problem that now will never be solved. She knew her husband's police record even if she had no suspicion that he was a murderer; she was intensely respectable as only a lower middle-class woman of her time could be; she made no pretense of being madly in love with him. She testified with him against Evans, and heard her husband accused during that trial without showing the least resentment. She left him once for nine years, and frequently for shorter periods, yet she always came back to him. She must have known of at least one of his extra-marital affairs, when he was named as co-respondent. She made no complaint, that anyone ever heard, of his unsatisfactoriness as a mate; perhaps she herself was undersexed and that was the reason Christie clung to her for so many years. According to some of her neighbors she was depressed and fearful (a doctor certainly treated her for 'nervousness'), but according to others she was cheerful and unconcerned. It would be rewarding to know what really did happen on that morning in December 1952 which ended with her death.

Christie's own account, given at his trial, was that he awoke on the morning of December 12th and found his wife choking, with her face blue. He was sure, he said, that she was dying, and if he went for a doctor (they had no telephone) she would be dead before he could get back to her. So he 'put her to sleep' by strangling her with a stocking, purely as an act of mercy! He told a proved lie about her having taken pheno-barbitone: there was no evidence of a drug when she was autopsied.

For a while he kept the body in the bed because he 'couldn't bear to be separated' from her! When that became too unpleasant, he wrapped her in some of her clothing and hid her under the floor-boards of the front room. Meanwhile he had taken from her, her gold wrist-watch and her wedding-ring; the ring, he said, he had wanted to keep in remembrance of her—but he sold them both three days later. He explained that he needed the money to buy food.

He did other things that argued full consciousness of his crime. Ethel had a sister and a brother who might visit her, so he wrote a Christmas card in her name, altered the date on a letter from the 10th to the 15th, wrote that she had rheumatism in her fingers so that he had to write for her, told a neighbor that he had had a telegram from her in which she sent 'love to Rosie' (the neighbor), told several persons that she had gone to Birmingham for 'a woman's operation.' He also withdrew her savings account from a bank, forging her name to secure the money.

Truly, as his lawyer had to concede, if Christie was insane 'whenever he committed a murder,' he was both technically sane, shrewd, and dishonest at other times!

The true motivation of Christie's murder of his wife is puzzling. Was he afraid she had become suspicious and might inform on him? There is no evidence of it. Did he really believe she was dying and kill her in mercy? He could not clearly explain it to himself. Undoubtedly there was some emotional stress so devastating that he could not bring it to consciousness. He could never speak of her without tears.

He kept on living in the flat, with his wife's corpse under the floor and two others of his victims buried in the garden.

He kept on living there after first one, then two, then three dead bodies had been crammed into the kitchen alcove. He said he 'never thought about it'—and that seems to be true, for on March 13th, posing as the owner of the house, he calmly rented the flat—for which he owed his own rent—to an unsuspecting couple named Reilly, who paid him rent in advance. (He told them, falsely, that he was being transferred by the British Road Services to the Birmingham office.) They noticed a horrible stench, which all Christie's assiduous disinfecting could not hide. But they thought 'it might be the dog.'

Part of the time at least, Christie actually may have forgotten that his home had become a morgue. But when he thought of it at all, living as he did with the dead must have given him a horrible perverted pleasure. Nevertheless, he must have realized that things could not go on in this way forever, for he sold his furniture (keeping the fatal deck-chair!) and did finally depart. To his unrealistic mind, going away may have meant wiping out the whole business; he never seems to have considered that eventual discovery was inevitable.

The medical testimony at his trial was contradictory, as is the case in most trials. Dr Matthew Odess, his family physician, who testified that he had treated him for eczema, insomnia, enteritis, and fibrositis, called him 'very nervous' and 'unfit,' but had never thought him insane—though he had recommended psychiatric treatment, which Christie refused.

Dr Jack Abbott Hobson, consultant in psychological medicine at Middlesex Hospital, called by the defense, said Christie suffered from 'gross hysteria' and 'falsification of memory'; that 'in an embarrassing situation he described things as though it was someone else.' But he too said that it would be 'inappropriate' to call Christie actually insane.

Dr John Cameron Matheson, principal medical officer of Brixton Prison, where Christie was confined before the trial, testified that exhaustive tests had shown 'a hysterical personality. . . . [But] I think he is sane. . . . He is a man of weak character, immature, who in difficult times tends to act in a hysterical fashion.'

And Dr Desmond Curran, psychiatrist at St. George's Hospital—called, like Dr Matheson, by the prosecution—denied outright that Christie had any 'defect of reason or disease of the mind'; he was only 'abnormal and conceited, an inadequate personality.' Christie, said Dr Curran, kept a photograph of himself in his cell, boasted of his killings, and compared himself with the 'blood-drinker,' Haigh. (Incidentally, Dr Curran remarked that Christie had told him he had always been opposed, on principle, to the death penalty!)

Curtis-Bennett had stated at the outset that no attempt would be made to deny Christie's guilt, that what he wanted was to prove his client insane. The prosecution's concern, therefore, was to disprove any legal insanity. Mr Justice Finnemore made it plain that, in his opinion of this 'horrible, horrifying case,' John Christie, though exceedingly abnormal, was not psychotic in the sense required by the McNaghten Rule. That was the salient issue in the entire trial.

The jury took just eighty-four minutes to bring in its verdict of guilty as charged. Then, with the black cap over his white wig, the judge sentenced the white-faced man who 'could not remember' how many people he had killed to 'suffer death by hanging' and to be buried in the prison precincts.

It may be noted, by the way, that the trial consumed just four days, and that Christie was hanged just sixteen weeks after the first bodies were discovered—a striking demonstration of the comparative speed of English and American justice.

Christie waived appeal but asked through the Home Secretary, Sir David Maxwell Fyfe, for the 'royal prerogative of mercy.' It was denied him. Then two Labor members of Parliament, one of them the representative of the Notting Hill District, brought up the question of Evans's possible innocence, and a motion was put for suspension of the death penalty in general. It failed, though once before a bill for the abolition of capital punishment had been carried in the House of Commons only to be defeated in the House of Lords. (And the present, almost complete abolition act was carried six years later, in 1959.) Meanwhile every attempt was made to keep Christie alive as 'a very material witness.'

Scott Henderson was then appointed as head of a special committee of investigation of the Evans case. His final conclusion, as said, was that the case against Evans had been overwhelming, that he was satisfied that Evans had killed both his wife and his daughter, and that Christie's confession of killing Mrs Evans was untrue.

And so at nine o'clock on the morning of Wednesday, July 15, 1953, after a visit from an Anglican priest, two wardens (guards) hurried John Reginald Halliday Christie to the scaffold. He was terrified but silent. His spate of inaudible speech had dried up at last.

Four minutes after the trap was sprung he was pronounced dead, and the crowd waiting outside Pentonville Prison saw the great doors open and the black-edged death notice posted. An inquest revealed that death had been instantaneous.

A family with small children moved into the Christies' flat. The new tenants said they were 'thrilled' to live in so 'historical' a spot. Then the owner put the house up for sale, but the only bidder wanted to make a museum of horrors of it and exhibit it for pay to the morbid public. The authorities took a dim view of this, and took action to have the house condemned and demolished. Now even the name of the street has been changed to Ruxton Close.

One hour after the hanging, Christie's effigy was already on display at Madame Tussaud's. A week later, the Royal Society for the Prevention of Cruelty to Animals, which had taken charge of Christie's pet cat, decided the animal must be destroyed. It was a one-man cat, they said; it was too wild and too savage for anyone else to handle.

How please Christie would have been if he could have known that!

LEONARD GRIBBLE

Nemesis in the Nude

On the 15th of October, 1958, before the crowded court-room of the Seine Assize Court, Maître Fouquin, making his closing speech for the prosecution, turned from facing the presiding judge, Counsellor Bonhoure, to stare at the pale-faced woman in the dock, watching him with wide eyes.

'This is the wild beast,' Maître Fouquin declared, stabbing a forefinger at the prisoner. 'She killed Marie-Claire Evenou in the manner of a beast using its claws.'

Almost everyone in court that day, listening to the finely drawn mixture of horror and contempt blended in the prosecutor's voice, shuddered.

But Simone Deschamps did not shudder. She did not blink her wide eyes. Although she must have realized she was listening to the voice of her personal doom, she gave no sign. It was as though something inside her had died. Perhaps it had. Crushed by the weight of a new sanity that had come to her while listening in the past days to her own dreadful story, one that had blazoned her name across Europe as 'the demon lover'.

She was forty-eight, a woman whose life had touched no memorable height and sunk to no significant depth before she met Yves Evenou, and through the smoke rising from his cigarette saw his small dark eyes, with their feral glint, staring at her with interest.

To look back to that day she had to pierce the miasma created by five years of incredible folly. It was in 1953 that she sat in Dr Yves Evenou's waiting-room, wondering how much she should tell the man of medicine, when she was summoned to his consulting-room. She was not a woman with pretensions to physical grace or beauty. Her face was thin, her hair was dark and rather lustreless, and she had little money to spare for good cosmetics or costly clothes. Not that she could not envy women who dressed to captivate susceptible males. Simone Deschamps was a dressmaker. Her fingers were deft with a needle. They knew the texture of good materials and had often lingered lovingly over a particularly well-turned hem or a well-nigh invisible seam that had the effect of making a garment she had made appear moulded to the feminine curves of its fortunate wearer.

She sat in the waiting-room turning her fingers, coarsened with countless needle pricks, over and over, wondering if it would be wiser to rise and leave before she incurred this expense she could not really afford, for to her a doctor was a luxury. She was still in two minds about staying or leaving when the door of the consulting-room opened, and Yves Evenou stood there looking at her, the half-smoked cigarette in the corner of his lean mouth with the bitterly twisted underlip, his balding head presenting an unnaturally high forehead, with two slits of dark eyes watching her.

He nodded to her, turned, and went back into the consulting-room, leaving the door open. She rose and entered after him. There was no longer any thought in her mind about leaving. When the door of the consulting-room closed after her a die had been cast.

Two curiously potent human forces had moved within the field of each other's deadly magnetism. How long the woman remained in the consulting-room is not known. It is not known, even, if she spoke to him about the malady that had brought her to the waiting-room. But it is certain that when she left Dr Yves Evenou's consulting-room the first overture had been made in an evil bargain.

The next meeting was outside the consulting-room.

Yves Evenou's breath carried the sour-sweet odour of port wine. The hand he placed about the woman had possessive fingers. They ate in a restaurant, and he smoked throughout the meal, and his speech became slurred, which was just as well when it is remembered that Yves Evenou, under the influence of the port wine he imbibed so freely, had a foul tongue.

However, its foulness did not appear to contaminate his table companion. She listened to his suggestions, and far from finding them outrageous was attracted by their bestial tone. Yves Evenou was a man with degrading sexual instincts. Their appetite was sharpened by the wine he drank. He explained in his slurred speech what he could offer the woman for her sharing.

She opened her eyes wider and smiled.

So a man of medicine with a depraved mind met a woman who was prepared to accept that depravity and match it with her own inner craving for satiety.

The two evil forces were not only in each other's field of magnetism by this time. They had become inseparable and were flowing together.

Simone Deschamps, the dowdy dressmaker with dark sexual instincts that required satiating, had found the depraved lecher who could provide the demanding animalism that would make her a dutiful slave to desire.

She became the drunken doctor's mistress.

In its more public aspects the liaison was a shabby one. Evenou treated her badly. He was a brute who took baneful pride in displaying his brutishness. He bullied her when they sat in restaurants and mocked her in the hearing of stone-faced waiters. Upon occasions we are assured he even forced her to pay for their meals.

Yet such manifestations of dark power were merely means of assuring himself that she was his creature. That was apparently all-important to him. For Yves Evenou was a man with two separate and distinct personalities. At home, if he was not the loving husband a Frenchwoman could naturally expect in the man she had married, certainly Marie-Claire Evenou found no reason to complain to her close friends, for Yves appeared to be a devoted father to their daughter Françoise, who was twelve.

But away from his wife and out of his consulting-room Dr Evenou was a creature obsessed with the brooding dictates of his baser nature. He demanded dark satisfactions he could not morally claim from his legal wife. He came to demand them from Simone Deschamps.

As their association continued she came to satisfy those demands in ways that reached the extreme in moral degradation and the total destruction of self-respect.

They indulged in what came to be described in print as 'sadistic orgies'. In time satiety demanded other expressions of the woman's sexual submissiveness to the demanding male. Evenou came to his mistress's room accompanied by Algerians, and when he told her to make love to them she complied, while he watched the performance like a perverted priest overseeing some satyric rite.

He introduced her to flagellation. She submitted to his callous insistence.

He forced her to undertake semi-public strip-tease acts. Again she offered no opposition to his growing demands. Month by month the bond between these two depraved lovers became braided into shackles from which neither could break free, not the man because he had no desire, not the woman because she had lost her last semblance of will.

His orgiastic demands, to which she was invariably the acquiescent partner, moved with terrible logic towards a culminating violence. Every depraved act of these so-called demon lovers was a step towards an eventual act which would climax their sordid relationship with overwhelming disaster.

Yet Yves Evenou, throughout this period of moral decay, continued to turn two faces towards the world.

One of his female patients later declared he was 'a gentle and a charming man'.

Another said, 'He used to tell me that his wife was a saint on earth.'

A neighbour firmly believed that Yves Evenou was passionately devoted to his daughter.

'He was always kind to his wife,' insisted a friend of the family.

But Madame Porrée was a shrewder person. She saw beneath the veneer and behind the façade of the respectable doctor who laboured to assuage the ills and pains of his fellows. She was almost vehement in her denunciation of the man who had lost her respect.

'He was a depraved creature,' she declared bitterly.

True, at the time she could have been viewing a man brought low by his wanton excesses with some measure of hindsight, but her words have a ring of conviction.

'I used to call him Dr Port Wine,' she admitted, 'because he drank so much of it.'

Well, she was in a position to know, for she was the proprietor of a restaurant where Evenou and his sad-faced mistress frequently ate an evening meal.

'He used such disgusting language,' Madame Porrée added, 'that I have had to send a young waitress out of the room. And as to that Simone Deschamps—well, he treated her like dirt. She was absolutely dominated by him.'

It was the observant and disapproving restaurant proprietor who reported that upon occasion the doctor mockingly told his mistress to pay for their meal.

It was at Madame Porrée's restaurant that Yves Evenou and Simone Deschamps had a meal on the day the drunkard dreamed up a way of forcing Simone Deschamps to commit the last act that would make her his creature beyond redemption. These incredible lovers had brought themselves to discussion of murder.

The victim was to be Madame Evenou.

She was sick, and had been an invalid for some considerable time. Her death was to be a sacrifice to their own perverted passion, and the crime was to be enacted in the name of love that was a mockery of all human tenderness.

It was during the lunch at Madame Porrée's that Simone Deschamps learned she and her perverted lover had come to a crucial crossroads in their depraved association. Indeed, she must have been prepared for his ultimatum, for they had been progressing with harsh logic towards the eventual elimination of Madame Evenou. Simone Deschamps had moved into the block of flats in the Avenue des Allies where the Evenous had an apartment on the first floor.

'I want you where I can get at you when I want to get at you,' Evenou had said with characteristic lack of subtlety.

Simone Deschamps had moved into a ground-floor flat, the

cost of which strained her resources.

Thereafter the love sessions of this strange pair became more frequent, and with proximity Evenou became even more demanding. Their wayward passion was indulged in the knowledge that the unsuspecting wife sat in a room or lay sleeping just above their heads.

There were times when the ailing Madame Evenou appeared to take a turn for the better, and under the medical treatment of her husband her health gave no sign of recovering its lost bloom with any degree of permanence. For the truth was the sadistic husband took pleasure from his wife's physical helplessness.

Until contemplation of her helplessness palled. That was when he decided he had to be freed of her presence in his home. His wife must be removed by his mistress. That was the ultimatum he gave Simone Deschamps across the lunch table in Madame Porrée's restaurant.

'We can't go on,' he said, 'unless she is removed. You must remove her. You have taken her place. You have a duty to me.'

This was the kind of distorted argument that had helped to make the woman with the large eyes and slightly bent nose his chattel.

'Marie-Claire must die today,' he insisted. 'You must kill her. I will make preparations of course. I shall see that everything is made ready. I think it would be as well if you stabbed her. Yes, that would be best,' he added dreamily, a happy man at the thought of his wife's blood being shed.

The meal had not been finished when Simone Deschamps, after much whispering across the table, rose and left the restaurant. Evenou lit a cigarette and waited. He presented the picture of a man with time on his hands, a man who could afford not to become impatient. He smoked and smiled contemplatively and sipped his wine, which, each time he held the glass level with his eyes, looked so much like blood.

Twenty minutes passed before Simone came bustling back to drop into her chair at the table. Evenou gave her a sharp glance, poured her some wine, watched her drink, then leaned closer across the table to ask a short question. Her reply was to produce the object she had just purchased in a shop in a neighbouring street. She placed it on the table.

The article she had left her lunch to purchase was a stout clasp-knife with a horn handle.

Evenou smiled, picked it up, hefted it against his palm, and put it down again. He nodded approval. Several persons at other tables saw the knife. When it was returned to Simone Deschamps' handbag the couple continued with their interrupted lunch.

Neither had lost an appetite.

When the meal was over they left the restaurant together. They went for a walk before turning into a café for some more drinks. Apparently details had to be agreed. Or maybe they had to find a suddenly flagging courage.

However that may be, when Simone Deschamps returned to her ground-floor apartment she was a ruthless woman without room in her mind for niggling doubt. She knew what she was going to do and was prepared to do it. The only bad patch was the waiting. Evenou had told her they must not be over-hasty. It had to be that night, but haste could spoil things. He had to prepare for the killer's visit.

Marie-Claire Evenou was also a good cook, and the gourmet who was over-partial to port wine found no satisfactory reason for denying himself the dinner his wife would have cooked. After all, it would be the last she would prepare for him.

But he found he could not face her across the dinner table, and took the easy way out. He gave her a barbiturate and talked quietly to her until she fell asleep. Then he tiptoed out of the room and, alone at the dining table, attacked the dinner prepared and cooked by the woman he had condemned to death sure in his knowledge that Simone Deschamps would not fail him.

Indeed, Yves Evenou's thoughts as he forked food into his lean mouth must have been of a curious quality. As a man of medical training he must have appreciated that in Simone Deschamps he was dealing with a woman who doubtless had a schizophrenic make-up. The seamstress who squinted for hours at needle and thread was one person. The ravenous sex-hungry lover was virtually a different person. Both inhabited the same body. Both obeyed him.

This obedience gave him the satisfactory sense of power that was as warming to his blood and as heady as the port wine that pleased his palate.

Over that lonely meal he felt like a Frankenstein about to test his ultimate control over a monster he felt was largely a creature of his own creation. After all, he had unleashed the evil in Simone Deschamps. He had taught her to revel in the obscene, he had helped her over five crazy years to acquire his own sense of being utterly without shame or remorse, to feel freed of normal inhibitions and to be ready at any time he ordered her to plunge into libidinous gratification of his own perverted desires.

As he sat back, listening to the ticking of the dining-room clock, it must have seemed that the short time remaining to his wife could be measured by her own heart-beats. He sat there obsessed by the thought of steel entering his wife's heart, and his concentration of mind made him restive for the time to pass more quickly.

He rose, went to his wife's side, stared at her passive face as he listened to her regular drugged breathing, then he looked at his watch, went out of the room, and collected his hat.

The flat seemed stifling.

There was still sunshine in the street outside, and heat rose from the pavements. He looked at his watch again, and decided he could go out for a breath of air. He could garage his car. It was an excuse.

He was out of the flat for half an hour, walking around the streets, trying, as it were, to grow sober. Not that he was drunk in any real alcoholic sense. But the culmination of his association with Simone Deschamps, as time for their fatal rendezvous approached, seemed to cloud his mind like wine fumes.

Or did his nerve fail, and did he have to take that walk to steel himself to go through with what he had planned?

Whatever the truth, when he returned to his flat at the end of that lonely half-hour spent in the streets that June evening he was ready to give the signal that would bring an armed murderess to his wife's door.

He picked up the telephone and dialled Simone Deschamps' number.

At the other end of the line Simone Deschamps sat in a chair awaiting the ringing tone. She was naked except for the high-heeled shoes on her feet and the black gloves covering her steady hands.

Her face was carefully made up. There was a glazed look about her large eyes.

Beside the telephone was the horn-handled knife.

At the first pealing ring she snatched the piece of black sensitized plastic from its cradle and held it to her ear.

'Now,' said a voice that always sent a strange tingling sensation through her, and had ever since the time of that first meeting when Yves Evenou had stared at her through his cigarette smoke in his consulting-room.

The line went dead. She replaced the receiver and, moving like someone in a dream state, reached for the overcoat she had ready. She shrugged into it, feeling its sleek lining cool against her warm nudity, and tugged it tight around her. She reached for the knife, slipped it in the coat's pocket, and turned to leave.

This was as arranged.

There was no hesitation on her part, no shrinking, and the steps she took towards the door did not stumble. In fact, after the door had snapped shut behind her she was able to run lightly up the flight of stone stairs to the Evenou apartment, her shoes tapping harshly until she reached the landing, where her heels beat a staccato tattoo to the door, which opened at once.

Evenou pulled her inside.

'No one saw you?'

She shook her head. 'No one.'

She took the knife from the coat's pocket, and he took the coat as she slipped out of it. Evenou pointed towards a door. He opened it, and they went into the room.

Marie-Claire Evenou, eyes closed, was in bed, breathing as she had before her husband took his after-dinner walk, more than half an hour before. Evenou gestured to one side of the bed.

Simone Deschamps sat down there, holding the glinting knife in her black-gloved hands, a fresh flush heightening the colour in her rather flat cheeks. Her mouth was pinched into a small bright knot of colour that was very like blood.

Evenou stooped over the other side of the bed and raised the bedclothes. He pulled them down, exposing his sleeping wife's body. He raised his right hand, folded the fingers until only the forefinger was outstretched, pointing.

'Look,' he said in a cold, matter-of-fact tone. 'There is the heart. Now strike there.'

He might have been giving a student a lecture in anatomy.

Obediently a black-gloved hand raised the knife it held, and the bright new blade intended to help make a camper's life easy flashed down to where the husband had pointed. But there was little force behind the blow. Simone Deschamps was willing. Her purpose was deadly. It was just that she lacked skill in murder. The blade drew blood, but the wound was little more than a savage scratch.

However, it was painful enough to awaken the wife, who cried out in fear.

'Yves—Yves—'

She stared aghast into her husband's smiling face, bent close over her.

'I'm here. You were having a nightmare.'

Well, it was truth of a kind. The nightmare was to continue relentlessly. Yves Evenou seized his appalled wife, and wrestled her struggling body into a prone position as he called to the naked woman to strike with her knife.

What followed was brutal butchery.

There was now great strength in Simone Deschamps' blows. Eleven times the knife slashed at the drugged and captive victim held by her husband. Horrible wounds were opened in her body. Steel mutilated her face.

Sixteen months later, in that crowded court-room of the Seine Assize Court, Judge Bonhoure asked the woman standing in the dock charged with murder, 'Why did you go that night to the Evenous' bedroom, naked except for your coat and wearing black gloves and red high-heeled shoes?'

The judge paused, leaned over his notes, and added in a cold clear voice, 'Was not this crime a climax to sexual perversion?'

The crowded court was silent for one dragging moment, then it was as though a collective shudder ran through it, as all eyes turned towards the woman, munching her lips before she replied to the Bench.

The judge spoke again, in the same severe voice.

'To go into all the details I have of your depravity I would have to clear this court. But why did you go upstairs naked? Was it to avoid bloodstains or in a sexual frenzy?'

The woman in the dock spoke.

'He ordered me to do it.' She munched her lips again, and appeared to shudder. 'I didn't want to, but I was afraid of him. I loved him.' Her voice became stronger, rang through the court. 'He was everything to me, and I knew he would never agree to obtain a divorce.'

Judge Bonhoure was ready with the next point for clarification.

'After the stabbing,' he told her, 'the doctor went into the bathroom, but you sat there watching his wife's death agonies.'

Again her voice was lowered.

'I never meant to do it. I never thought I would,' she said. 'I hesitated because I did not want to, but he screamed: 'You're just scared. Stab, stab!' I was afraid, and after that I do not know what happened.'

The whole sordid story was unfolded like a roll of stained bed-linen in the three days of the hearing. The all-male jury heard how Simone Deschamps had carefully cleaned the camper's knife after Marie-Claire Evenou had shuddered out her last breath. They frowned over the evidence of the demon lovers quarrelling after the pitiful remains of the wife had been seen by the police. First one of the accomplices had accused the other, then there had followed a counter-charge.

Yves Evenou, his health ruined by his excessive self-indulgence and dissipation, had died in prison while awaiting trial. His death left the woman who had wielded the camper's knife to stand alone in the dock.

But evidence had been obtained before Dr Evenou collapsed and died of the incredible orgies of lust in which the demon lovers had indulged. Judge Bonhoure had the court cleared as he had intimated when this evidence was offered In the judge's words the kind of sexual relations revealed in that evidence were 'beyond imagination'.

Such evidence made tantalizing and speculative reading, but it was not unhelpful to the defence's plea that Simone Deschamps was a woman 'bewitched' by her married lover. The sordid butchery was dressed up by the defence as a *crime passionnel*.

The jury sat impassively through the arguments, the claims, and the counter-claims. Judge Bonhoure was not quite so passive. His questions were penetrating and decisive in destroying the *crime passionnel* claim. The result of reconstruction of the crime, held by Paris detectives, left no one in doubt about the quality of the passion working in Simone Deschamps when she ran up the stairs in her red shoes, black gloves, and fur coat to kill a woman whose only injury to her had been her marriage to Yves Evenou years before.

Maître Fouquin demanded the guillotine for the woman in the dock.

Brushing aside, almost contemptuously, the claims of the defence, he insisted: 'She washed the bloodstained knife and gloves, and went to the trouble of sewing them into her mattress. That is not the attitude of a bewitched woman.'

But the counter-claims tried to undo the harm done by this picture of a woman whose actions had been deadly and remorseless. The defence strove to reveal another aspect of the woman in the dock, a woman with grey in her hair who had been normal until her meeting that day with Yves Evenou in his consulting-room. She had been destroyed by the evil in the man.

Simone Deschamps listened to both prosecutor and defending counsel with few signs that the arguments reached her. Occasionally she chewed her lip as she had when answering the judge's questions. But no tears welled in her eyes at the pitiful descriptions given by heated advocates. She remained dry-eyed throughout the entire three days. Even the demand for the guillotine did not make her flinch visibly. She seemed terribly resigned after giving her own direct answers.

But she did on one occasion voice regret for her terrible deed of blood. It was after the brother of the dead woman had given his evidence that she said in a choked voice: 'I am terribly sorry for what I did. I shall always feel the remorse.'

Those words saved her neck.

The charge was premeditated murder, and only extenuating circumstances could save her from the guillotine, and the jury had to find that there had been such extenuating circumstances.

'There are none,' the prosecutor declared roundly.

However, the jury in closed conclave remembered the words of regret, and decided that the woman who had uttered them might have been a woman of decent habits and honest affections before she met the man who unquestionably was her dark fate. They decided that, although she had committed a brutal murder, she had been dominated by the evil genius of the man who had died before he could stand beside her in the dock to share the awful weight of her crime.

They returned the verdict of guilty with extenuating circumstances.

Simone Deschamps remained dry-eyed when the verdict was proclaimed. Soberly she looked at Judge Bonhoure when he solemnly sentenced her to hard labour for life.

Her only sign of emotion was when her left hand stole to her right, on which she wore a small metal amulet.

The Paris reporters at the trial had referred to it as her goodluck piece or lucky charm.

The dry-eyed woman in the dock was superstitious and had carried her superstition into the place where she faced an ordeal that could conclude in an order for her death.

When she stepped from the dock, flanked by guards, she took her superstition with her. It was likely to prove very chill solace in the years ahead, for she looked like a woman in whom the spirit had died, leaving only a dry shell capable of enduring pain and the bitterness of memory.

Part 6

KILLING FOR SELF-PRESERVATION

J.H.H. GAUTE AND ROBIN ODELL

'If Only I Could Have Foreseen. . .'

London's streets were lashed with heavy rain and blued with lightning as a violent summer storm thundered overhead. The more timid of the city's inhabitants could have been forgiven for thinking that it was the end of the world – for one princely visitor, it really was. In the early hours of 10 July 1923, at the height of the storm, Prince Ali Kamel Fahmy Bey was shot dead by his wife in the Savoy Hotel. Fahmy was a wealthy young Egyptian who held a nominal diplomatic post at the Egyptian Legislation in Paris. He had been in England four days, having travelled from Paris with his beautiful French wife Marie-Marguerite, and his male secretary, Said Enani.

The Prince was not of royal rank. His title had been granted by virtue of his charitable work in Egypt where he had inherited the massive wealth of his father, a noted engineer. He had married Marie-Marguerite, a striking Parisienne beauty ten years his senior, in Cairo the previous December. Fahmy had a reputation as a playboy and with the enormous wealth at his command lived in great style and luxury. The couple engaged a suite of rooms at the Savoy overlooking the river where a staff of a valet and two maids looked after them. They danced every evening in the hotel ballroom and found a welcome in exclusive West End social circles. During the course of 9 July, the Fahmys quarrelled and their disagreement continued over dinner in the hotel restaurant. The room was crowded with diners when the quarrel spilled over into angry words. Speaking in French Madame Fahmy angrily told her husband, 'You shut up. I will smash this bottle over your head.' When the leader of the orchestra came to the table and asked her if she wished the band to play any particular request, she replied, 'I don't want any music – my husband has threatened to kill me tonight.' The musician withdrew tactfully. 'I hope you will be here tomorrow, Madame,' he said. The quarrel concerned medical treatment which a specialist had prescribed for Madame Fahmy and which necessitated going into a nursing home for an operation. Her husband refused to recognise the necessity for this and said he would not pay the bill. In between the ebb and flow of their disagreement Fahmy twice asked his wife to dance with him but she declined, although she did dance with his secretary, Said Enani.

The Fahmys retired to their fourth floor suite about 1.30 a.m. as the thunderstorm outside was reaching the peak of its fury. Shortly afterwards the Prince, dressed in his pyjamas, was seen by the hotel hall porter, John Paul Beattie, who was wheeling some luggage along the corridor outside his suite. Fahmy said to Beattie, 'Look at my face! Look what she has done!' The porter noticed a small red mark on the man's left cheek. Then Madame Fahmy appeared. She was dressed in a white beaded evening gown and spoke excitedly in French. The porter politely asked the couple to go back into their rooms and not create a disturbance in the corridor. As he walked away the porter heard a whistle, and looking behind him saw Fahmy snapping his fingers at a small dog which had emerged from his room. Moments later he heard three shots fired in rapid succession. As he ran back he saw Prince Fahmy lying in the corridor bleeding from the head. His wife threw a pistol onto the floor and said over and over again, 'What have I done?' When the night manager arrived on the scene she told him, 'I lost my head! I lost my head!' She telephoned Said Enani who had retired for the night, urging him, 'Come quickly! Come quickly! I have shot at Ali!' The young secretary hurried to the fourth floor and joined the knot of people bending over his injured master. Prince Fahmy was taken to Charing Cross Hospital where he died twenty-five minutes later from bullet wounds.

Detective Inspector Grosse questioned Madame Fahmy in her hotel room at about 3.00 a.m. She was calm and collected and told him simply that there had been an accident. There were bloodstains on the bottom of her evening dress and an examination of the corridor outside the suite revealed three bullet holes. Grosse took charge of the .25 Browning pistol and asked Madame Fahmy to go with him to Bow Street Police Station. Dr Gordon, the London physician who had been treating her for her complaint which precipitated the quarrel with her husband, had been called to the hotel. In answer to his question on French, 'What have you done?' she replied, 'I have shot at my husband.' The doctor accompanied her and Grosse in a taxi to Bow Street. Madame Fahmy wrote later, 'While we went the storm was still going on, and there were violent thunderclaps and flashes of lightning.' She was detained for the rest of the night and put in the care of two elderly wardresses. Although the atmosphere was warm and humid, Madame Fahmy was shivering and her teeth chattered. Her distress communicated itself to her kindly guardians who fetched her some tea – there could be no effective conversation as Madame Fahmy only spoke French.

After daybreak she was interviewed with the help of an interpreter and had her fingerprints taken. At about 11.00 a.m. she was charged with murdering her husband and appeared before the Bow Street magistrate in the afternoon. Her slim, elegant figure attracted considerable attention and the expensive jewellery she was wearing spoke for her wealth background. Detective Inspector Grosse read out the charge and after she had answered a few questions put by Madame Fahmy's solicitor, Mr Freke Palmer, she was remanded in custody for eight days. The proceedings were interpreted for her benefit and then she was taken by car to Holloway Prison. Madame Fahmy later described her memories of the scene: 'I can still see outside Bow Street the insistent photographers and the crowd standing silently gazing at the car.'

The Coroner's Inquest was held at Westminster and to the disappointment of the crowd gathered outside Madame

Fahmy did not appear. The newspapers had taken up the story of the Savoy shooting with great vigour. After all it was not every day that a wealthy Prince was shot dead by a beautiful woman. There was also a whiff of scandalous behaviour in the air which was fuelled at the inquest by statements made by Said Enani, the dead man's secretary. The couple were known to have quarrelled frequently and publicly and it was alleged that they assaulted each other. Said Enani said, 'They quarrelled about every trifle. I remember a great dispute between them in Paris in the hall of the Majestic Hotel. He was with his two sisters and his two brothers-in-law, and husband and wife were insulting each other in front of them.' Asked if Fahmy had ever struck his wife with his fist, Enani replied, 'Only once,' adding in rather quaint language that 'They smack each other'. It also came out that Fahmy and his wife were in the habit of keeping firearms in the bedroom. As the Coroner put it, '. . . each of them had a pistol, one each side of the bed.' Evidence was given about the shooting on the night of the thunderstorm and what had led up to it. Dr Gordon said Madame Fahmy told him in French that her husband had been ill-treating her that evening and had tried to force his attentions on her. After they had retired to their rooms he threatened her and she took up an automatic pistol which she fired at him as he advanced on her. She lost her head when her husband fell and believed he was shamming. It was only when she saw blood that she realised that the pistol was loaded. Dr Gordon said she told him that after she had fired one shot she did not know another would come up from the magazine. The Coroner remarked somewhat acidly, 'That does not help us very much when she fired three shots.' Mr Freke Palmer replied, 'No, but she did not know what she was doing – she lost her head.'

The medical evidence was that Fahmy had died from severe laceration of the brain tissue due to the bullet wound in the head. In all there were seven wounds, four being caused by one bullet. Inspector Grosse told the court that when charged Madame Fahmy replied in French, 'I told the police I did it. I told the truth. It does not matter. My husband has assaulted me in front of many people since we were married. He has told me many times to kill him . . . I lost my head.' Mr Freke

Palmer told the Coroner that he did not propose putting up a defence in that court. The jury brought in a verdict of 'Wilful Murder against Madame Fahmy' and the Magistrate's Court similarly concluded that there was a charge to be answered, so Madame Fahmy was commited for trial.

In the weeks leading up to the trial, and during the trial itself, enough words were written about Madame Fahmy to fill several volumes. The lady herself, because of her elegant background, captured the public imagination. From the start she was pictured sympathetically: 'A beautiful brunette, slim, and graceful, she was nevertheless a very pathetic figure in the dock . . . at times she pressed a small handkerchief to her eyes . . .' This was how her appearance at Bow Street Court was described. The fact that she had shot her husband, who was young, oriental and wealthy with suggestions of beastliness in his character, was sufficient to ensure her immortality in the annals of crime reporting. Marie-Marguerite was born in Paris on 9 December 1890, she had a sister and two brothers, both of whom were killed, one in an accident and the other in the First World War. She was educated at a Convent School: 'I was very devout myself, in a mystic way, as young sensitive girls sometimes are. I was, of course, a Roman Catholic.' Marie-Marguerite, or 'Maggie' as she later became known to her friends, left home when she was sixteen, and her father died a year or two later, heart-broken it was said, at the loss of his children. She became a mother at the tender age of sixteen, giving birth to a daughter, Raymonde, who was adopted by her grandmother and aunt. Maggie spent a great deal of her time with her godmother whom she acknowledged as inspiring her with a love of art and music. Her experience of life was broadened when, still in her early teens, she became engaged to a man of twenty-eight whom she had known since childhood. This was André Meller, brother of a wealthy racing stable owner. They were never married, but in his mature company Maggie learned to ride and dance and she acquired those social graces which turned an awkward girl into an elegant young woman. She already had many admirers and began to move in distinguished social circles. 'My nature was mercurial and under my love-sorrow my life quite changed.' She left the care of her godmother and went to live at Bordeaux where she met and fell in love with another older man. He was waiting for his marriage to be annulled and in 1913 Maggie's wedding plans were announced, only to be suddenly dashed when the divorce failed to go through.

Maggie returned to Paris and served with the Red Cross during World War One. She drove an ambulance and sang at charity concerts. In 1919 she was admitted to hospital for an operation and there met Charles Laurent who was also a patient. 'During our convalescence, we fell in love,' she said. They were married in April but marital bliss did not follow. Laurent worked as an interpreter at the Japanese Consulate in Paris, and when the opportunity arose he wanted to work in Japan and take Maggie with him. She did not wish to do this and the disagreement ended with Laurent going alone and Maggie subsequently divorcing him. Her ex-husband made her a generous allowance and left her a flat in Paris and a motorcar. Thus set up, the world of high society was Maggie's oyster. She was the talk of Paris and of all the fashionable watering places throughout France and Europe.

During a visit to Cairo in January 1922, Maggie was introduced to a handsome young Egyptian, Ali Kamel Fahmy Bey. They were mutually impressed – Maggie thought him to be a 'magnificent individual' and Ali told a friend, 'Tell her I will give a *fête Vénitienne* on my yacht in her honour.' She declined to be fêted on this occasion but was obviously intrigued by the man. Ali Kamel, at twenty-two was blessed with a great fortune. His father, a distinguished Egyptian engineer, had died when Ali was a mere lad, leaving his son immense wealth, made chiefly out of growing cotton. Estimates of Ali's income varied but a hundred and fifty thousand a year was widely suggested. He lived in a grand manner, employed hundreds of servants to run his numerous homes and was a familiar and, no doubt, welcome participant at the gaming tables of Monte Carlo. Ali also did charitable work making grants available for Egyptian students to receive higher education in Europe and putting up the money to build much-needed hospitals in his own country. In recognition of this work a grateful government allowed him to use the title of 'Prince'. This 'spoiled child of fortune', one of the many epithets subsequently used to capture the essence of the man, followed Maggie to Paris in the spring. They met a few times and she began to feel that she could not go anywhere 'without sooner or later finding the steadfast gaze of this foreigner fixed yearningly' upon her. In July, while entertaining some friends in Paris, Maggie received a mysterious telephone call from a woman she knew who said, 'I have a friend who absolutely must make your acquaintance. He says that it is his sole ambition while he is in Paris.' A rendezvous was arranged at the Majestic Hotel and there when she walked into the lounge Maggie found fixed upon her, 'the large dark eyes of the man I knew as Ali Fahmy'. Ali suggested going to the Château de Madrid and Maggie agreed. They walked to the hotel entrance and pointing to two limousines standing outside, one of which was a Rolls Royce, Ali asked his companion, 'Which one do you prefer?' This was the first of many meetings and Ali pursued his lady love with telephone calls, telegrams and visits, sometimes driving halfway across Europe to see her. There were high-speed drives through the French countryside with Ali at the wheel, despite the presence in his entourage of a chauffeur whom Maggie called 'a chocolate-coloured Colossus'. He liked to drive fiercely and no doubt enjoyed scaring his companion. He also initiated Maggie, no mean driver herself, into the mysteries of double de-clutching.

Ali was a persistent suitor with a great advantage – nothing was too expensive. As Maggie was to describe it: 'Money was poured out lavishly. Nothing was too good, too beautiful, or too dear for me.' He gave her presents of the most marvellous jewellery bought from Cartier and other exclusive houses. But with all this wooing and spending and dashing about, Ali occasionally showed flashes of temper which were to bode ill for the future. On one occasion when Maggie declined to go with him to Italy, he blazed angrily at her, 'I count on your coming with me tomorrow.' Maggie stuck to her decision, preferring the attractions of a season at Biarritz, and Ali went alone to Milan, but she had seen a hardened glint in his eyes and a set in his jaw that made her afraid. From Milan there came a stream of letters from Ali phrased in passionate terms and when he moved on to Egypt there were telegrams: 'I am dying. Your name alone is on my lips.' Not surprisingly, Maggie succumbed to the entreaties and in November travelled to Egypt. She arrived by boat to be met by Ali who swiftly whisked her away in one of his many cars to his villa on the coast, a few miles from Alexandria, from there they travelled by train to Cairo and to Zamalek on the River Nile.

Although Maggie had visited Egypt before, she was about to enter an opulent palace like something out of the Arabian Nights. Servants in gold-braided uniforms greeted the couple on the steps of the marble palace at Zamalek, the interior of which echoed Fontainebleau. The walls were hung with tapestries, the floors covered with Persian carpets, and the rooms furnished with Louis XVI pieces. The palace housed a film theatre and there were servants, cars and boats for every occasion. Maggie's room had been designed for the King of Serbia. Its walls were decorated with rich blue and gold hangings and the bed, shaped like a boat, was raised on a dais surrounded by bronze figures. The bathroom, in white marble, was a Greek temple in miniature with a solid silver bath, lace drapes and onyx fixtures. This was Maggie's 'Wonder House of the Nile' which she said contained '. . . so many solid gold cigarette boxes that they got in the way . . .' Now that he had dazzled the light of his desire with his fairy tale world, Ali told her, 'You are to become my wife; you are my only happiness.' Maggie, overwhelmed, simply begged for time to reflect.

The next month was taken up with trips and fêtes and further unfolding of wondrous events. There were also a few insights into the unstable and despotic side of Ali's nature. He had already shown an enthusiasm for fast driving in France such that Maggie had dubbed him a 'Velocimaniac'. In his native country and with the considerable prestige which his wealth and rank afforded him, he was a dangerous menace on the roads. One of his favourite hobbies seemed to be to terrorise the pedestrian population of Cairo with his erratic driving. He made it a point of honour to overtake every other car and frequently had arrogant confrontations with other drivers. Maggie said, 'In like fashion, some young bloods of the town made it a point of honour to try to stop him overtaking them. Then a frenzied race would begin. Terrified people would dash to the pavement, and stalls would be scattered all over the place . . .' Ali was fined repeatedly for exceeding the speed limit, not that the fine was any penalty to him. He merely laughed about it; 'I fear neither God nor the Devil,' he joked. His antics on the River Nile in his powerful motor boats were no less inconsiderate. The wash from his 450 h.p. aero-engine-powered speed boat played havoc with the normal, peaceful river traffic.

Maggie still refused to accept his proposal of marriage but her vacillation spurred Ali on to provide even more luxurious delights. Finally the combination of passionate expressions of love and the prospect of unrivalled riches swayed her. Ali gave a great feast in her honour at Shepheard's Hotel and their intention to marry was announced. 'Truly at this hour I was intensely happy,' said Maggie. 'Ali unfolded before my eyes the life of "A Thousand and One Nights".' The civil marriage contract was enacted on 26 December and Maggie agreed to adopt her husband's religion. This involved a number of legal formalities, including a statement from the French Consul in Cairo that Maggie was free of any bond of marriage. Her Roman Catholic adviser tried to dissuade her from the conversion but she decided to see it through. On 11 January 1923, by declaring 'There is one God and Mohammed is his prophet' she renounced her former faith and became a Moslem. The convert signed the documents in the name of Munira, in honour of Ali's mother.

Next came the religious marriage but instead of the traditionally magnificent ceremony, Maggie wanted it to be a simple occasion. This took place at Ali's mansion in Cairo. Maggie dressed in black with a black head-dress and wearing a heavy veil, appeared before the priest. Some of Ali's relatives were present together with his lawyer and secretary, Said Enani. A number of preliminary formalities were completed and then Maggie was asked an unexpected question – she was requested to waive the right of divorce.

This she was reluctant to do for she knew that, under Moslem law, her husband could cast her aside by saying before two witnesses 'I put away this woman', whereas his wife had no redress if he took three other wives as was his right. The marriage ceremony was adjourned while the parties argued about the divorce question and Maggie was put under great pressure by the Fahmy family to accept their wishes. After four hours of confrontation, Maggie eventually agreed, and she and Ali became man and wife under Moslem law. With all arguments cleared away, another great celebration took place at Shepheard's Hotel and the happy couple prepared for a voyage up the Nile to Luxor in Ali's yacht. The journey took ten days, intoxicating days for Maggie with new scenery and a new life opening ahead for her.

But again, the happiness was tinged with other emotions – suspicion, spitefulness and anger, all on Ali's part. He censored Maggie's letters, counting the sheets of note-paper and examining the blotter to see to whom she had been writing. It was a few days into this river journey that Maggie witnessed one of Ali's mad rages. A tug-boat on the river approached their yacht coming quite close in a manner to which Ali took exception. At the time he had been taking his siesta reclining in a pair of black silk pyjamas. Suddenly he leapt up, frantically blowing a whistle, and, summoning three of his seamen, jumped into the motor boat which was towed behind his yacht, and raced off in pursuit of the tug which had simply gone on its way down river. He soon caught up with the vessel and, having boarded it, commanded the two native pilots to get into his motorboat. He then raced back to his yacht where they transferred and he accused them of trying to sink his boat. While his own crew stood by gaping he thrashed the two seamen with a stick until they grovelled at his feet. When he had finished he gave instructions that the beaten men were to be left marooned on a sandbank as their final punishment. It was an extraordinary scene and Maggie protested to her husband. 'That's the way they ought to be treated,' he told her, 'I must teach them who I am.'

'Grim forebodings may have clutched at my heart,' said Maggie, 'but I found solace in the wonders that surrounded us.' One of the wonders was the yacht itself which carried twenty-five seamen, a chef and six cooks, two stewards and a maid. Dinner usually consisted of twenty courses in this floating palace. During their passage down the Nile, they passed many poor villages where some of the men would dive spectacularly into the water in the hope of obtaining money – baksheesh. But Ali, Prince of the Nile, reviewing these performances from his motorboat, would rap the knuckles of the swimmers as they came alongside begging for money. 'The man who could spend thousands of francs on a single article never gave a piastre to a beggar,' said Maggie.

As they approached Luxor, home of some of the great monuments built by the Kings of Ancient Egypt, Ali was impatient to get ashore. In order to reach the city quickly, especially as dusk was falling, he used his motorboat to make better time. There was a crowd waiting to greet him but their welcome did not seem to please him. Apparently what troubled him was that his motorboat did not afford him sufficient style, so he returned to his yacht in order that he could make an adequately regal arrival the next morning. Fahmy and his bride spent three days at Luxor visiting the temple at Karnak and the Valley of the Kings. The untouched tomb of Tutankhamun had been discovered the previous November and Ali played host on his yacht to Lord Carnarvon, one of the discoverers, and other distinguished guests including a Maharajah and a General. During a visit to the Valley of the Kings, Ali made a slightly macabre request of Maggie – he wanted her to lie down in an ancient stone sarcophagus, whose previous occupant had been a long dead king, so that he could photograph her. Maggie responded to this weird request and the picture went into the album of honeymoon snapshots.

Ali continued to display extraordinary traits of behaviour which turned the honeymoon into disillusionment for Maggie. On an occasion when he was abusing his seamen, Maggie interceded. 'Oh, well,' said Ali, 'I will leave you with the sailors and go away.' With that he stopped the yacht and went ashore. He returned about three hours later and his next tantrum was to forbid his wife to leave the boat. 'Surely,' asked Maggie, 'you will not imprison me on my honeymoon?' 'The yacht is beautiful,' he said, 'you have many servants. Stay here.' And he meant it. When he went ashore he had the gangplanks pulled up behind him and left four black servants to guard her. Ali also constantly mistreated his crew either with tongue lashings or by making impossible demands. He seemed to delight in it all and Maggie was pleased when the honeymoon cruise was over.

They returned to Cairo and according to Maggie, 'My husband's character underwent a further change.' Ali took to going out on his own, absenting himself from meals and often returning extremely late. His wife suspected that he visited Arab theatres 'which no self respecting woman can visit' while she languished at home as a Moslem lady which meant that former pleasures such as horseriding were denied her. She was a virtual prisoner in her palace and her movements were closely watched by black guards. 'There were evenings when I felt thoroughly worn by grief,' said Maggie and she supposed, 'he was making me pay for my disdain, my refusal, my resistance of the first month of our meeting.' She missed her parents, her friends and, above all, her freedom. 'Oh, how I longed for the return to Europe.' The attempt to make the transition from West to East had failed and she was broken-hearted. Ali promised a return to Europe and the date for the departure was fixed for 18 May 1923. When the time came to leave for Alexandria Ali inevitably played up. First of all he announced that he had changed his mind about going and then, once on their way, he refused to name their destination. Happily for Maggie, they ended up in Paris where they took a suite at the Majestic Hotel. She was able to see her friends, ride her horses and attend the theatre and dinner parties as she had before her marriage. Ali still behaved strangely if perhaps slightly less despotically now that he was not in his own country. He had taken to decorating himself with jewellery and accommodated an Algerian guard in his suite. This man, whom Maggie called a 'Black Hercules', was known as Le Costaud because of his size. His presence terrorised her and of this period of her life Maggie was to write, '. . . our return to Paris was shortlived. Indeed, it consisted in the temporary joy of renewed associations rather than any change in the relations between Ali and myself, such as could bring permanent joy.' And so the Paris episode came to an end and Prince Ali and his wife travelled to London for a short holiday and for their final quarrel.

Maggie appeared at the Old Bailey on 10 September. The case against her was overwhelming and, recognising this, her solicitor knew she needed the best defence advocate he could find. He retained two famous counsel, Sir Edward Marshall Hall and Sir Henry Curtis-Bennett. These great advocates, who had often appeared in opposition, now spared no effort in preparing Madame Fahmy's defence. Their client's statements after the shooting left no room for doubt that hers was the hand which discharged the fatal shots. While the background had all the ingredients of what in mitigation the French called a *crime passionnel*, that was not a condition easily recognised by British courts. What was obvious from the start was that Maggie had been provoked and it was the circumstances of that provocation which the defence was busy researching. Marshall Hall advised his colleagues, 'Take any opinion from anyone you like, this lady's life is in peril. Three shots were fired – three shots, remember that. We are entitled to procure *any* evidence to get at the truth and save her life.' At least part of the truth was that Prince Ali Fahmy was a homosexual and Marshall Hall had two youths with painted faces brought from Egypt to support that contention. It was also clear that Ali made perverse sexual demands on his wife which to a person of her sensitivity were at the very least undignified if not painful. Defence enquiries into the character of the dead man and his behaviour towards his wife built up into a powerful case which Marshall Hall would unleash at the trial. There were also practical considerations and with his passion for thorough preparation Marshall Hall paid a visit to Whistler's, the gunshop in the Strand, and asked to see a Browning automatic. He was well-known to the proprietor and his request was readily met. Taking the pistol he examined it in great detail and learned its handling characteristics. There were daily conferences with Sir Henry

Curtis-Bennett and his other advisers to build the defence and
decide the tactics which would save Madame Fahmy.

The trial opened before Mr Justice Rigby Swift and
Marshall Hall immediately asked to have the proceedings
translated into French so that Maggie could follow what was
going on. She wrote later that she had '. . . always regretted
not having learnt English. Never has my regret been keener
than during my sad detention and trial.' H. Ashton-Wolfe
described in his reminiscences the thrill he experienced at
being asked to act as interpreter. 'I have rarely seen a
court at the Old Bailey so packed with notabilities,' he
wrote. He described Madame Fahmy's appearance as pale
and dressed in deep mourning. Under the eyes of a packed
court, which included her sister-in-law and several Egyptian
lawyers, Ashton-Wolfe asked the defendant in French how
she pleaded. *Non coupable* was the answer. Mr (later Sir)
Percival Clark opened the case for the prosecution. He placed
an emphasis on the unhappiness of the Fahmys' marriage:
'He is said to have been a quiet, nervous sort of man . . . and
she a woman rather fond of a gay life.' Counsel pointed out
that Madame Fahmy always slept with a pistol close to hand
after she was married, 'whether to protect her jewellery, of
which she had plenty, or for some other reason, I am unable
to say.' He recounted the events of that stormy night at the
Savoy Hotel and re-iterated Madame Fahmy's admissions.
'Coming to this country persons are bound by the laws which
prevail here,' he concluded. 'Every homicide is presumed to
be murder until the contrary is shown. From her own lips it is
known that she it was who caused her husband's death. And,
in the absence of any circumstances to make it some other
offence, you must find her guilty of murder.'

Said Enani, the late Prince's secretary, was called to give
evidence on the first day of the trial. For four hours, during
cross-examination, Marshall Hall teased out of this man an
account of Prince Fahmy's life with his European wife. 'Did
you say he was an Oriental and rather passionate?' 'Yes.' 'You
had a great deal of influence with him?' 'No not influence.'
'Was he a bully?' 'He was rather shy.' 'You know what a
bully means? Was he a man in the habit of beating women –

not only one woman, but women?' 'No sir, he would dispute with them, but I have never seen him beat them.' 'You have known of his intimacies with many women?' 'Yes sir.' 'Do you know he treated them brutally, one and all?' 'No sir, I cannot say brutally.' Defence Counsel was at pains not to spare Ali's reputation but Said Enani wa steadfastly loyal. Switching to Ali's methods for inducing Maggie to go to Egypt, Marshall Hall said he used feigned illness as a ruse to persuade her. 'Was he infatuated with her at that time?' he asked Said Enani. 'Yes, much in love with her.' 'Just look at this letter sent from Cairo,' said Counsel, and he went on to read it: 'My dear little Bella, I have landed on Monday and my first letter is to you. The crossing was delicious and more delicious still was that indefinable fragrance radiated from your entire self. Your presence everywhere pursues me incessantly. These are not memories I am invoking, they are realities . . . Sincerity – it is so difficult to find . . . Confidence and sincerity, cause and effect. I believe I have obtained it and I believe I have merited it. I believe I have proved sufficiently that I was worthy of it. How can one fail to recognise qualities which stand out so blindingly clear? Torch of my life . . . you appear to me surrounded by a halo. I see your head encircled by a crown which I reserve for it here. It is a crown I have reserved for you on your arrival in this beautiful country of my ancestors. If you abandon your journey scheme, you will have made my life aimless. Envy and jealousy should never have any weight with any of us. Come, come quickly and appreciate the beautiful sun of Egypt. My only consolation is you. Believe me I love you very much. From your faithful Little Baba.' Marshall Hall elicited from Said Enani that the reference in the letter to envy and jealousy was a warning from Fahmy (Ali Baba) to Maggie not to pay heed to any scandal she may have heard about him. Referring to telegrams he sent the defendant saying that his master was ill, Said Enani was told by Marshall Hall, 'You and Fahmy conspired together to make these statements in order to induce this woman to go to Egypt?' The loyal secretary's denial was firm enough but it seemed inadequate set against the text of a telegram sent on 7 October which read: 'Desperate. Still grave dying today.' and another two days later: 'Baba better today. First word your name. Always asking for you. Your presence necessary.'

Moving on to Maggie's arrival in Egypt and the period after her marriage to Prince Fahmy, Marshall Hall now taxed the luckless witness with questions about his master's cruel and threatening behaviour. 'Do you know that on February 21 he swore on the Koran that he would kill her?' 'No.' 'Do you know that she was in fear of her life?' 'I never knew.' 'I suggest that from that moment Fahmy began to treat her with persistent cruelty?' 'I cannot say cruelty. He was a bit unkind.' Defence Counsel went on to draw out some of the incidents of the Nile boat trip and the episode in which Ali thrashed the boatmen. Regarding Ali's behaviour to his wife, Said Enani was unable to remember whether he smacked her face or kicked her.

An illustration of how well the Defence had prepared the case came when Marshall Hall read out a letter which Fahmy had written to his sister about his bride: 'Ha! ha! ha! Just now I am engaged in training her. Yesterday, to begin, I did not come in to lunch or to dinner, and I also left her at the theatre. This will teach her, I hope, to respect my wishes. With women one must act with energy and be severe.' Counsel invited Said Enani to recall other threats which Fahmy had made against his wife, including seizing her by the throat during a visit to the Folies Bergères and punching her in the face, causing her mouth to bleed, in the Hotel Majestic. 'Had every bit of life been crushed out of her during these six months?' 'I do not know.' 'From an entertaining and fascinating woman, had she become miserable and wretched?' 'They were always quarrelling.' 'Did she say that you and Fahmy were always against her, and that it was a case of two to one?' 'Yes.'

Marshall Hall's final contribution to the first day of the trial was to hold up in court a large coloured cartoon which had appeared in 'Kachkoul', a Cairo comic weekly. This showed three profiles and was entitled 'The Light, the Shadow and the Shadow's Shadow' with text describing Said Enani as 'The evil genius of Fahmy'. Counsel suggested that the association between Enani and Fahmy was notorious – Enani denied it and the Judge observed duly that the cartoon did not reflect on anyone's moral character 'except perhaps the artist's'.

On the second day, Robert Churchill, the well-known gun expert, gave evidence for the prosecution. His testimony was factual and straightforward. He identified the pistol alleged to have been used in the shooting as a .32 Browning of Belgian manufacture with an eight cartridge magazine. Sir Edward Marshall Hall informed the court when he rose to begin his cross-examination: 'I want you to give me your careful attention. A great deal depends on this witness's evidence and I shall be some time with him.' He asked the gunsmith to explain the manner in which an automatic pistol worked with special reference to the recoil mechanism which feeds a new round of ammunition into the breech. Counsel suggested that when the pistol was gripped tightly a small pressure on the trigger would fire several shots. He also contended that an inexperienced person might easily reload the gun thinking that in reality he was emptying it. The witness agreed that someone unfamiliar with firearms might do this. 'A lot of people think these pistols are like Lewis guns,' said Churchill, 'They are not. Each bullet requires separate pressure. If by accident a series of shots were fired it would sound as one.' The gunsmith was followed in the witness box by the doctor. Dr Gordon was called out on the night of the shooting and found Madame Fahmy 'dazed and frightened'. She told him at Bow Street of the quarrel with her husband and said that he refused to pay for an operation which had been arranged. 'Later in the evening,' said the doctor, 'Fahmy brutally handled her and pestered her.' She had a scratch about an inch and a half long on her neck, 'probably caused by a fingernail'. Dr Gordon testified that when he had seen Madame Fahmy on 4 July, she had bruises on her arms and leg which she said had been caused by her husband. Marshall Hall asked, 'Was the mark on the neck consistent with a hand clutching at her throat?' 'It was. Madame Fahmy complained that her husband was very passionate and that his conduct had made her ill. Her condition was consistent with conduct she alleged against her husband.' The unspoken illness from which poor Maggie suffered was haemorrhoids, a complaint made more painful and unbearable by the perverse demands of Fahmy.

When the tall figure of Marshall Hall rose on the third day to begin his opening speech for the defence, the court was to be awed by the powerful oratory of one of the greatest of English advocates. He told the jury that three verdicts were possible, murder, manslaughter or not guilty. 'If this woman was in fear of her life, if Fahmy had threatened to kill her, if, on the early morning of this July 10 he had hold of her in such a way that she believed he intended to strangle her, and she, believing the pistol to be unloaded, presented it at him for the purpose of preventing him killing her, and discharged it and killed him, that would be a verdict of Not Guilty. When you have heard the evidence we shall ask you to say that the last is the proper verdict in this case.' He said that Madame Fahmy made a terrible mistake in her estimate of Fahmy's character and only found out after they were married that he was abnormal, '. . . this was a man who enjoyed the sufferings of women. He was abnormal and a brute.' Clearly, Marshall Hall was in no mood to spare the feelings of any in court who cherished the memory of the dead man. He went on to illustrate Fahmy's behaviour after the marriage, how he had sworn on the Koran to kill his wife, how he had threatened her by firing a pistol over her head and how he posted a guard of black men to watch her. Fahmy was a man who heaped every sort of indignity on his wife. 'She was a poor wretched woman suffering from the tortures of the damned, driven to desperation by the brutality and beastliness of this man, whose will she had dared to oppose', she thought that he was carrying out the threat he had always made, and that when he seized her by the neck he was about to kill her'.

Before resuming the defence on the next day of the trial, Marshall Hall raised a legal point which was discussed in the absence of the jury. It concerned the Prosecution Counsel's intention of asking Madame Fahmy whether she had led an immoral life with the result that she could be considered a woman of the world and well able to look after herself. Mr Percival Clarke said he wanted to show that the defendant's word could not be relied on, but that she had associated with other men and that the fault was not all on her husband's side. Mr Justice Rigby Swift pointed out that Sir Edward had already said that she was an immoral woman, '. . . but he said it in such a way that he gave the impression to everyone who listened to his speech that she was an innocent and most respectable woman. It is a difficult thing to do but Sir Edward, with all that skill we have admired for so long has done it.' The judge ruled that Mr Clarke would not be entitled to ask the defendant about her relations with any other men. This was an important point to have won for the protection of his client and Marshall Hall no doubt felt buoyant as Madame Fahmy walked in to the dock. Her progress was slightly unsteady and she was supported on the arm of a wardress as she ascended the steps of the witness-box.

Talking to her through the interpreter, Marshall Hall led Maggie through her early life and first meetings with Ali Fahmy and then questioned her on their life together. 'Did you notice any change in your husband's attitude after you left Cairo to go to Luxor?' 'The last day he tried to frighten me, and fired a revolver several times above my head.' 'Why did you not leave him when you reached Luxor?' 'Every time I tried to leave him he cried and begged me to stay, and said that he would not do it again.' 'When you went back to the yacht, what was your husband's demeanour and behaviour?' 'He began to strike me. On several occasions, he struck me and kicked me.' She said that when she threatened to leave him, her husband, in an obvious reference to the fact that she could not divorce him, said, 'You can never leave me anymore.' Choking with emotion, Maggie went on, 'During the three days' journey to Luxor, he made a terrible scene, locked me in my cabin, and quarrelled violently during the whole journey.' Because of these experiences, Maggie wrote to Maître Assouard, her lawyer in Cairo, telling him of her predicament. Marshall Hall read the letter out in court and its contents amply supported her testimony from the witness-box: 'For the last three days I am a prisoner on board. I am absolutely unable to get out. He has forbidden me to leave my room. I have on my arms marks of my husband's gentleness.'

Maggie described her horror of the black valet who followed her everywhere and of her husband's huge Algerian bodyguard 'Costaud'. Fahmy threatened he would order Costaud to disfigure her. Sobbing now with her head down on her black-gloved hands, Maggie said, 'My husband threatened me every day and said Costaud would do anything he wished to me.' 'Did you think you would be safe in London?' asked her Counsel. 'I passed from despair to hope and from hope to despair,' was the sobbed reply. Marshall Hall now moved quickly to the evening of the shooting. Maggie described the scene when she returned from an afternoon shopping trip with Said Enani. They got back about 7.30 p.m. and found Ali in a furious temper because Maggie had packed in readiness to go to Paris. 'He took his photograph from the table,' she said, 'tore it into pieces and threw them in my face . . . he was pale and aggressive and repeated, "You will see; you will see." His attitude was threatening.' Counsel asked her, 'Did you do something with the pistol?'

'I took the pistol from the drawer . . . I tried to look into it to see if there were a bullet. I tried to do as I had seen him do to bring the cartridge out of it.' Marshall Hall had demonstrated earlier, by handing the defendant an automatic pistol, that she was unable to pull back the breech cover. Now Maggie described her attempt in the Hotel suite 'to make the cartridge fall out, but I did not have the strength to pull sufficiently', 'Why did you want to have the cartridge out of the barrel?' 'Because he said he was going to kill me, and I thought I would frighten him with it—I thought there were no more cartridges to fire and that the revolver was inoffensive.'

Maggie told how she went to the theatre later that evening with her husband and Said Enani. When they returned there was a quarrel and Fahmy's temper flared—he told her, 'I will disfigure you and after that you can go to the devil.' She retired briefly to her bedroom and then Fahmy returned and renewed the quarrel. He pulled at her and she hit him on the face. At this point her husband went out into the corridor and 'showed his face to the porter'. Then he was back again banging on her door. 'I saw the revolver,' she said, 'which I put in my bag next to the door. When I saw him at the door I was frightened and felt weak.' As she relived those dramatic moments, Maggie sobbed convulsively and her cheeks were wet with tears. Fahmy advanced on her and said,

'I will revenge myself.' Maggie had picked up the pistol by this time and, moving towards the door of the suite and out into the corridor, she told him, 'I will say that you have threatened me,' With that he seized her by the throat. 'His thumb was on my windpipe and his fingers pressed my neck.' Husband and wife, as if engaged in some weird dance, moved back into the bedroom and there Maggie said, 'He crouched to spring at me and said "I will kill you".' Maggie's voice broke and, tapping her forehead with her left hand, she closed her eyes and sobbed, 'I now lifted my arm in front of me and without looking pulled the trigger.'

Maggie had been in the witness-box for three hours but before the court adjourned for the day, she had to face cross-examination by Mr Clarke. He went over some of her earlier history and asked if her father was a Paris cab-driver. Mr Justice Swift quickly intervened, 'Does it matter whether he was a cab-driver or a millionaire? I do not want a long inquiry into her ancestry . . .' Prosecuting Counsel next asked the defendant, 'Can I correctly describe you as a woman of the world?' The interpreter had some difficulty translating this phrase but Maggie replied, 'I have had some experience of life.' The impact that she had made in the witness-box could not be weakened and when the day's proceedings were concluded she fainted and was helped away by attendants. A tightly-packed court had listened, riveted, to a domestic story told with stunning sincerity.

In a shrewd move to help his client, Marshall Hall secured the services of Maître Odette Simon, a young woman barrister from Paris, as interpreter. This appeared to reflect some criticism on the previous interpreter but Marshall Hall, who was himself fluent in French, was not happy that Maggie understood all the questions put to her. There could be no room for doubt and Mr Justice Swift allowed Mlle Simon to be sworn. Mr Clarke then returned to his cross-examination covering much familiar ground. Asked if she hated her husband in view of his objectionable behaviour, Maggie replied, 'I loved my husband and when he had been so bad I despaired and told him I hated him. I did not hate him, but only what he wanted me to do.' There

were further distressing moments for her when Prosecuting
Counsel went through the routine with the automatic pistol
and then produced her torn evening gown. 'Did you know
that your husband was absolutely unarmed when you pointed
the revolver at him?' 'I did not know,' she answered, 'he often
had a pistol in the jacket of his dressing gown.' Maggie was
asked about a letter she had written to her sister which was
sent to her lawyer to be opened in the event of her death.
This document, written on 22 January at Zamalek, provided
further corroboration of the world of fear in which she lived.
'I Marie Marguerite Alibert (her maiden name), of sound
mind and body, formally accuse, in the case of my death,
violent or otherwise, Ali Bey Fahmy, of having contributed
to my disappearance. Yesterday, January 21st, 1923, at three
o'clock in the afternoon, he took his Bible or Koran – I do not
know how it is called—kissed it, put his hand on it, and swore
to avenge himself upon me tomorrow, in eight days, a month
or three months; but I must disappear by his hand. This
oath was taken without reason—neither jealousy, nor bad
conduct, nor a scene on my part. I desire and demand justice
for my daughter and my family.' Mr Clarke asked, 'Is that
letter here?' 'Yes. It is the exact truth,' replied Maggie, at the
end of nearly four hours in the witness-box. There followed
a brief succession of witnesses: Maggie's sister Yvonne, her
maid and her chauffeur. They all spoke of her unhappiness, of
seeing bruises on her and of her husband's callous attitude to
her. Eugene Barbay, the chauffeur, said he heard Fahmy use
bad language to his wife which he repeated in French to the
court but the interpreter said it was so bad that it should not
be uttered—the offending word was denoted in the records
by its initial letter.

In his address to the jury, Sir Edward Marshall Hall said,
'There are really only two issues before you. Either this was
a deliberate, premeditated and cowardly murder, or it was
a shot fired by this woman from a pistol which she believed
was unloaded at a moment when she thought her life was in
danger. She made one great mistake,' he said, 'possibly the
greatest mistake any woman can make—a woman of the West
married to an Oriental.' Marshall Hall paid tribute to ancient

Egypt civilisation and supposed there were many magnificent Egyptians today, 'but if you strip off the external civilisation of the Oriental you have the real Oriental underneath as it is common knowledge that the Oriental's treatment of woman does not fit in with the idea the Western woman has of the way she should be treated by her husband.' He relegated Said Enani to part of that 'Eastern duplicity' and believed him to have been 'hostile to this unfortunate woman'. Then there was Costaud, 'that great black Hercules, who came day after day for orders and was ready to do anything'. He spoke of the indignities placed on Madame Fahmy and referred to the sex question which is one of mystery: 'It is the abuses and not the uses of that great natural function that are the curse of mankind,' boomed Marshall Hall. There were sidelong glances at the two youths brought to England in case the dead man's homosexuality needed proving. Marshall Hall was winding himself up for the final crescendo of his speech. He emphasized the effect of the thunderstorm would have on a woman of nervous temperament who for six months had been 'outraged, abused, beaten and degraded'. With the court hushed and tense, Defense Counsel stooped in imitation of the stealthy advance of Ali Fahmy. 'In sheer desperation as he crouched for the last time, crouched like an animal, like an Oriental, retired for the last time to get a bound forward – she turned the pistol and put it to his face, and to her horror the thing went off.' Holding up the pistol in full view of the jury, he paused dramatically and then let the gun clatter to the floor. It was an electrifying moment; 'Was that,' he asked, 'deliberate wilful murder?'

'The drama over, Marshall Hall told the jury, 'I do not ask you for a verdict: I demand a verdict at your hands . . . You will open the gate and let this Western woman go back into the light of God's great western sun.' The great advocate's *tour de force* had lasted two and a half hours—he felt back into his seat exhausted. Mr Justice Swift summed up the important points in Madame Fahmy's favour and reminded the jury that there were three verdicts which could be found, 'murder', 'manslaughter' and 'not guilty'. 'I cannot say that no provocation existed,' he said. 'I should

think that it would not be right for you to return a verdict
of manslaughter against this woman if you believe that he
actually seized her by the throat.' The judge referred to
certain aspects of the case which he described as 'shocking,
sickening and disgusting'. The story of the defendant's life in
Paris was, he pointed out, corroborated by her sister and her
chauffeur. Finally, Mr Justice Swift told the jury, 'A person
who honestly believes that his life is in danger is entitled to kill
his assailant if that is the only way he honestly and reasonably
believes he can protect himself. But he must be in real danger,
and it must be the only way out of it.'

The jury had been out for just over an hour when they
returned and Maggie was brought up, her face pale and heavy-
eyed behind a veil, to her verdict. The jury foreman's
words, 'Not Guilty', were almost drowned by a great outburst
of cheering in court which was picked up and echoed by a large
crowd waiting outside. Mr Justice Swift ordered the court to
be cleared and then, turning to Mlle Simon, said, 'Tell her that
the jury have found her not guilty and that she is discharged.'
It was an unnecessary instruction, for Maggie knew from the
spontaneous and noisy public approval of the verdict that she
was free. She was carried swooning from the dock while men
and women alike clapped and laughed and cried by turns.
When Maggie's sister, Yvonne Alibert, left the court, she was
mobbed by the crowd who mistakenly called out, 'Princess'. A
woman in the mob embraced her in a gesture which personified
the enormous public feeling there was for the woman who had
stood alone in the dock. Mlle Alibert was in tears as she was
driven away—she blew kisses to the crowd and called out, '*Les
Anglais sont très bien.*'

Maggie, after being seen by her doctor, was whisked out
through a side entrance of the court, and driven away
practically unnoticed. She was taken to a West End hotel
to rest.' All I want now is just to be forgotten by everybody
except my own friends,' she said, adding, 'I want to thank
everybody whose sympathy has been with me throughout
my terrible ordeal . . . I am very touched . . . I think British
justice is too wonderful for words.' In recognition of the great
debt she owed to Sir Edward Marshall Hall, she sent him a

telegram expressing her gratitude and followed it the same evening with a letter of thanks. The day after the trial was Marshall Hall's sixty-sixth birthday. Good wishes from his family and friends combined with world-wide congratulations to make the occasion a personal triumph. One well-wisher wrote simply to 'Marshall Hall, The Greatest Lawyer on Earth'—the Post Office had no difficulty in locating the addressee. His final speech in defence of Madame Fahmy was unsurpassed for its dramatic eloquence, an opinion shared by the *Daily Express* which called Marshall Hall 'the last of the orators'. But the Egyptian Government was not amused by his derogatory remarks made about Orientals and a long cable of complaint was sent to the Attorney-General by the Egyptian Bar Association. To the charge that 'it is unjust and disloyal to judge a whole nation on the conduct of a single individual' Marshall Hall replied that his attack was made 'on the man Ali Fahmy, and not on the Egyptians as a nation'.

After she had recovered from her ordeal Maggie celebrated her acquittal with a small gathering of friends and began to recover her good spirits. Her room was filled with flowers which had been sent from far and wide in tribute and her table was covered with letters from well-wishers. She spoke movingly of the strength she had derived from the expressions of encouragement sent to her during the trial by many unknown English women. 'My faith in British justice never faltered even during the blackest hours of that awful cross-examination,' she said. 'All along my legal advisers assured me that I had a strong case, and I trusted them. I knew I was in good hands.' Her acknowledgement of Marshall Hall's contribution to her freedom lay in subsequent correspondence to the advocate and, during trips to London, she would always visit him if possible. Of her time in the witness-box she said, 'It looked so like a pulpit in a church. I thought I should not be able to speak when I got there. I had to speak. I had to defend myself. My heart beat until I felt it would burst.' She was outspoken in her praise of her young wardress who attended her during the trial and who lifted her spirits. 'Often she uttered a phrase which will ring in my ears for the rest of my life—Courage, Fahmy!' The young widow, whose thirty-three years had encompassed such passion, wealth, delight, despair and hope, as most women fail to experience in a whole life time, was left with her memories. 'My reflections,' she said, 'make me very sad. It was a terrible thing for me to become a Moslem . . . I loved Ali, and no sacrifice seemed too great for me. If only I could have foreseen . . .'

BERNARD O'DONNELL

The Vampire of Kansas City

It was a strange premonition of death which came to Dr Zeo Zoe Wilkins some forty-eight hours before she was discovered with a knife in her throat. Amidst a scene of wildest disorder she lay dead in the sumptuous office in Kansas City, from which she ran her osteopathic business.

Just two days before an assassin's hand struck her down, Zeo told Mrs Eva Grundy, a patient and friend, 'I have but forty-eight hours to live.'

Almost to the very hour her prophecy came true.

Prior to that she had confided to her attorney, Jesse James, 'At least four persons have threatened to get me . . . I'm worried—terribly afraid.' And well she might be, for murder, suicides and the wrecks of human lives and fortunes had been the milestones of her life; indeed she had been guilty of pretty well every crime in the calendar.

The tragic discovery was made by Mrs G. L. Palmer when she made a personal call upon the osteopath. She noticed that newspapers lying in the porch of the premises had not been taken in for two or three days, and that uncollected letters were poking out from the over-filled letter-box. To repeated knocking she obtained no reply, so Mrs Palmer got a little boy to clamber through a side window. He soon came out, a look of terror on his face as he cried, 'She's dead—she's been killed—there's blood all over the place.'

When the police forced the door and entered the room which had been used as a consulting room, they found Zeo Wilkins lying on the floor in a welter of blood. A great hole had been burned in the thick pile of the Turkish rug on which lay the body, clearly indicating that the murderer had tried to set fire to the place in order to destroy traces of his crime. There was evidence too that the dead woman had put up a terrific fight for life. Her gown was torn to shreds, and her injuries indicated that great violence must have been used. In addition to the wound in her throat her neck and forehead had been bruised and lacerated. The room was strewn with papers, and every drawer had been thoroughly ransacked.

Who had murdered Dr Zeo Zoe Wilkins? And why?

Those were the two questions to which the police tried to find answers. Three people were suspect! Charles Wilkins, a brother of the victim, B. F. Tarpley one of her patients, and Dillard Davis, the coloured janitor in the home of the dead woman. They were all subjected to the fiercest grilling and proved innocent, so to this day the murder of the osteopath remains shrouded in mystery.

Not so the lurid story of her life, for the glare of publicity which was concentrated on her death revealed the hideous spectres of her past in all their revolting details.

It was perhaps an unlucky omen that she should have been the thirteenth child of her parents who lived in the little township of Lamar, Montana, U.S.A. They were humble in circumstances, dealing in butter and eggs, yet they managed to scrape up enough to send fifteen-year old Zeo to the School of Osteopathy at Kirkville, in the same state. They did not know that their daughter had decided on osteopathy as a profession, simply because it would be the means of putting her in touch with men and women of wealth—particularly men. She wrote to a schoolgirl friend that she intended to use her beauty to this end.

Thus early she had decided on a vampire career, and how utterly and unscrupulously she carried out her plans will be seen. She did in fact become one of the best known feminine practitioners of the science, and, because she was a woman, and a very beautiful woman at that, she gathered around her a clientele of wealthy patients among whom the male sex predominated.

Of Junoesque figure, with a wealth of crisp curly hair and a pair of dark flashing eyes, she had a striking appearance, and from the very outset of her career Zeo Wilkins cashed in on her physical charms.

In a way she was a female Jekyll and Hyde, for in a diary which she wrote even before she began her studies, she described her two personalities. 'Helen was the better self,' she confessed in this document, 'Zeo the evil. My family always liked Helen the better but Zeo developed so readily that I soon grew too fond of her and Helen found less and less favour in my mind.' an illuminating admission you may think in view of subsequent developments.

At the school of Osteopathy, Zeo applied herself to her studies with zest for she had determined to make a success of her career. One of her fellow students chanced to be Richard Dryer, the son of a prominent banker in Montana. 'I intend to marry him,' wrote Zeo to her girl friend at Lamar. 'I shall get enough money to finance my start in osteopathy and then divorce him.' which was further early evidence of her cold and calculating mind.

She carried out her intention, and the young man had scarcely got to know his bride upon whom he had settled a large sum of money, when she blandly told him that she was going to divorce him and return to school to continue her studies. She was as good as her word. Some weeks later she received a heart-broken letter from the boy's father to say that his son had taken his life because of her desertion.

Displaying not the least remorse or sorrow at the tragedy she had brought about, she promptly set her cap at a young doctor, C. K. Garring, who was adding osteopathy to his other medical qualifications. As well as being captivated by Zeo's beauty, he was also impressed by the brilliance of her work, and the combination made him a ready victim to her wiles. On the very night following their graduation in 1905, they eloped and after a brief but passionate honeymoon, young Garring proudly took his wife back to San Antonio, Texas, where he lived with his extremely wealthy parents. They settled down in one of the most fashionable quarters of the town in a fine house purchased for them as a wedding present by the bridegroom's doting parents. Every luxury that her heart could desire was lavished upon Zeo, who became one of the most popular women in San Antonio social circles. Had she so desired, she could have lived a life of ease and pleasure. But the Zeo (or Hyde) in her, gradually rose to the surface. She could not resist the adulation of men, and there was one in particular who capture her imagination. They became lovers, and during one of his surreptitious visits to her, tragedy for the second time entered Zeo's life.

She was in the arms of her lover when she heard her husband's car drive up to the front of the house. Without a moment's hesitation Zeo seized a revolver, and crept downstairs into the hall to await the entrance of her husband. The moment he opened the door, she fired a fusilade of shots at him. He staggered out of the door and fell bleeding on to the lawn. In the meantime the lover made his escape.

When the police arrived, Zeo was still standing over Garring, the smoking revolver grasped in her hand. Her husband alive, unconcious, was rushed off to hospital.

'I heard noises downstairs and saw a shadowy figure moving about,' Zeo told the police in answer to their questions. 'I thought it was a burglar and I fired.'

Her plausible explanation was accepted by the police, but evidently the husband had other views. When he had recovered and was discharged from hospital, he brought an action for divorce and succeeded. In court he declared that his marriage had been 'a foolish mistake', and that his young wife was 'too temperamental and hot headed'. An understatement, one may think.

For a time Zeo faded from public sight and knowledge, until one day the newspapers came out with a sensational story of the arrest of a prominent Oklahoma banker on a charge of embezzlement. It was revealed that this elderly Romeo, had fallen beneath the spell of Zeo Wilkins (she had reverted to her maiden name) and had loaded her with jewels, furs and other extravagant gifts including vast sums of money. It was only when his bank failed and he was brought to the verge of ruin, that his folly and his crime came to light. A typical entry in Zeo's diary read:- Without a scratch of the pen I got 17,000 dollars.'

The banker was sent to gaol, and Zeo turned her attentions to Leonard Smith, a druggist in Kansas City who completely lost his head when this Jezebel focussed the battery of her charms upon him. For the time being she was eschewing matrimony having found that she was able to wheedle money from her victims without becoming a bride—at any rate dispensing with the marriage ceremony.

In all, she obtained over 15,000 dollars from her lover Smith which fact was duly recorded in her diary with the brief note, 'He gave me all his money and went to get more . . . poor man.'

The sympathetic comment arose from the fact that her lover was accidentally shot dead during a street fracas while going to his bank for further money to squander on his beloved. In this case Zeo must be absolved from direct responsibility for her lover's tragic fate.

One would think that with all these thousands of dollars simply falling into her lap Zeo Wilkins might have concentrated on her osteopathic career, and left romance behind for a time. But she was a girl of great ambition, and was determined that once she *did* start it would be on such spectacular lines and on such a sumptuous scale that only the wealthiest patrons would seek her services.

It was through her picture appearing in the newspapers as a result of her connection with the banker in Oklahoma that Zeo entered the matrimonial stakes for the third time. In Oklahoma City lived a prosperous furniture dealer, Grover Burcham. He saw the photograph which was published, and—like countless others who are drawn to anybody achieving notoriety—he wrote to her. Zeo made discreet enquiries ere committing herself, and having discovered that the writer was a man of repute and substance, she replied to his letter and cupid took charge.

They were married and again a long and happy union might have ensued but for the wanton extravagance of Zeo. There appears to have been a certain amount of mutual affection but her spendthrift ways would have ruined any man no matter how wealthy. Only a few years after their marriage Zeo awakened one morning to find her husband gone. He had risen, packed a few things and disappeared without a word or note by way of explanation. This was a reversal of the usual procedure with a vengeance since it was Zeo, who, as a rule, performed the deserting act. She could not understand it, but was forced to the conclusion that her wild extravagance must have been partly the cause when she discovered that her husband had sold his business, realised all his available assets, and taken practically every dollar he could lay his hands on, leaving her stranded.

Of course, Zeo was not without money, for she took good care that wherever she happened to be somebody would be around to provide her with considerably more than the bare necessities of life. A couple of weeks went by, and the deserted wife was just making up her mind about her next move and her next victim, when there came a brief note from the missing Burcham. 'Join me at Houston, Texas', it said. 'Say nothing to anyone as to my whereabouts.'

Her immediate problem thus solved. Zeo blithely set out to rejoin her husband. He was living in a nicely furnished house on the outskirts of town, and clasped her fondly in his arms when she arrived.

'You nearly broke me', he told his wife. 'I just had to get away before I got into trouble. But I missed you darling—and I simply had to send for you.' For a few months Zeo tried to restrain her extravagance, but eventually she broke out again, and it was not long before her infatuated husband found himself up against the old problem of finding enough money to satisfy the inordinate demands of his wife.

The climax came one night when the Houston police shot and killed a robber whom they caught red-handed in the process of burgling a mansion in the town. The intruder had put up a stiff fight until a bullet found its mark. It was Burcham! He had resorted to crime in order to keep his wife in luxury. Zeo was arrested in the belief that she had been at least the instigator, if not an actual partner in her husband's crimes. For *crimes* it was, as a search of the home in which they lived made clear. The fine clothes and furs which had bedecked the statuesque figure of Zeo, as well as the costly furnishings which had decorated their love nest, were either the proceeds of burglaries far and near, or else had been bought with stolen money.

Although Zeo pretended to be greatly upset and protested her innocence about her husband's activities, there can be no doubt that it was she who had driven him to crime. At the same time it must be admitted that she did genuinely grieve the loss of this husband—probably the only man of whom she was ever really fond.

The police could do nothing to her, and to get away from the scene of her sorrow she journeyed to Colorado Springs, the playground of the idle rich. Among the visitors there, was seventy-two-year-old Thomas W Cunningham, a retired millionaire banker who cast an appreciative if rheumy eye upon the physical charms of the alluring widow Zeo. It was the first time for twenty-five years that this aged Romeo had taken a holiday from his native Joplin in Montana where he owned a big estate.

Zeo was quick to notice the ardent glances the old man cast upon her figure as she disported herself in the sunshine, clad in the latest fashion beach wear. She made discreet enquires and from the moment she learned his identity, old man Cunningham became her target. She displayed tender solicitude towards him, and acted the old man's darling to such effect that before a month had passed, the banker was begging her to become his wife. Zeo though not eager for matrimony, had nothing against wifehood provided its dividends were substantial. She first made sure that there was to be no slip betwixt cup and lip so to speak, and even before their marriage she succeeded in obtaining from her lover, dollars to the equivalent of £80,000.

This nice cash-down advance payment was sufficient to convince the insatiable Zeo that this elderly bridegroom was a most attractive investment. Coyly she professed that her love for him was growing, and he could name the happy day. So December and May were married at Colorado Springs, and as a further token of his love, the husband—President of Joplin's most prosperous bank, bear in mind—promptly gave Zeo 300,000 dollars worth of bank stock which she as promptly sold for the equivalent of £60,000. He also settled upon her certain landed property of which he was possessed. Their honeymoon over, the bride thought she would like to visit Chicago before settling down in Joplin.

Motor-cars, town and country homes, jewellery of immense value, these were the offerings which Cunningham laid upon the altar of love and in return his goddess did not stint him the kisses he craved. But alas! his dreams of love were soon destined to turn into nightmares.

The first shattering blow to the romance came when a Mrs Tabitha Taylor, seventy-year-old housekeeper of Mr Cunningham, declaring that she was his common law wife, brought an action against Zeo for alienation of the old man's affections. She had tended him for twenty-five years, she averred. Then, Joplin friends of the aged bridegroom brought an action for the annulment of the marriage on the grounds of the old man's insanity. They even went so far as to kidnap him, snatching him from the very arms of his young bride while the trial of the action was pending.

Once away from the wiles of Zeo, and back again in Joplin Mr Cunningham had leisure to repent his hasty marriage,and he consented to divorce proceedings being instituted. Zeo also compromised and consented to yielding up all her husband's property with the exception of assets to the value of £60,000. All in all, her net total of £120,000 was generous compensation for a few months of married life to an old dotard.

And among the tangible assets included in the settlement was an exceptionally handsome young man, Albert Marksheffel, who had been employed by the Cunninghams as chauffeur. Handsome Albert had qualifications beyond those necessary to a driver-mechanic and often when Mr Cunningham was enjoying his afternoon siesta, Zeo and Albert would enjoy the intimate delights of each others company. To put it plainly they became lovers and Albert was already earmarked as husband number five when the brief—but profitable—encounter with Banker Cunningham came to an end.

This time, however, Zeo had picked a partner who was less amenable to her whims than her previous husbands or lovers.

Albert was unable to give her anything but love, so it fell to Zeo to provide the material things of life and this she did with unwanted profligacy.

She embarked on an orgy of spending, and opened a banking account for her husband with £5,000 to his credit. They occupied a fine house in Colorado, and she set him up in a motor business. In return, he fulfilled the role of a spouse without the rapturous adoration that she had known from all her other men. There were no extravagant presents from him, not even a few flowers on occasion, and Zeo loved flowers.

Once she lay in bed for three days pretending to be ill, in order to arouse some sympathy in her husband's heart. But all in vain! From her 'sick-bed' she demanded flowers and she wept when he refused even a posy. Then Zeo staged a macabre scene to shake him our of his indifference.

One night when Albert returned home from the garage he found a bow of black crepe tied round the knocker of the front door. His heart missed a beat! Was Zeo really ill after all? Had something terrible happened to her? Yes! he was shaken all right, and his feet could not carry him quickly enough up the stairs to his wife's bedroom. As he got to the door he noticed the sickly sweet odour of some disinfectant. All was silent within. He called her name but there was no answer. Almost fearing to turn the handle of the door he paused for some seconds before he pushed it open and took a frightened glance towards the bed. He nearly dropped in his tracks at what he saw. The blinds were drawn and in the dim light of four flickering candles, two at each end of the bed, lay Zeo her face white with the pallor of death, her lovely body shrouded with a sheet.

With slow faltering steps, and with horror gripping his very soul, the stricken husband made his way towards the bed to look down upon all that was mortal of his wife, or so he thought. As he approached the lids of her eyes flickered upwards, and she gazed at him with reproach. And then her body rose from its recumbent position, her outstretched hand pointed towards him, and her croaking voice echoed his name.

Poor Albert! He simply fell flat on his face in a dead faint while Zeo wiped the chalk-like powder from her face. It had taught him a lesson however, and he never ceased to bring her flowers—even without her asking—for the rest of their married life. But their married life didn't last long.

It was in 1917 that they were married, and in 1919 Zeo obtained a divorce from her husband. It must be a matter for conjecture as to which of the pair was the most relieved by the dissolution.

Following her divorce from Marksheffel, Zeo embarked with zeal on her osteopathic career. She opened her fabulous surgery in Kansas City, where with one or two love affairs mingled with business, she carried on a lucrative practice.

Her 'manipulative surgery' was not the only activity in which she indulged however. After her death the police discovered documents which proved that many of her patients, whose trust she had gained, had been cleverly blackmailed by the resourceful Dr Zeo Zoe Wilkins, the name by which she was professionally known. Some of her victims had been her lovers and as such—her slaves. She wormed from them guilty secrets which gave her the power to levy tribute upon them under pain of exposure.

By way of variant too, her osteopathic skill provided an ample if sinister cloak for carrying out abortions on wealthy women anxious to avoid motherhood, who thus also became prey to her blackmailing wiles. And if this was not enough, drug-peddling was another side line which Zeo added to her shameful accomplishments.

Perhaps hidden deep somewhere in these nefarious exploits there is the clue to the murder of this fickle, fascinating and vile woman. But it has never been found. The secret is locked in the dead black heart of the Vampire of Kansas City.

SOURCES AND ACKNOWLEDGEMENTS

'The Case of the Burning Bride' by Alan Hynd from *The Case of the Burning Bride and Eleven Other True Crime Cases* (New York: Avon, 1952), copyright © 1952 by Alan Hynd. Reproduced by kind permission of Noel Hynd.

'Landru – A Real Life Bluebeard' by H. Russell Wakefield from *The Fifty Most Amazing Crimes of the Last 100 Years* (London: Odhams, 1936).

'Cordelia Botkin's Candy' by Edward H. Smith from *Famous American Poison Mysteries* (London: Hurst and Blackett, n.d.).

'The Passion that Passed for Love' by Leo Grex from *Mystery Stranger than Fiction* (London: Hale; New York: St. Martin's, 1979), copyright © 1979 by the Estate of Leonard Gribble. Reproduced by kind permission of Lois Gribble.

'Death at her Elbow' by Stanley Ellin from *My Favourite True Mysteries* (London: Heinemann, 1956), copyright © 1956 by Stanley Ellin. Reproduced by permission of Curtis Brown Limited.

'Doctor Finch and Miss Tregoff' by Eric Ambler from *The Ability to Kill* (London: Boddley Head, 1963), copyright © 1963 by Eric Ambler. Reproduced by permission of the author.

'The Buck Ruxton Case' by Colin Wilson, copyright © 1990 by Colin Wilson. Reproduced by permission of Colin Wilson and David Bolt Associates.

'Jealous Woman with a Gun' by Rupert Furneaux from *They Died by a Gun* (London: Herbert Jenkins, 1962), copyright © 1962 by Rupert Furneaux. Reproduced by permission of Random Century Limited.

'Conman, Casanova, Killer' by Norman Lucas from *The Sex Killers* (London: W.H. Allen, 1974), copyright © 1974 by